Travel agency practice

I wish to dedicate this book with love to my husband Bob.

Travel agency practice

Pauline Horner

LONGMAN

Addison Wesley Longman,
Edinburgh Gate, Burnt Mill, Harlow,
Essex CM20 2JE, England
and Associated Companies throughout the World.

© Addison-Wesley Longman 1996.

First printed 1996

ISBN 0582-28856-8

British Library Cataloguing-in-Publication Data
A catalogue record for this book is available from the British Library.

Set by 30 in 9.75/12 pt Sabon
Produced by Longman Singapore Publishers Pte
Printed in Singapore

Contents

Acknowledgements

We are grateful to the following for permission to reproduce copyright material:

Dr Caroline Allen for Figure 4.4; Eurolines for Figures 2.6, 2.7 and 2.8; Fleishmann-Hillard © Sea World, 1995 for Figure 8.2; Jamestown-Yorktown Foundation for Figure 8.6; Mr Anthony LaRoche for Figure 11.1; National Express for Figures 2.1 and 2.5; P & O Cruises (UK) Limited for Figures 12.2, 12.3 and 12.4, Pauline Gillett for Figure 8.9; Reed Travel Training (ABC Hotel and Travel Index, ABC World Airways Guide) for Figures 3.8, 3.9, 5.8, 5.9 and 5.11; and Thorpe Park, Chertsey, Surrey for Figure 6.19.

Whilst every effort has been made to trace the owners of the copyright material we take this opportunity to offer our apologies to any copyright holders whose rights we may have unwittingly infringed.

Preface

This book covers the syllabus for ABTAC, the ABTA Travel Agent's Certificate of Competence for travel agents, as well as much of the underpinning knowledge for the Travel Services NVQs levels 1, 2 and 3. The author is an External Verifier for City and Guilds Travel Services NVQs and has over ten years' experience in training travel agents.

Aimed specifically at trainee travel agents, whether in the workplace or in college, the first half of the book examines the components of the travel industry, namely transport, accommodation and travel services, and considers the main holiday destinations which appeal to UK tourists. The second half of the book deals with package, specialist and tailor-made holidays and the role of the travel agent in booking those holidays, together with the administrative issues involved in keeping track of a travel agency business.

The book is illustrated with diagrams, maps and photographs, many of which have been taken by the author to illustrate the text. Sample ABTAC style questions are provided at the end of each chapter at both the Primary and Advanced levels and acceptable solutions for all questions are included at the end of the book.

Pauline Horner

Part one

The travel industry

1 An overview of the UK travel industry

By the year 2000, the largest industry in the world is likely to be tourism supported by the network of organisations and people in the travel industry. For many British tourists their primary link with tourism is through their local travel agent (Fig. 1.1).

The travel industry and the economy

Between 1970 and 1990 the world arrivals expanded from 160 million to 430 million, an increase of 169 per cent in the people travelling. Receipts from tourism worldwide for the same 20 years rose from $18 billion to nearly $250 billion. Such figures indicate many jobs in tourism and in Western Europe, according to the World Travel and Tourism Council, travel and tourism actually accounts for 9.6 per cent of employment.

In 1985, according to the figures of the Employment Department, there were 1.38 million people employed in tourism in the United Kingdom alone, and this had risen to 1.5 million by 1990. By 1993 the overall figures had dropped slightly to 1.47 million

Figure 1.1 Thomas Cook travel agency, Southport

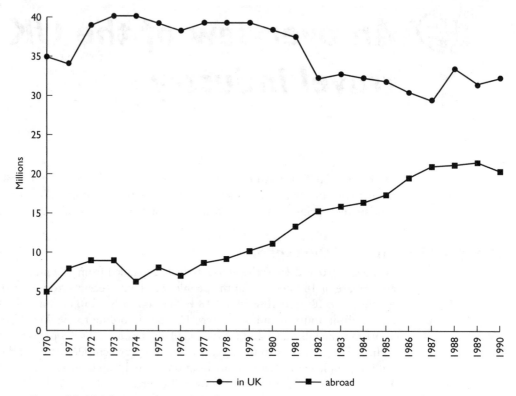

Figure 1.2 Holidays over four nights taken by UK citizens

but in the same period the numbers of people employed in museums in the UK had risen by 4%. This rise can be explained by the fact that many social history museums linked to local culture and customs opened in the early 1990s, and established open air museums, such as Beamish in Gateshead and Ironbridge near Telford, extending their appeal to visitors from far beyond their own local boundaries.

Figure 1.2 shows the number of holidays over four nights taken by UK tourists in the 20 years from 1970 to 1990. The figures are based on the results of the annual British Tourist Authority (BTA) national travel survey and show a steady increase in the number of holidays taken abroad by UK citizens.

Figure 1.3 shows how the data of the International Passenger Survey demonstrate that North America in particular gained in popularity with British tourists in the early 1990s. This popularity can be accounted for by the fact that British tourists became more used to travelling abroad and the cheaper cost of living in the USA made it very attractive financially. In fact there was a massive 19 per cent increase in UK tourists to the USA between 1991 and 1992 when the exchange rate was almost $2.00 to the pound. The popularity of a destination in large numbers is usually regarded as mass tourism.

Mass tourism

The four essential conditions for mass tourism to exist are

- cheap, easy travel
- availability of leisure time
- opportunities for pleasure and entertainment
- the travel industry.

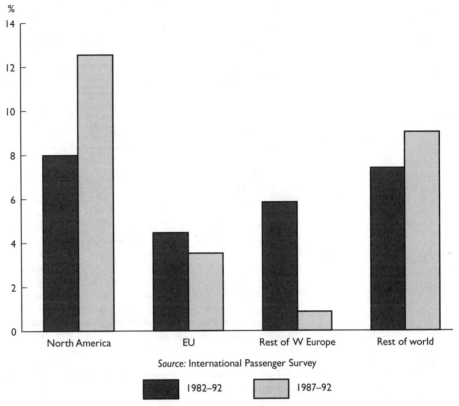

Figure 1.3 UK residents travelling abroad (average annual growth)

Tourism has expanded over the centuries as different types of travel have become more widely available (Fig 1.4). In the earliest times people travelled on foot to hunt, explore or to make pilgrimages. The development of roads in the UK saw the growth of spa towns such as Bath and Scarborough and in the mid-1800s, as railway networks spread across the country, seaside towns such as Brighton and Blackpool flourished. After the Second World War the availability of aeroplanes saw the start of charter flights and package holidays to Spain and the Mediterranean and in the 1970s the introduction of wide-bodied jets meant that journeys to the USA and the Far East came within the reach of many British people. We will consider transportation in Chapter 2.

Tourism has also expanded as people's leisure time has increased. In the 1700s and 1800s leisure time was available only to the richer people in the UK; indeed they were sometimes referred to as the 'leisure classes'. At the beginning of the twentieth century, Bank Holidays were introduced and in the 1930s paid holiday time was more widely available. In the latter half of the twentieth century paid holidays are accepted as a norm and package holidays are within the reach of most people.

British people become tourists for a variety of pleasurable reasons such as

- a break in the sun
- cultural or historical interest
- relaxation in a different environment
- a religious pilgrimage
- to visit friends and relatives and meet other people (VFR).

Anglo-Saxon times	on foot	hunting exploring, making pilgrimages
Roman times	roads	spa towns
1815	steamboats	UK seaside resorts with piers
1850s	railways	UK seaside resorts
1950s	charter aircraft	package holidays to Spain
1960s	wide-bodied jets	long haul holidays to USA and the Far East

Figure 1.4 Means of travel over the centuries and the development of tourism

Statutory leisure time in the UK

1871   Bank Holidays were introduced
1890s   Half-day closing was introduced in some local areas
1901   Factory Act gave six days' holiday a year to women and young people
1938   Holidays with Pay Act

Indeed many people become tourists for more than just one of these reasons. In Part Two we consider the destinations which attract various categories of travellers.

Wherever tourists spend their holidays they will usually expect to find certain facilities. These facilities are supplied by the travel industry and they include

- help from a travel agent or reservations staff at an airline, coach or ferry company to reach their destination
- a hotel, apartment or caravan in which to stay
- a restaurant or cafeteria in which to eat
- information about the place where they are staying
- some entertainment during their stay.

All of these facilities imply jobs in the travel industry for those who are willing to meet the needs of the modern holidaymaker or business traveller. Companies such as airlines and ferry operators are referred to in the travel industry as principals.

Package holidays

Tourists can book each component of their holiday themselves or they can book a package holiday which consists of

- transport to the holiday destination
- accommodation throughout the holiday
- transfers from the airport or ferry to the accommodation.

Package holidays are put together by tour operators who charge an all-in price for the whole holiday and provide couriers to look after their clients during the holiday. We consider brochures, tour operators and their activities in Part Three. Holiday flights may be scheduled, meaning that they fly to a published timetable, or chartered, which is a means of hiring the aircraft. Further information about airlines and other forms of holiday transport is in Chapter 2. Holiday accommodation may vary from a five star hotel to a self-catering break in a caravan and we will learn more about selecting the appropriate accommodation for clients in Chapter 3. Clients should also be given advice about insurance, passports, visas, health regulations and foreign exchange and further details can be found in Chapter 4.

Part Four of this book deals with the role of the travel agent in providing information, identifying the needs of clients and making holiday and travel bookings. The Association of British Travel Agents (ABTA) is the principal trade organisation for travel agents in the UK, but there are also the Guild of Business Travel Agents (GBTA), the Guild of European Business Travel Agents (GEBTA) and the National Association of Independent Travel Agents (NAITA).

Organisations in the travel industry

Other organisations within the travel industry include the following:

- The tourist boards set up in the UK by the Development of Tourism Act 1969, namely the British Tourist Authority (BTA), the English Tourist Board (ETB), the Wales Tourist Board (WTB) and the Scottish Tourist Board (STB). Within local areas, tourist information centres (TICs) provide information about attractions, travel accommodation and local entertainment (Fig. 1.5).
- English Heritage and the National Trust, both of which protect traditional buildings of interest in the UK. The National Trust also protects the environment of large stretches of coastline and countryside. English Heritage, whose official title is the Historic Buildings and Monuments Commission for England, is under the directorship of the Department of the Environment whereas the National Trust is a voluntary organisation founded in 1895 by a Victorian group which included the writer Beatrix Potter.
- Airline organisations such as the International Air Transport Association (IATA) formed in 1945, which draws its members from over 80% of the world's airlines, and the Civil Aviation Authority (CAA), which was founded by an Act of Parliament in 1971 to approve and license air carriers in the UK. British tour operators who sell foreign package holidays which include charter flights are required to obtain from the CAA an Air Travel Organiser's Licence (ATOL).
- Professional associations for travel employees such as the Institute of Travel and Tourism (ITT) and the Tourism Society, both of which are concerned with educational and professional standards in the tourist industry providing lectures, seminars and a forum for discussion on topical tourism issues.

● Marketing organisations such as the Association of National Tourist Office
Representatives (ANTOR), a voluntary non-political marketing organisation
which represents over 80 worldwide national tourist offices which provide
information about their destinations to UK tourists and travel agents. The British
Incoming Tour Operators' Association (BITOA) was founded in 1977 to
represent the interests of tour operators who provide holidays, tours or tourism
services for visitors coming into the UK from overseas. The Pacific Asia Travel
Association (PATA) is a marketing organisation which was founded in Hawaii in
1952 to facilitate and promote tourism in Asia and the Pacific area. The
Passenger Shipping Association (PSA) exists for the benefit of its members, who
are passenger ship owners. PSA promotes travel agency links through its
subsidiary the Passenger Shipping Association Retail Agents' Scheme (PSARA)
through which travel agents can attend seminars, training programmes and
educational visits about cruising.

Figure 1.5 Southport Tourist Information Centre

Summary of the travel industry

Transport	Accommodation	Services		Attractions
air	hotel	**public sector**	**private sector**	stately homes
coach	• full board	• passport	• travel agents	theme homes
rail	• half board	• visa	• tours operators	museums
cruise ship	• bed and breakfast	• tourist boards	• insurance	art galleries
ferry	self-catering	• tourist offices	• car hire	zoos
• hovercraft	• tent	• port authorities	• financial services	ancient monuments
• jefoil	• caravan	• CAA	• travel trade press	activity centres
• seacat	• apartment	• IATA	• guides	
• car	• villa	• English Heritage	• travel trade manuals	
• private car	• gîte	• education and training	• training establishments	
• chaffeured car	guest house	**voluntary sector**	• travel trade associations	
		• National Trust	• restaurants and cafés	
		• guides		

Revision Questions

Primary level

1 Name FIVE different jobs to be found in the travel industry.

2 What are the THREE parts of a holiday which are normally included in the price of a package holiday?

3 Name THREE tour operators which offer package holidays to the Mediterranean.

4 Name THREE tour operators which offer package holidays to the USA.

5 In connection with British tourism what do the letters ETB stand for?

6 Which is the largest trade association for travel agents in Britain?

7 Name TWO professional associations for employees in the travel and tourism industry in Britain.

8 What do the letters CAA stand for?

9 Other than ABTA, name ONE trade association to which a travel agent specialising in the business market might apply for membership.

10 What is the more commonly known name given to the Historic Buildings and Monuments Commission for England?

Advanced level

1 What are the FOUR main conditions for the growth of mass tourism?

2 Name TWO major marketing organisations in the travel industry which could supply a travel agent with information about holidays in the Far East.

3 In connection with the travel industry, what do you understand by the letters VFR?

4 Give THREE reasons why a British tourist might wish to take a holiday or short break to an area, other than London, within 50 miles of your own home.

5 Give THREE reasons why a French tourist may wish to take a holiday or short break in London.

6 What do you understand by an 'ATOL' and from where can one be obtained?

7 Which Act of Parliament set up a domestic structure for tourism in Britain?

8 For a travel agent specialising in the cruise market, which organisation might offer useful information and support, including educational visits to ships?

9 Which organisation represents the interests of tour operators who provide tours and holidays for incoming tourists visiting this country from abroad?

10 Name a voluntary organisation in Britain which is concerned with environmental issues and tourism in the countryside.

2) *Transportation*

Transport, an essential ingredient of travel for tourism, may be provided by

- surface travel by coach or rail
- vehicle carrying services by rail or sea
- air travel by scheduled or charter services
- car hire.

Surface travel

Journeys within the UK, or from the UK to the rest of Europe, can be booked through travel agents by coach or rail.

Coach travel

Coach travel is supplied by a variety of private companies but a scheduled European network is provided by the sister companies of

- National Express
- Scottish Citylink
- Eurolines.

All three companies are members of the Bonded Coach Holidays Group of the Confederation of Passenger Transport, with a bond to protect customers in the event of the collapse of the company. Such bonding is required under the EC Directive on Package Tours for all companies, used by travel agents or others, for overnight stays of groups of tourists.

National Express and Scottish Citylink

These companies offer a wide range of routes to over 1,200 destinations which can be booked for regular fare-paying passengers or as part of all-inclusive holidays in Great Britain (Fig. 2.1).

On many long-distance routes the Rapide service offers extra comfort on the coach (Fig. 2.2) with:

- courier
- hot and cold drinks
- snacks
- toilet and washroom facilities
- relief driver
- no smoking on buses or in segregated areas
- reserved seats.

Children aged 5–15 years of age travel at a discounted rate with up to 30% reduction. Reductions are offered to families, young people and senior citizens through discount

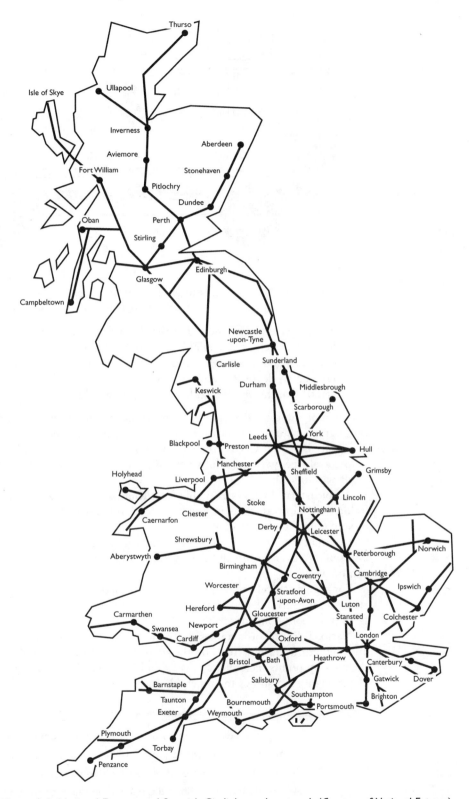

Figure 2.1 National Express and Scottish Citylink coach network (*Courtesy of National Express*)

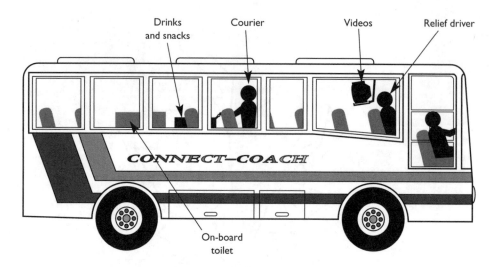

Drinks and snacks   Courier   Videos   Relief driver

On-board toilet

Figure 2.2 Coach travel

cards which entitle the holders to child rates of travel. In 1995 these discount cards cost £7.00 for twelve months or £18.00 for three years. Discount cards include:

- Young Person's CoachCard available to those between 16 and 25
- Student CoachCard available to full-time students aged 16–25 or mature students over 26 years of age who study in a recognised establishment for at least 15 hours a week for 20 weeks in a year
- Senior CoachCard available to persons over 55.

When applying for a discount card the applicant should present a passport-sized photograph with the application form and appropriate fee.

Family Discount Cards are available for up to two named adults and two children who travel free, with the adults paying regular fares. The scheme also applies to one adult with one child.

A Tourist Trail Pass is available for UK citizens or overseas visitors and entitles the holder to unlimited travel in England, Scotland and Wales for a given number of days as shown in Fig. 2.3.

Discounts on Tourist Trail Passes are available for children, young persons, students and senior citizens. On valid days there is no limit to the number of journeys which can be made.

For regular travel on National Express or Scottish Citylink, there is a wide price structure for fares, depending on the day of travel. Figure 2.4 summarises the types of fares most commonly available.

National Express timetables show the outward journey times on the left of the chart and the return journey times on the right. Routes through the day can vary as regards the pick-up points included, so care should be taken when recommending a route to a client. Figure 2.5 shows the timetable for the National Express routes between

Figure 2.3
Validity of National Express Tourist Trail Passes

1 any three days unlimited travel within three consecutive days
2 any five days unlimited travel within ten consecutive days
3 any eight days consecutive travel within sixteen consecutive days
4 any fifteen days unlimited travel within thirty consecutive days

Southport and London and it can be seen that

- the only through bus is the 09.15 which arrives in London at 14.50
- the 07.30 bus from Liverpool does not stop at Golders Green
- the overnight 23.25 bus from Liverpool does not stop at any of the in-between points
- some of the buses going to London drop off at Marble Arch, but all of the return buses can be boarded only at Victoria Coach Station or Golders Green.

Abbrev.	Explanation	Day of travel
SR	Standard Return	Fridays, some Saturdays and other peak travel
dSR	Discount Standard Return*	Standard day with up to 30% discount
ER	Economy Return	not a Standard day
dER	Discount Economy Return*	not a Standard day, with up to 30% discount
EAR	Economy Advanced Purchase Return	tickets booked 7 days in advance for travel on a day other than Friday, some Saturdays and other peak times
SAR	Standard Advanced Purchase Return	tickets booked 7 days in advance for travel on standard days
* for Discount CoachCard holders and children aged 5 to 15 inclusive		

Figure 2.4 National Express fares

To London						**From London**				
550	550	550	550	421	Service number	550	550	550	550	421
D	D	D	D	D	Days of operation	D	D	D	D	D
......	0915	......	......	......	SOUTHPORT, Eastbank St, Tourist Info Centre ❷	......	1845	......	......	......
......	0935	......	......	......	Ormskirk, Bus Stn	......	1825	......	......	......
......	0938	......	......	......	Ormskirk (Edge Hill College), A570 Bus Stop o/s College	......	1820	......	......	......
0730	1030	1300	1700	2325	LIVERPOOL, Coach Stn, Norton St	1445	1750	2025	2245	0545
	1055				Widnes, Victoria Rd, Kingsway Hotel ❷			2000		
	1105				Runcorn, Old Town Bus Stn			1950		
0800		1330	1730		WARRINGTON, Bus Stn	1415	1720		2215	
					via M6/M1 Motorways					
		1655	2050		Golders Green	1055	1355			
1135	1440	1710	2105		London (Marble Arch) (E) ❷					
1145	1450	1720	2115	0610	LONDON (Victoria Coach Stn)	1030	1330	1600	1830	2300

Figure 2.5 National Express Southport–London timetable (*Courtesy of National Express*)

National Express tickets should be completed with the customer's name and address and date of sale on the top line. The departure point and arrival points should be shown clearly in the left hand boxes, with a line drawn through any unused boxes and the word VOID inserted. The service number, departure time, day and date of travel should be shown in the boxes in the centre of the ticket and the fare type and price are shown in the box on the right. Any hotel or other relevant information is shown in the small box at the bottom of the ticket. All tickets should be validated with the agency stamp, agency number and the name of the sales person (Fig 2.6).

'Minifill' quick issue National Express tickets can be used in the case of regular customers and here the ticket would contain the departure and arrival points, date of travel, service number, fare type and fare calculation as well as the agency validation. Within the airline style ticket there are four pages and if some sections are unused and VOID has been entered in the boxes, the corresponding ticket pages should be removed. The rear cover of the ticket booklet is the customer receipt and shows full details of the sale.

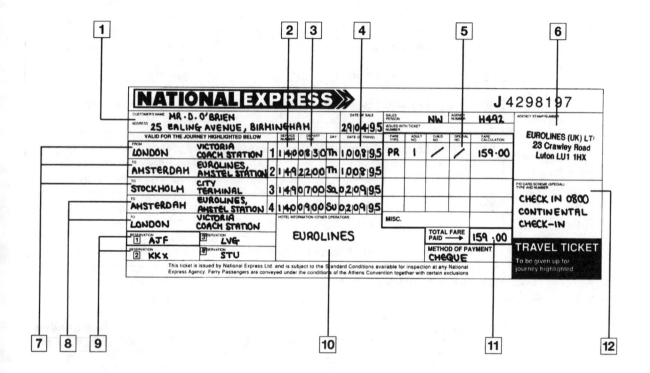

1	PASSENGER NAMES AND ADDRESS
2	CORRECT SERVICE NUMBER
3	CORRECT DEPARTURE TIME
4	CORRECT DATE OF TRAVEL
5	TO BE USED WHEN A YOUTH OR SENIOR CITIZEN FARE IS CHARGED
6	ISSUING AGENT STAMP AND NUMBER
7	DESTINATION AND FULL DEPARTURE POINT DETAILS MUST BE SHOWN
8	ALL UNUSED SECTIONS OF THE TICKET MUST SHOW 'VOID'
9	CORRECT BOOKING REFERENCES MUST BE SHOWN
10	NAME OF OPERATING COMPANY MUST BE INDICATED IN THIS BOX, AS EUROLINES CONDITIONS ARE DIFFERENT TO THOSE OF NATIONAL EXPRESS
11	CORRECT FARE MUST BE SHOWN
12	DETAILS OF CHECK-IN MUST BE SHOWN, WHERE RELEVANT

Figure 2.6 National Express ticket (*Courtesy of Eurolines*)

Airport and ferry port links are provided by National Express and a special arrangement with a number of airport hotels enables the Airport Stopovers scheme to operate. Fares are based on nine departure zones in England, Scotland or Wales and for an all-in price the client receives:

- return coach travel to the airport hotel
- overnight bed and breakfast accommodation before or after the flight
- courtesy transport from the hotel to the airport.

Eurolines

Travel to over 250 European destinations can be booked through Eurolines with departures in the UK from Victoria Coach Station in London. Check-in is at least 30 minutes before departure and the check-in desk closes 10 minutes before departure.

Timetables for Eurolines are similar in layout to National Express but with long distance routes the second or subsequent days of travel are indicated by -----. The sample timetable shown in Fig 2.7 demonstrates how it can take two days from London to reach Rome.

Eurolines has a special arrangement with the Ibis group of hotels to provide economic accommodation en route and the Euro Explorer tickets provide fifteen different combinations of the more popular routes at a discounted rate. The cheapest Euro Explorer is to Ireland with stopovers in Dublin, Galway and Cork. The most expensive Euro Explorer is number 6 which allows stopovers in Paris, Amsterdam, Rome and Barcelona. The tickets are valid for six months, except for the Republic of Ireland, which is valid for three months, and only the first leg of the journey must be booked before departure.

LONDON • MILAN • ROME

151	151	SERVICE NUMBER			151	151
1/4- 30/3 WED SAT	3/7- 29/9 MON FRI	**euro◆lines**			2/7- 27/9 WED SUN	3/4- 29/3 MON FRI
		EUROLINES UK, FRANCE & ITALY				
0900	0900	Check-in	**Eurolines Desk**			
0930	0930	Dep.	**LONDON**	Arr.	1615	1615
1115	1115	Check-in	**DOVER**	Dep.	1415	1415
1500	1500	Dep.	**CALAIS**	Arr.	1245	1245
1845	1845	Arr.	**PARIS**	Dep.	0900	0900
2000	2000	Dep.	**PARIS**	Arr.	0830	0830
0200	0200	Arr.	**LYON**	Dep.	0200	0200
			Via Frejus Tunnel			
0645	0645	Arr.	**TURIN**	Dep.	2115	2115
0900*	0900	Arr.	**MILAN**	Dep.	1830	1830
0930	0930	Dep.	**MILAN**	Arr.	1800	1800*
1230	1230	Arr.	**BOLOGNA**	Dep.	1500	1500
1415	1415	Arr.	**FLORENCE**	Dep.	1315	1315
1815	1815	Arr.	**ROME**	Dep.	0900	0900
				Check-in	0830	0830

* Passengers change coaches in Milan.

CHRISTMAS & NEW YEAR ARRANGEMENTS
No Service ex Rome 25 December & 1 January.
Extra Service ex London 5 January.
Extra Service ex Rome 21, 28 December & 3 January.

LUGGAGE One medium sized suitcase per person plus hand luggage is carried free of charge. Additional items may be carried subject to availability of space.

FARETABLE

LONDON & DOVER	ADULT SINGLE	ADULT RETURN	YOUTH/ SENIOR CITIZEN SINGLE	YOUTH/ SENIOR CITIZEN RETURN	CHILD SINGLE	CHILD RETURN
LYON	53.00	85.00	53.00	85.00	41.00	67.00
TURIN, MILAN	72.00 **77.00**	109.00 **119.00**	66.00 **71.00**	99.00 **109.00**	42.00 **47.00**	62.00 **72.00**
BOLOGNA, VERONA PADOVA, VENICE	79.00 **84.00**	119.00 **129.00**	72.00 **77.00**	109.00 **119.00**	46.00 **51.00**	69.00 **79.00**
FLORENCE	83.00 **88.00**	126.00 **136.00**	76.00 **81.00**	115.00 **125.00**	49.00 **54.00**	73.00 **83.00**
ROME	85.00 **90.00**	129.00 **139.00**	79.00 **84.00**	119.00 **129.00**	50.00 **55.00**	75.00 **85.00**

Bold Type = Peak Fares 1 July - 2 Sept. (Outward date determines fare to be charged.)

One infant 0–3 yrs travels free, when accompanied by fare-paying passenger over 17 yrs.
Child Fares 4–12 yrs.
Youth Fares 13–25 yrs.
Senior Citizen Fares 60 yrs and over.

SERVICE SUMMARY

LONDON–MILAN ROME | MILAN– VENICE | DOV–CAL 1¼ hrs | RECLINING SEATS | ON BOARD TOILET | SMOKING SEATS/ NO SMOKING SEATS

☾ No smoking allowed between 2200 hrs–0600 hrs.

Figure 2.7 Eurolines timetables (*Courtesy of Eurolines*)

Rail travel in the UK

This is provided by British Rail and InterCity with the rail lines and stations managed by Railtrack. Under the provisions of the Railways Act 1993, as from 1996 British Rail will be privatised into 23 subsidiary regional companies and two InterCity companies. Figure 2.8 shows the 1995 rail routes in the UK.

Facilities on board the trains

These depend on the class of travel booked.

- First class accommodation includes
  - wide adjustable seats
  - large tables
  - restaurant seats where applicable
  - telephone
  - complimentary InterCity First Class Magazine.
- First Class Pullman on selected trains has the above facilities plus a choice of a restaurant meal or light refreshments at the customer's seat with complimentary tea or coffee.
- Silver Standard is for customers with full standard tickets and the service includes complimentary tea or coffee with biscuits.
- Sleepers are provided on long distance journeys to Scotland or the West Country with single berth cabins for first class passengers and twin berth cabins for standard class.
- Some long distance routes also have Motorail so that cars as well as passengers can be transported to the destination.

Facilities for disabled passengers

These are provided when railway staff are informed. After privatisation the provision for disabled passengers throughout the network becomes the responsibility of the Office of the Rail Regulator. Railway staff can usually arrange to meet disabled passengers at the departure station, accompany them onto the train and arrange car parking and portable ramps where appropriate. Standard sized wheelchairs can be carried in the spaces provided on most trains although large outdoor runabout vehicles cannot be carried. Induction loops are fitted at many ticket office windows to help hearing-aid users and guide dogs can be taken into all areas of both stations and trains, including the buffets and restaurants.

Special discounts apply to persons who are visually impaired or remain in their own wheelchair for a rail journey. The discounts also apply to a companion, and the wheelchair is carried free of charge. The discounts which apply are:

- single journey   34% off
- first class/standard day return   50% off
- first class/standard open return   34% off

Discounts

Discounts of up to 33% are available through railcards which include:

- Young Person's Railcard for those aged 16–25 or mature students over 26 years of age who study in a recognised establishment for at least 15 hours a week for 20 weeks in a year

- Senior Citizen's Railcard for those over the age of 60
- Family Railcard for adults travelling with children.

The minimum group size for use of a Family Railcard is one adult and one child whereas the maximum group size is four adults and four children. The 'family' group need not be related but they must stay together for the journey. Discounts apply to the adult fares but all children in the group travel for a standard £2.00 fare, regardless of the length of journey.

Discount cards cannot be used for

- special excursions
- rail-air coach links
- some boat trains
- shipping services, except those to the Channel Islands
- the London or Glasgow Underground
- Tyne and Wear Metro.

In 1995 these rail discount cards cost £16 for twelve months for young persons and senior citizens or £20 for a Family Railcard.

For regular travel on British Rail or InterCity there is a wide structure of fares and discounts depending on how much notice can be given for travel and which days and times are chosen. Some examples of the types of fares are shown in Fig. 2.9.

British Rail and InterCity timetables always show direct journeys in bold print and connecting services in light print. Where a departure time is shown in light print, the client will have to change at the next station whose time is printed in heavy type. Where the arrival time is shown in light print, the client will have to change at the station whose time is listed in bold print immediately above the arrival time.

Where there is a connecting service shown in two separate columns in the British Rail (BR) timetable this is indicated by arrows as shown in Fig. 2.10.

A service that does not run for the full length of the timetable is shown by a wavy line down the column and details are given in the appropriate footnote. Where trains run to a regular schedule over a period of time in a day a wide column is used to indicate the pattern of frequency with words such as 'and at the same minutes past each hour until'.

Most BR timetables include small letters with footnotes and these indicate changes of train or particular times when the service is available. All footnotes should be read carefully. Other commonly used symbols in BR timetables include:

MO   Monday only
MX   not on Mondays
p   overnight service
R   reservations recommended

Figure 2.11 indicates the London stations and the directions from which trains will arrive. Waterloo is the main station for arrivals from the Channel Tunnel services.

British Rail tickets show the departure and arrival points with any connecting stations; the class of travel and a description of the fare type and validity; the number of adults and children travelling with the fare calculation; and the date travel will commence.

Figure 2.8 UK rail routes in 1995

Tickets with no restrictions

First Class ticket	valid on any train for a single or return journey in First Class on the date of the ticket
Standard ticket	valid on any train for a single or return journey on the date of the ticket
Season tickets	available for the period of validity from one week to one year
Saver	valid for travel on any day with return within one calendar month

Tickets with travel restricted to off peak times

Cheap day return	usually valid only after 9.30 am with return any time that day
Supersaver	not valid for travel on Fridays, summer Saturdays or Bank Holidays
Super Advance & Apex	purchased in advance of travel but valid only on certain days and services

---

Figure 2.9 Sample fares and ticket types on British Rail and InterCity

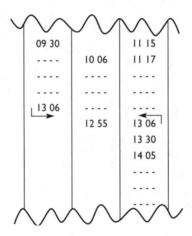

Figure 2.10 Arrow showing connections in BR timetable

Rail-air links

Rail-air links exist for the following UK airports:

- Birmingham
- Gatwick
- Heathrow
- Luton
- Manchester
- Southampton
- Southend.

The link may be provided by train or through a rail and coach link. In Birmingham the service is provided by an independent people mover system (MAGLEV) which operates between Birmingham International station and Birmingham airport terminal buildings at frequent intervals with a journey time of only two minutes.

Eurostar

The Eurostar cross-Channel rail services depart from London to Paris, Brussels and Lille with high speed connections from Paris to Disneyland, Lyon and Avignon and from Brussels to Bruge, The Hague and Amsterdam. Departures are from Waterloo International Terminal in London which was specially designed to handle up to 6,000 passengers per hour. The air conditioned Eurostar trains are equipped with buffet cars for standard fares, and a meal is included in the price for first class passengers. The journey takes 2 hours to Lille, 3 hours to Paris and 3 hours 15 minutes to Brussels.

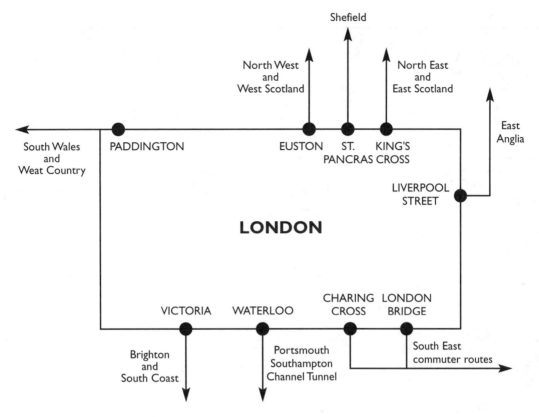

Figure 2.11 London mainline stations

Vehicle carrying services

Motorail services in the UK

These are provided from Euston to Carlisle, Edinburgh, Aberdeen, Inverness and Stirling, as well as from Paddington to Penzance, and Bristol to Edinburgh. The times of operation vary throughout the year and these should be checked carefully. The price on the Motorail usually includes

- the car
- three adults or two adults with two children
- tray meal
- rugs and pillow overnight
- a sleeper lounge car on some services.

Berths are normally available 2–3 hours before departure time and cars must be checked in at least 2 hours before departure.

French Motorail

Most areas of France are easily accessible for the motorist through the French Motorail system (Fig. 2.12). The trains travel through the night from Boulogne, Dieppe or Calais to take clients and their cars to Bordeaux, Biarritz, Narbonne, Avignon or the Côte d'Azur. Connecting services can take clients and their cars on to Lisbon, Madrid or Milan.

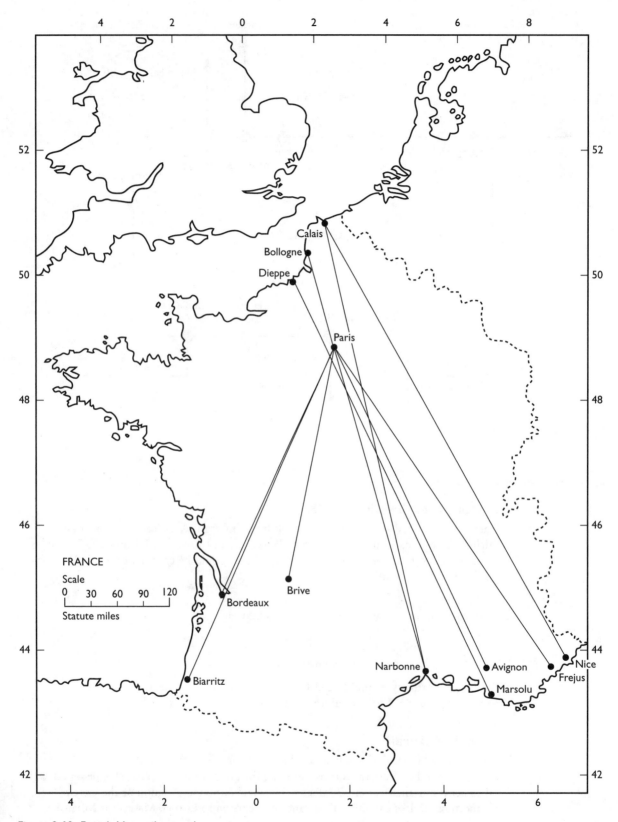

Figure 2.12 French Motorail network

Passengers must book overnight sleepers on the French Motorail and these vary according to the class of ticket booked. All accommodation is air conditioned.

- First class accommodation may be in:
  - single sleeper which is a single bed compartment fitted with a washbasin and shaver point
  - special sleeper which is a smaller compartment having a single bed
  - double sleeper which has an upper and lower bed with a washbasin and shaver point.
- Second class accommodation may be in:
  - tourist T2 compartments which have berths for two persons, either one above the other, or in the case of Upper T2 compartments side by side but reached by a ladder; both types of T2 have a washbasin
  - tourist T3 compartments which have an upper, middle and lower bed plus a washbasin and shaver point
  - couchettes which are bunk berths in a compartment designed for four in first class, or six in second class. There are no washing facilities in couchettes; passengers are not segregated according to sex.

On French Motorail, vehicles are generally loaded up to one hour before departure and are usually available for collection half an hour after the train arrives. However, the collection time can vary with the Paris–Grenoble collection being the following day and the Paris–Lisbon collection two days after loading. The details should therefore be checked for each client. Reductions are available for clients who hold BR Senior Citizen or Family Railcards and published rates normally apply to single journeys.

French Motorail markets its advantages over driving through France as

- less hassle than driving
- savings on petrol, wear and tear and motorway tolls
- savings on hotel bills and travelling time
- arriving relaxed.

Ferries

Car ferries are the traditional way for UK travellers to cross the Channel and in recent years they have marketed strongly against the threat posed by the Channel Tunnel. Car ferries may in fact be regular ships, hovercraft or the newer designs of the seacat and high speed sea-service (HSS).

Car ferries are generally purpose built with substantial passenger facilities including:

- lounges
- cabins
- restaurants and bars
- children's play areas
- casinos, arcade machines and discos
- cinema
- foreign exchange facilities
- duty free shopping.

Details of all car ferries and cruise ships are published in the *ABC Cruise and Ferry Guide*. The index is cross-referenced so that information can be obtained through the names of the ships, their operators or the ports they serve. Days of operation are shown, as in airline timetables, by numbers with 1 representing Monday, 2 Tuesday and so on. Air conditioned ships are indicated with an A and stabilised ships are shown with an S. Stabilisers are horizontal fins on the side of the ship which can be extended out from the bows below the water line. The fins have the effect of reducing the roll of the ship so that the ship moves more smoothly. However, sailings still have to be cancelled when the weather is very bad.

Hovercrafts travel on a cushion of air so that they ride above rather than on the waves. However, hovercraft cannot operate in rough weather and are liable to be damaged by heavy seas. In good weather the journey is generally smooth for passengers and the timing is faster than that of a ship on the same route. Both types of car ferries usually have drive-on/drive-off facilities, with vehicles loaded at one end of the craft and driven off at the other end. Some ships also incorporate an extra floor, with the higher level cars loaded first and ramps removed so that the lower deck can be loaded.

The seacat is a catamaran service which operates from Stranraer to Belfast, and Denmark to Sweden. The Stena Sealink HSS is the latest in ferry technology and draws heavily on airline design to offer increased speed and comfort on its two routes between Stranraer and Belfast, and Holyhead and Dun Laoghaire in Ireland.

Car ferry timetables, which use the 24-hour clock and always show local times, normally highlight different season and fare bands by colour coding and most fares are published for single journeys. However, car ferry companies usually offer reduced rate travel for three or five day trips, children, youth fares and senior citizens. The dates of a client's booking should be checked carefully to see if the client can qualify for these discounts. Passenger accommodation in reclining seats or cabins is paid for in each direction of travel and, as on cruise ships, berths indicate beds one above the other. All berths in a cabin must be paid for. The cost of transporting vehicles depends on the length and overall height of the vehicle. Tickets are similar to those for airlines and care should be taken to complete all passenger and travel details in the required boxes. The ticket booklets can have up to seven pages for:

- accountancy counterfoil
- agent's copy
- up to four passenger counterfoils, depending on the journey booked
- the client's receipt on the back page.

Le Shuttle

Le Shuttle Holidays is Eurotunnel's tour operator which takes clients through the Channel Tunnel in drive-on/drive-off trains designed to carry passengers in their own cars. The journey between Folkestone and Calais takes 35 minutes and, once fully operational, the trains will run for 24 hours a day each day of the year (Fig. 2.13).

Both British and French customs formalities are completed prior to departing and tax and duty free shopping is provided in both terminals.

Air travel

Air travel is the first choice of about 85% of UK holidaymakers, in spite of delays at airports and tight security measures. Tour operators use both charter and scheduled flights in their package holiday arrangements.

Scheduled services

A scheduled service operates to a timetable and is committed to fly whether or not the aircraft is filled. To offset the fixed costs of flying on scheduled routes, the airlines offer

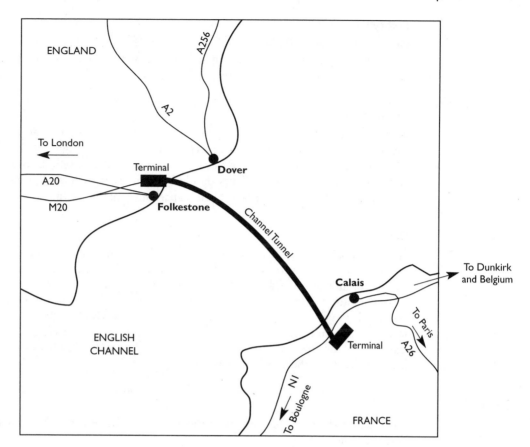

Figure 2.13
Channel Tunnel

special group inclusive tour rates (SGITS) to the tour operators. Package holidays which make use of seats on scheduled aircraft are referred to as Inclusive Tours by Excursion (ITX).

Charter flights

A charter flight is commissioned for a specific period of time and usually flies a full load of passengers to a given destination. Package holidays which make use of chartered aircraft are referred to as Inclusive Tours by Charter (ITC).

Aircraft may be chartered for a specific flight or over a period of time, such as six or twelve months. This type of charter is know as *time charter*.

Flight series

More commonly in the package holiday trade an aircraft will be chartered for a *flight series*, making it available for example at the same time each week for specific flights.

Back to back

By using flight series charters, tour operators can reduce costs and aim to fill their aircraft to a destination. They can book clients who are going to different resorts and hotels, but in the same locality, on the same aircraft. This type of operation is known as *back to back* as the flight out is filled with holidaymakers and the flight back will bring other holidaymakers home.

Empty legs

One disadvantage of flight series charters is that inevitably there will be an empty flight home at the beginning of the season and an empty flight out at the end of the season. These empty flights are referred to as empty legs.

Consolidation

Sometimes, if bookings are poor from a specific airport a tour operator will require clients to take a flight from another airport. This way of changing flight arrangements is known as consolidating. Some travel agencies specialise in selling consolidated flights at a reduced rate. However, clients should be aware that such bookings carry restrictions and it may be impossible to cancel and obtain a refund.

Flight only

Flight only sales using charter seats are also sold to individual clients. However, international airline agreements define that charter flights should be sold in conjunction with accommodation and it is for this reason that flight only sales include minimal accommodation. Such accommodation is really provided only to fulfil the letter of the law and is in no way intended for occupation. Clients who book flight only charter seats should also be made aware of the fact that they need to arrange their own transfers to and from the airport at the resort and they should always reconfirm their flights at least 24 hours before departure.

Car hire

Car hire bookings can be made with the major companies through computerised booking systems on

- AMADEUS
- APOLLO
- GALILEO
- SABRE
- SYSTEM ONE
- WORLDSPAN.

The types of cars used by most international car hire companies are shown on the SIPP (Standard Inline Passenger Procedures) car matrix in Fig. 2.14.

For example EDAR indicates an economy sized, four-door car with automatic transmission and air conditioning. STAN indicates a standard convertible with automatic transmission but no air conditioning.

Renters should normally be over the age of 21, but those who are under 25 years of age usually have to pay a daily supplement. The normal maximum age for hiring a car is 70 years of age. Drivers need to produce a valid driving licence which is at least twelve months old and in some cases they may also have to give information about their driving record. Where the licence is in a foreign language drivers will be required to produce an international driving licence in addition to their own.

Additional charges may be made for

- child seats
- luggage racks
- ski racks
- mileage
- one way rentals
- drop off in another country in Europe or state in USA
- local taxes.

Car class	Car type	Transmission	Aircond
M Mini	B 2 door	A Automatic	R Yes
E Economy	C 2 door or 4 door	M Manual	N No
C Compact	D 4 door		
I Intermediate	S Sports Car		
S Standard	T Convertible		
F Full Size	W Wagon		
P Premium	V Van		
L Luxury	F 4 Wheel Drive		
X Special	J All Terrain		
	P Pick Up		
	L Limo		
	T Truck		
	R Recreation Vehicle		
	X Special		

Figure 2.14 SIPP (Standard Inline Passenger Procedures) code to identify car types

The price of car hire should be checked carefully to ensure how much insurance cover is included in the price. Insurance can cover

- damage to the vehicle
- claims for bodily injury
- claims for property damage
- injury or death for the driver or occupants of the car.

The following are the main types of insurance which are offered by the car hire companies:

CDW Collision Damage Waiver covers the renter for the cost of repair to the car in the case of an accident

PAI Personal Accident Insurance covers the renter for the rental period, and all occupants of the car while travelling in the car, for death and medical expenses

LIS Liability Insurance Supplement raises the limit of both personal insurance and liability for damage to others to $1 million

SLI Supplement Liability Insurance is the same as LIS

PEC Personal Effects Insurance covers the personal property of the renter and members of the renter's immediate family who are household residents, against loss or damage caused by fire, theft, explosion, lightning or accident to the rental vehicle.

Loss Damage Waiver (LDW) is not insurance, but is offered by some car hire companies as an optional waiver of the renter's responsibility to pay for damage to or loss of the rental vehicle, including costs and expenses resulting from collision, theft or vandalism.

Car hire companies also vary in the procedures used for refuelling the car. The main procedures in use are

- the renter pays for the petrol in the car and brings it back with an empty fuel tank
- the fuel tank is full when the renter receives the car and the renter should bring it back full
- the fuel tank is full when the renter receives the car and the renter pays to fill up the car's fuel tank when returning it.

The travel agent either can charge the client in full for the car hire or can give a recommendation voucher to the client which ensures that the appropriate commission is paid to the travel agent when the client hires the car at the destination. Car hire companies take credit cards in preference to cash for payment. In fact clients who wish to pay in cash are normally required to pay a substantial deposit in addition to the estimated cost of the hire and sometimes a return airline ticket may be requested as security.

The process of returning hired cars is made as simple as possible with rapid return procedures whereby clients simply record the mileage and return the keys in an envelope, having already signed their credit card payment when they took the car. Automated rapid return is used by some large companies where a hand held computer is used to record the details on each car as it is returned to the parking bay. Again this type of rapid return is dependent on the client having paid by credit card. In the more popular resorts car hire is available at the airports or a coach transfer is provided to the car hire depot.

Revision Questions

Primary level

1 In connection with car hire what do you understand by
   CDW
   PAI

2 According to SIPP, what type of car is represented by
   CBAN
   IDMR

3 A client wishes to book a car for two adults and three children aged 6, 8 and 9 for a touring holiday in Portugal. If price is not an issue, which car would you recommend and why?
   (a) IDAN
   (b) FRAR
   (c) LFAN.

4 State FIVE differences between charter and schedule flight operations.

5 (a) When using a Family Discount Card on National Express, how many children would be entitled to free travel?
   (b) What type of discounted fare on National Express could be offered to clients in their 40s who were not entitled to apply for a Family Discount Card?

6 On a National Express Rapide service from Liverpool to London
   (a) name THREE services which should be provided on the coach
   (b) state the approximate journey time
   (c) identify the destination in London.

7 State FIVE provisions which are made by British Rail to accommodate persons who are disabled.

8 Name the following
   (a) the InterCity station immediately north of York
   (b) the London station for travel to Harwich
   (c) the London station for travel to the east cost of Scotland
   (d) the station furthest west on the south coast of Wales line
   (e) the most northerly InterCity station in Great Britain
   (f) the London station for travel to the south west point of England.

9 Which two services use the Channel Tunnel?

10 On the same route which would be the fastest mode of transport?
   (a) regular ferry
   (b) hovercraft
   (c) HSS
   (d) seacat.

Advanced level

1 In connection with car hire, what do you understand by
   LIS
   PEC

2 Use Fig. 2.15 to calculate
   (a) the cost of a compact auto car with a luggage rack for two weeks, starting 15 February in Malta
   (b) the cost of a ten day rental in Portugal, starting 24 January, of a four-door economy car with a child's car seat, if the driver is aged 22
   (c) the cost of a 23 day rental in Spain of a mini, starting 21 December.

MALTA

Rental period		daily 3–5 days	one week	extra days	2–4 weeks	extra days
ECMN	Economy	14	80	12	75	12
CCMN	Compact	15	85	13	77	12
CCAN	Compact auto	18	105	15	94	14
IWMN	Intermediate Stw	21	120	18	12	17
MVMN	Mini Van	24	138	21	129	19
IFMN	Intermediate 4x4	24	142	21	134	20

PORTUGAL

Rental period		daily 3–5 days	one week	extra days	2–4 weeks	extra days
MCMN	Mini	15	86	13	80	12
EBMN	Economy	17	100	15	93	15
EDMN	Economy	19	110	17	103	15
CCMN	Compact	25	143	21	135	20
ICMN	Intermediate	27	156	23	145	23

SPAIN

Rental period		daily 3–5 days	one week	extra days	2–4 weeks	extra days
MBMN	Mini	17	96	15	89	15
ECMN	Economy	19	112	17	103	16
EXMN	Economy	23	132	20	123	18
CCMN	Compact	26	152	22	140	21
ICMR	Intermediate A/C	28	166	25	154	23
SXMR	Standard A/C	36	210	31	196	29

Rates include: Unlimited mileage, CDW, PAI, Theft Protection and Local Tax

Extra charges: Luggage rack 55p per day, Child Car Seat 50p per day,
Airport Charges may apply for rental commencing from airports – please check at time of reservation

Surcharges: for drivers under the age of 25 £10 per day
Peak Season 20–27 December £12 per week, or part of a week, for the entire duration of rental

Figure 2.15 Car hire rates: valid 1 November to 31 March

3 A client, who will travel by AMTRAK train from Florida to Hilton Head in South Carolina, wishes to hire a car for a week. At the end of the week the car will be returned to Atlanta airport. Savannah or Charleston railway stations are equally convenient for Hilton Head but which would be the better location for the car hire to commence? Give TWO reasons for your answer.

4 Name ONE car ferry company which serves EACH of the following routes

(a) Plymouth to Santander
(b) Dover to Calais
(c) Harwich to Gothenburg
(d) Portsmouth to Cherbourg.

5 In relation to French Motorail briefly describe the following types of accommodation
T2
T3
couchette.

6 List THREE factors which can determine the cost of travel on a car ferry.

7 State FIVE on-board facilities (excluding bars and restaurants) normally available to passengers travelling on a cross-Channel ferry.

8 Calculate the total commission earnings from the following sales
   (a) car hire for three days @ £74 per day at 20% commission
   (b) ferry crossing for a couple and their car costing £345.00 at 9% commission
   (c) Le Shuttle two night short break for a group of four friends costing £105 per person for the first night and £30 per night for extra nights at 10% commission.

9 In relation to air travel what do you understand by the following
   ITX
   SGITS
   ITC
   flight series
   empty leg
   consolidation.

10 Name TWO computerised reservations systems which could be used to book both car hire and hotel accommodation for a client.

3) *Accommodation*

Holiday accommodation needs to cater for a full range of tastes and circumstances. It is the role of the travel agent to point out distinctions between the different types of accommodation and assist the client in making a suitable choice. At the time of booking the client's main concern will possibly be the resort or the flight time, but once the client has arrived in the resort, the accommodation will assume new importance.

The client has several choices of accommodation:

- hotels (with a bedroom and possibly some meals included in the price)
- self-catering (with rooms but no meals included in the price)
- private accommodation
- holiday centres.

Hotels

Rating schemes

Hotel star ratings are awarded in many countries by various organisations and sometimes by tour operators according to the facilities offered in the hotels. Within the UK, star ratings are awarded by the Automobile Association (AA) and the Royal Automobile Club (RAC); furthermore the tourist boards offer crown ratings.

AA and RAC ratings

The AA and RAC one to five star ratings are based on the facilities offered in the main areas of the hotel and within the bedrooms. For instance a hotel rated as one star by the AA would need to have, among other facilities, a lounge with some seats and a cooked breakfast for residents, whereas an AA five star hotel would be required to have, among other facilities, public rooms with an atmosphere of luxury and a cooked breakfast with a choice of hot dishes for residents and non-residents. A list of facilities in relation to each AA star rating is shown in Fig. 3.1.

Tourist board schemes

The ratings of the tourist boards in England, Scotland and Wales are somewhat different from the AA and RAC in that these ratings take into account not only the facilities offered but also the standard of those facilities. It is for this reason that the tourist boards offer both crowns and a statement of recommendation. Accommodation in hotels or guest houses is classified with crowns for the facilities offered and is also graded with a recommendation from approved to highly commended for the standard of those facilities and the service offered. The grading of the tourist boards indicates the quality of the warmth of welcome, the atmosphere, personal comfort of guests,

	1 star	2 star	3 star	4 star	5 star
all bedrooms with hot and cold water, electric shaver point and at least one other power point	●	●	●	●	●
adequate bath and lavatory arrangements	●	●	●	●	●
meals provided for residents	●	●	●	●	●
private bathrooms for at least half of the bedrooms		●	●	●	●
WC on each floor and at least one bathroom to serve every four bedrooms without private facilities		●			
telephone and colour television in bedroom at no extra charge		●	●	●	●
wide choice of meals for residents		●	●	●	●
more spacious accommodation and higher standards of furnishings			●	●	●
private facilities in all bedrooms, with 80% having a bath			●	●	●
separate facilities for ladies and gentlemen toilet facilities for non-residents			●	●	●
lifts			●	●	●
telephone and colour television in all bedrooms at no extra charge			●	●	●
full meal facilities for residents and non-residents daily			●	●	●
high standard of comfort, cuisine and service				●	●
spacious bedrooms with superior furnishings				●	●
private bathrooms with shower facility in all bedrooms				●	●
luxurious room furnishings and a variety of additional facilities such as bookstall, flower shop, hairdressing salon, business and/or recreational facilities					●
uniformed staff available to drive guests' cars to and from garages, storage room for luggage					●
wide selection of meals, including à la carte menu					●

The above is a selection of the requirements for AA classification. Those hotels which have approved status are recommended establishments which do not meet the minimum classification requirement in respect of porterage, reception facilities and choice of meals.

Figure 3.1 AA star ratings for hotel accommodation

efficiency and friendliness of staff, condition of decorations and furnishings, the appearance of the buildings and the tidiness of the grounds and gardens. The three grading awards are

- approved, which indicates an acceptable quality standard
- commended, which indicates a good quality standard
- highly commended, which indicates a high quality standard.

A highly commended two crown establishment offers a higher quality than a commended four crown establishment, although not offering as many facilities and services. Therefore, in certain circumstances a two crown hotel may be better for a particular client than a three or even four crown hotel. Details of the facilities required for tourist board crown ratings are shown in Fig. 3.2.

Jersey Tourist Board has similar ratings to those in the UK but these are based on suns for hotels and diamonds for guest houses and the Northern Ireland Tourist Board has a classification system based on letters (A, B, C). Other European countries have their own national system of classification of hotels, with letters used in the Republic of Ireland and Greece, and stars in Belgium, France, Italy, Luxembourg, the Netherlands and Spain. There is no classification of hotels in Germany, Denmark or Portugal.

Tour operators' ratings

Many tour operators list their own hotel ratings, often using a system associated with the name of the company. Thomson Holidays has a T rating which works in a similar way to the AA star rating, with the higher number of Ts indicating a better hotel standard. The ratings are from one to four Ts and the hotels which are known to Thomson for their particularly high standard of food, service and comfort are classified as 'Blue Ribbon' hotels.

Other schemes

The Michelin system indicates comfort by house symbols, restaurants by the number of crossed knives and forks and cooking excellence by stars. Egon Ronay stars are also awarded for excellence in cooking and crowns indicate luxury in restaurants. Les Routiers plaques are placed on selected establishments with a charge for inclusion in their guide.

Rating systems are provided only as a guide for clients and it is sometimes worthwhile comparing the descriptions of an apartment or hotel abroad in more than one brochure. Travel agents can also refer to the agents' *Hotel Gazetteer* which provides a frank 'warts and all' description of accommodation offered in the tour operators' brochures. Clients booking directly with a hotel can normally be provided with an illustrated brochure or leaflet from the hotel.

Meal arrangements

Hotel meal arrangements may be

- bed and breakfast basis, sometimes called Continental Plan (CP)
- half board, sometimes called Modified American Plan (MAP)
- full board, sometimes called American Plan (AP).

Package holidays in many brochures provide a choice of half board or, for the payment of a daily supplement, full board.

	listed	1 crown	2 crown	3 crown	4 crown	5 crown
clean and comfortable accommodation with adequate heating at no extra charge	●	●	●	●	●	●
clean towels, fresh soap and no extra charge for baths and showers	●	●	●	●	●	●
breakfast	●	●	●	●	●	●
comfortable lounge or sitting area		●	●	●	●	●
a washbasin in the room or private bathroom		●	●	●	●	●
beds no smaller than 6'3" × 3' (single) or 6'3" × 4'6" (double), with no nylon sheets		●	●	●	●	●
cooked breakfast		●	●	●	●	●
use of telephone		●	●	●	●	●
tourist information		●	●	●	●	●
help with luggage			●	●	●	●
colour television in the lounge or bedroom			●	●	●	●
double beds with access and tables at both sides and bedside lights			●	●	●	●
early morning tea/coffee and a hot beverage in the evening			●	●	●	●
early morning call			●	●	●	●
private bathrooms for at least one-third of the bedrooms				●	●	●
easy chair, full length mirror, luggage rack and tea/coffee in the bedroom				●	●	●
hair drier, shoe cleaning equipment and ironing facilities available				●	●	●
public telephone or one in the bedroom				●	●	●
a hot evening meal				●	●	●
private bathrooms for at least two-thirds of the bedrooms					●	●
colour television, radio and telephone in the bedroom					●	●
room service with drinks and light snacks between 7 am and 11 pm					●	●
lounge service of drinks and snacks to midnight					●	●
evening meals with wine, last orders 8.30 pm or later					●	●
a quiet sitting area					●	●
laundry services, toiletries, message taking, newspapers on request					●	●

Figure 3.2 Tourist board crown ratings for hotels and guest houses

	listed	1 crown	2 crown	3 crown	4 crown	5 crown
all bedrooms with baths, shower and WC en suite						●
direct dial telephone, writing table						●
shoe cleaning and daily clothes pressing service						●
24 hour lounge service and room service with hot meals up to midnight						●
restaurant open for breakfast, lunch and dinner with last orders 9 pm or later						●
full liquor licence						●
night porter and porterage						●

Figure 3.2 cont Tourist board crown ratings for hotels and guest houses

Half board

Half board in the UK usually means bed, breakfast and the evening meal but in other European countries it is becoming more and more common for it to mean bed, breakfast and either the midday or the evening meal. The travel agent needs to check this with the hotel or the tour operator in order to be able to inform the client.

Full board

Full board means that all three meals are provided and, if the client wishes to go out for a full day, a packed lunch can be ordered. Packed lunches vary greatly from hotel to hotel, with the larger hotel chains providing excellent boxed picnics including soft drinks.

European plan

It should be noted that hotels in the USA and the Far East do not normally include any meals in the basic hotel price, although a restaurant is usually provided on site. This arrangement is known as European Plan (EP).

Rooms

Hotel rooms can be

- single rooms
- executive rooms
- double rooms with a double, king- or queen-size bed
- twin rooms with two single beds
- family rooms which may be described as three bedded, four bedded or simply large rooms.

Single rooms

Single rooms can be very small, without facilities such as a balcony, or they may be larger rooms which would normally take two or more people. In the UK, single rooms are usually smaller than average, but in some European resorts where the hotel's rooms may be all of a standard size, a supplement may be charged for the sole use of a larger room.

Executive rooms

Executive rooms are usually twin rooms which are furbished to a high standard for business people, who can expect to find a lounge and sleeping area, a desk with a supply of paper, a telephone and possibly a fax and a small fridge with drinks. Such executive rooms are most commonly found in four and five star hotels.

Double and twin rooms

A double room is almost always available in British hotels but is more unusual in the rest of Europe. The distinction may have to be made for the client between the implications of a double or a twin room. Sometimes a hotel will provide twin beds which are placed side by side or can be separated as required.

Family rooms

The standard family room varies but the hotel or the tour operator will have details on whether the rooms are genuinely large or if the hotel management will simply put a roll-up bed on the floor. Hotel rooms in the USA normally have two large double or king-size beds as standard, sleeping four people. As the price charged is for the room, this type of accommodation is very economical for a family, but not so much for a couple or a single person.

Self-catering

All self-catering accommodation should include living space, sleeping areas, the use of a bathroom, and cooking facilities so that clients can either cook for themselves or eat out.

Classification system

The UK tourist boards provide a classification system for self-catering establishments based on a number of keys. Figure 3.3 gives details of this classification system.

	1 key	2 key	3 key	4 key	5 key
full details of the accommodation and how to find it	●	●	●	●	●
thoroughly cleaned and checked before every letting	●	●	●	●	●
exterior and interior decorations, furnishings, etc. maintained in good condition	●	●	●	●	●
gardens (where present) maintained in good order	●	●	●	●	●
reasonable space for movement throughout, with adequate table and seating provision	●	●	●	●	●
television (may be extra charge)	●	●			
adequate heating and lighting throughout	●	●	●	●	●

Figure 3.3 Tourist board key ratings for self-catering accommodation

	1 key	2 key	3 key	4 key	5 key
full range of crockery, cutlery, etc., cooker (including oven and grill) and fridge	●	●	●	●	●
local tourist information	●	●	●	●	●
easy chairs or sofas for all		●	●	●	●
colour television (may be extra charge)		●			
bedside units or shelves		●	●	●	●
heating in all rooms		●	●	●	●
fridge with icemaker, automatic kettle		●	●	●	●
colour television (at no extra charge)			●	●	●
minimum adult beds 6'3" × 3' (single) or 6'3" × 4'6" (double)			●	●	●
bedside lights			●	●	●
linen and towels available (may be extra charge)			●	●	●
dressing table, wardrobe, etc. in adult bedrooms			●	●	●
vacuum cleaner, iron and ironing board			●	●	●
dressing table, wardrobe, etc. in all bedrooms				●	●
all sleeping in beds or bunks, i.e. no bed settees				●	●
supplementary lighting in living room				●	●
garden furniture – where patio or garden				●	●
automatic washing machine and tumble drier or laundry service					●
all rooms with automatically controlled heaters					●
bath and shower, with second bathroom and/or WC where more than six people					●
telephone					●
hair drier					●
food processor, microwave, dishwasher and fridge freezer					●

Figure 3.3 cont Tourist board key ratings for self-catering accommodation

As with hotels, the tourist boards indicate the quality of the facilities and services in self-catering establishments with a grading statement using the same approved, commended or highly commended statement. In Scotland and Wales there is also a Q Scheme which grades holiday parks with one to five ticks according to the quality of their provision. In England the Rose Award is given to those parks which not only provide facilities to a high standard but also have first class caravan holiday homes for hire.

Welcome pack

Many tour operators or apartment managers provide a 'welcome pack' of groceries on arrival at the request of the client. These packs either are included in the cost of the accommodation or should be paid for on arrival.

Types of accommodation

Self-catering accommodation can be provided for indoor and outdoor holidays in:

- studios
- apartments
- villas
- tents
- caravans
- barges
- boats.

Indoor holidays

A studio is usually a room containing the bed, sitting area and a small kitchenette. In the USA studios are sometimes referred to as 'efficiencies'. Apartments have at least one separate bedroom as well as a sitting and kitchen area. Villas can vary in size and sometimes come with their own private swimming pool.

Outdoor holidays

Outdoor holidays in tents, caravans, barges or boats are becoming very popular both within the UK and abroad. Some tour operators specialise in camping holidays, especially in France, where the tents are already put up on site and all necessary equipment is provided. Static caravans are also provided on many sites and in addition touring caravans can be hired in the UK. Bookings for canal holidays in the UK have risen steadily since the 1970s and it is now possible to hire barges and boats in most parts of the UK and travel at a leisurely pace along the networks outlined in Fig. 3.4.

Flotilla holidays abroad are also available where clients book a yacht which joins a group sailing in a specific area with a guide. Flotilla holidays are particularly popular in the waters off Turkey.

Private accommodation

Booking into private accommodation enables clients to mix more with local people. Examples of such accommodation are

- gîtes in France
- tavernas in Greece and pensions in the rest of Europe
- guest houses in New England, USA.

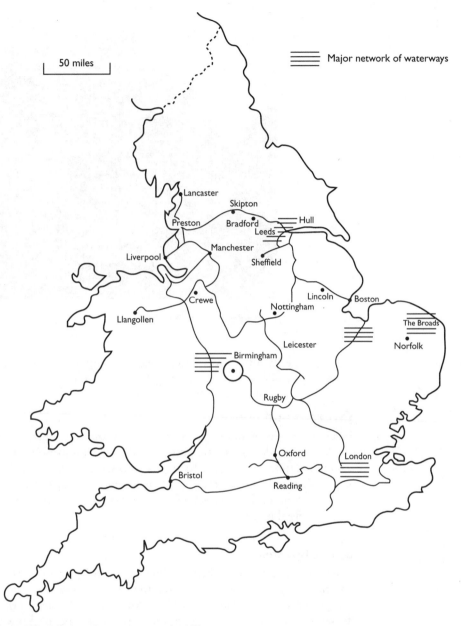

Figure 3.4 Canals and waterways in the UK

Gîtes are a system of privately owned self-catering units which are peculiar to France. These individual properties are modernised with the help of the French government and supervised by the non-profit making Fédération Nationale des Gîtes. The company can be contacted through its London address at 178 Piccadilly, London W1V 0AL. A gîte may be a small cottage, a village house, a flat in a farmhouse or rooms in a château. As they can be in quiet rural areas, they afford a good opportunity for clients who wish to observe and even become part of French life and culture. The added financial advantage is that when opting to eat in local bars and restaurants the

Figure 3.5 Gîte in St Just, Brittany, France

holidaymaker will find prices much cheaper than in the fashionable resorts. Figure 3.5 shows a typical gîte and the Gîtes de France symbol.

Tavernas and pensions

Tavernas in Greece and pensions in other European countries are rooms or bed and breakfast provided in private homes or above small local restaurants. Such accommodation is attractive to clients who wish to mix with the local community, eat local dishes and learn or improve their foreign language. The accommodation is usually very basic and meals in Greek tavernas are often taken in the open air patios surrounding the bar or restaurant.

Guest houses

Guest houses, which offer bed and breakfast (B&B) in family homes, have been a traditional type of accommodation in the UK for many years. In the first half of the twentieth century, the landladies of Blackpool could be sure of their clients throughout the season, as well as from year to year, because as one local town's holiday week finished so another would start. Recently guest houses have been offered as an alternative accommodation for visitors to the USA, particularly in New England. B&B signs are not generally displayed in the USA but most homes offering this service are listed in directories and Local Convention and Visitors' Bureaux can provide information.

Holiday centres

In the 1920s and 1930s private cars became fairly widespread in the UK and for those who could not afford a private car there were the coaches or charabancs. This new means of transport encouraged cheaper holidays by the sea, mainly in camps with tents or chalets. At this time the camps took up to 300 people but in 1935 Billy Butlin built his first holiday camp at Skegness in Lincolnshire to take 3,000 guests. Billy Butlin worked on the idea that he would make more money by taking a small profit from a lot of people, rather than a large profit from a few. This is an idea which still holds true in the travel industry today.

Entertainment

Once he had his first guests at Skegness, Billy Butlin could not understand why the faces around him were so glum when he had provided everything for their comfort and the beach was only a stone's throw away. It did not take him long to realise that these people were bored and so the famous 'red coats' were born when he persuaded a friend to don a red blazer and organise some entertainment. Ever since, entertainment with resident red, blue or yellow 'coats' has been a symbol of British holiday camps.

Holiday camps have changed their names and with it their image in recent years. They are now known as holiday centres or villages. Many centres have fun pools with slides and wave machines, and some have shed their family image and now appeal to adults only.

Butlins

Butlins holiday camps, now owned by the Rank Organisation, were totally updated during the 1980s. Five of the original camps have been renamed Holiday Worlds and the brochure also offers holidays in five hotels. The Holiday Worlds offer self-catering, half board or full board accommodation. Entertainment facilities include fairgrounds, fully equipped theatres, fun pools with slides and flume rides and clubs to occupy children of all ages (Fig. 3.6).

Pontins

Fred Pontin started his holiday camps in the late 1940s and today's brochure offers a choice of twenty Holiday Centres around England, Scotland and Wales, as well as

Figure 3.6 Butlins Holiday Centre

Plemont Bay on Jersey. Five of the mainland centres are Chalet Hotels with full table service as well as all the entertainment offered in the other centres. Five of the Pontins Holiday Centres offer adults only holidays which are very popular with older people, particularly during the summer months of the school holidays.

Center Parcs

Center Parcs has holiday villages in Sherwood Forest in Nottinghamshire, Suffolk in East Anglia and Longleat in Wiltshire as well as in the Netherlands, and each village has a central dome over the swimming area creating a subtropical paradise. The self-catering accommodation at Center Parcs is usually in well furnished log cabins and a variety of outdoor activities are provided on site.

Figure 3.7 summarises the different types of accommodation described so far.

ACCOMMODATION							
	bedroom	kitchen and living area	breakfast	breakfast plus one meal	breakfast plus two meals	entertainment included	alternative description
Self-catering						possibly	
studio		●					
apartment	●	●					
villa	●	●					
tent	●	●					
caravan	●	●					
boat/barge	●	●					
Hotels						possibly	
room only	●						European Plan (EP)
B & B	●		●				Continental Plan (CP)
half board	●			●			Modified American Plan (MAP)
full board	●				●		American Plan (AP)
Guest houses	●		●	possibly			
Tavernas	●		●	possibly			
Holiday centres	●	●	●	possibly	possibly	●	

Figure 3.7 Summary of types of accommodation

Accommodation bookings

Accommodation bookings can be made directly with the provider or through a tour operator. Bookings made directly with hotels and other accommodations can be confirmed by using a computerised reservation system, a pre-payment voucher or the client's credit card number. Guaranteed reservations made with a credit card or a pre-payment voucher will be kept for the client beyond the normal checking-in time, which is generally between 16.00 and 18.00 hours. For bookings which have not been guaranteed in this way, clients should be advised to inform the hotel if they are likely to be late checking-in, otherwise their rooms may be sold before they arrive.

Hotel rates

According to the type of booking, hotel rates may be

- rack rate
- corporate rate
- group rate.

Rack rate is the standard charge and will be the highest. Corporate rate is offered to companies and will vary according to the amount of business done with the hotel. Group rates are offered to parties of ten or more people booking together who are normally offered about 10% discount.

Extra facilities

Extra facilities can be booked at some hotels. Such facilities might be

- a balcony
- a sea view from the room
- a room on the ground or top floor
- a room over the swimming pool
- a room with facilities for a person using a wheelchair.

Some tour operators charge a supplement for extra facilities such as those above and this should be pointed out to the client at the time of booking. If such facilities are described by a tour operator as being 'available in most rooms' then the client's requirements should be noted and the request passed on to the tour operator. Supplements for extra facilities are normally charged per person per day and they may initially appear to be quite small. However a 75p supplement for a balcony in a family room for a family of four for two weeks would cost

$$75p \times 4 \times 14 = £42.00$$

Accommodation reservations and payments

Gazetteers

A variety of gazetteers are published giving details of hotels by area around the world. Figure 3.8 is an extract from the *ABC Hotel and Travel Index* and shows the main information to be found in the gazetteer.

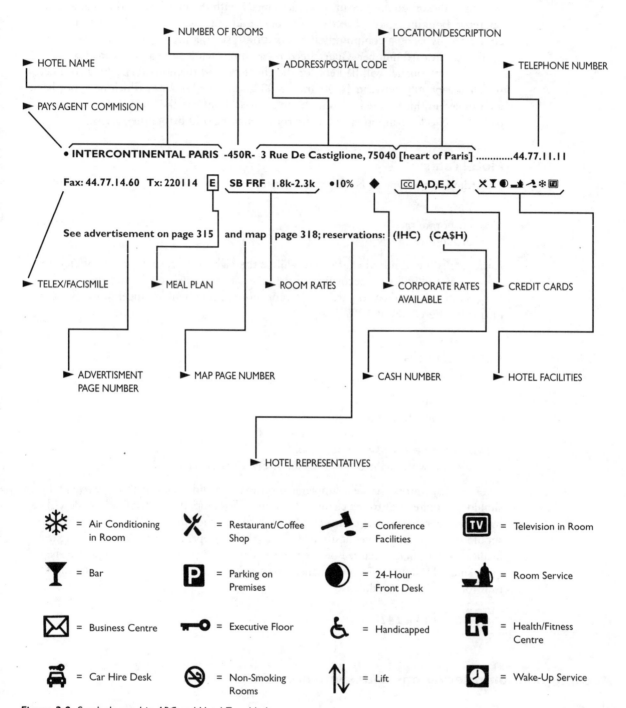

Figure 3.8 Symbols used in *ABC and Hotel Travel Index*

In a hotel gazetteer it is normal to find listed:

- name, address, telephone and fax numbers of the hotel
- number and types of rooms
- hotel facilities
- meal plans and room rates
- types of credits cards accepted
- agent's commission
- reference to any maps or advertisements in the gazetteer.

Figure 3.9 shows an extract from the *ABC Hotel and Travel Index* giving information about hotels in the area of Naples, Florida.

According to the gazetteer:

The Best Western Naples Inn is on Ninth Street North, only one minute from the beach. It has 80 suites with bedroom, living room, TV and bathroom costing from $49 to $119 per night which includes continental breakfast. The facilities in the hotel include a restaurant and bar; air conditioning and a car park; 24 hour room service and front desk with a wakeup service; no smoking rooms where required and facilities for handicapped people; a fitness centre and swimming pool; and golf course and tennis courts. The hotel will accept all credit cards except Japan Credit Bureau and they offer 10% commission to travel agents.

The World Tennis Center and Resort is on Airport Road in Naples, only five minutes from the beach. It has 124 single rooms with TV and bathrooms costing $75–$130 per night. Facilities in the complex include a restaurant and bar; air conditioning and a car park; 24 hour room service and facilities for handicapped people. Access, Visa and American Express cards are accepted and bookings can be made through the VIP Reservations in Calgary, Canada, with 15% commission to travel agents.

In fact the gazetteer fails to say that the World Tennis Center accommodation is in luxurious apartments, the tennis courts are more numerous than on any other site in Florida and five minutes from the beach would be in a very fast car! The gazetteers are a prime source of information but the travel agent should always clarify details when making reservations.

Making reservations

Hotel and other accommodation reservations can be made by the travel agent in a variety of ways including

- directly with the hotel
- central reservation office for a large hotel chain
- hotel representative or consortium

NAPLES   ☎ Int: 1 +813

Naples Municipal Airport (APF), 2 miles east of city.

- **BEST WESTERN NAPLES INN –8OR– 2329 Ninth St N. 33940 {1 mi to beach}** .... **(813)261.1148**
  Fax: (813)262.4684 Ⓒ STE $49-119 •10% ♦ CC A,B,C,D,E,X × ∗ ▣ Υ ➡◖ ⌁ ♿ TV ⊛ ☎ 🛄 🅿 🔄 ●
  See advertisement on page 231 and map pg 232; reservations: (BW) (CASH)
- Charter Club Resort on Naples Bay –33R– 1000 10th Ave S. 33940 .... (813)261.5559
  Fax: (813)261.6782 Ⓔ TB $695.1.4k •10% CC A,B,X × ∗ ▣ ⌁ TV 🚗 ☎
- Comfort Inn Downtown on the Bay –100R– 1221 Fifth Ave S. 33940 .... (813)649.5800
  Fax: (813)649.0523 Ⓒ SB $45.95 •10% ♦ CC A,B,C,D,J,X × ∗ ▣ Υ ➡◖ ⌁ ⊠•◖ (CCQ)
- **COVE INN –102R– 1191 8th St South, 33940 {On Bay of Naples}** .... **(813)262.7161**
  Fax: (813)261.6905 Ⓔ SB 60-135 •10% ♦ CC A,B,C,D,X × ∗ ▣ Υ ➡◖ ⌁ ♿ TV 🚗 ☎ 🅿
  See advertisement on page 231
- **DAYS INN & LODGE OF NAPLES –158R– 1925 Davies Blvd, 33942** .... **(813)774.3117**
  Fax: (813)775.5333 Ⓔ SB $44-115, TB 44-115 •10% ♦ CC A,B,C,D,X × ∗ ▣ ➡◖ ⌁ TV ⊛ 🚗 🅿 ●
  See advertisement on page 231 and map pg 232; reservations: (HCR)(DAY₁.₃)(CASH)
- Edgewater Beach –124R– 1901 Gultshore Blvd N, 33940 .... (813)262.6511
  Fax: (813)262.1243 Ⓔ STE $99-1200 •10% CC A,B,D,X × ∗ ▣ Υ ➡◖ ⌁ ⊠ (VIP₃)
- Fairways Resort Inc –38R– 103 Palm River Blvd. 33942 {3 mi from beach} .... (813)597.8181
  Fax: (813)597.5413 Ⓒ SB $40-95, TB 45-85 •10% CC A,B,E,X × ∗ ▣ ➡◖ ⌁ TV ⊛ 🚗 ☎
- Holiday Inn –137R– 1100 Ninth St, N, 33940 {7 blocks from beach} .... (813)262.7146
  Fax: (813)262.1809 Ⓔ SB $49-69 •10% CC A,B,X × ∗ ▣ Υ ➡◖ ⌁ ♿ TV (HOL)
- Howard Johnson Resort Lodge –101R– 221 9th St South. 33940 {In town} .... (813)262.6181
  Fax: (813)262.0318 Ⓒ SB $45-125, TB 55-125 •10% × ∗ ▣ Υ ➡◖ ⌁ ♿ (HOW)(TRT)(APS₂)(EXP₁)
- Inn at Pelican Bay –100R– 800 Vanderbilt Beach Rd, 33963 .... (813)597.8777
  Fax: (813)597.8012 Ⓔ SB $55-160, TB 55-160 •10% CC A,B,X × ∗ ▣ Υ ➡◖ ⌁ ⊠•◖ ⌁
- The Inn Of Naples –64R– 4055 Tamiami Trail, 33940 {3/4 mi to beaches} .... (813)649.5500
  Fax: (813)649.5500 Tx: 205839 Ⓒ SB $60-130 •10% CC A,B,D,X × ∗ ▣ Υ ➡◖ ⌁ ♿ TV (FTS)
- Keewaydin Island –45R– 260 Bay Rd, 33940 [Island] .... (813)262.4149
  Fax: (813)262.8235 Ⓐ SB $125-350 •10% CC A,B,X × ∗ Υ ⌁ 🚗
- **LA PLAYA BEACH & RACQUET INN –173R-9891 Gulf Shore Dr N, 33963** .... **(813)597.3123**
  Fax: (813)597.6278 Tx: 510-951-8531 Ⓔ Rates on request •10% ♦ CC A,B,X × ∗ ▣ 🛄 Υ ➡◖ ⌁ ♿
  See advertisement on page 231 and map pg 232
- Naples Bath & Tennis Club –60R– 4995 Airport Rd N. 33942 .... (813)261.5777
  Fax: (813)649.2045 Ⓔ STE $90-235 •10% CC A,B,X × ∗ ▣ Υ ➡◖ ⌁ ♿ TV
- Naples Beach Hotel & Golf Club –315R– 851 Gulf Shore Blvd N, 33940 .... (813)261.2222
  Fax: (813)261.7380 Ⓔ SB $65-215, TB 65-215 •10% CC A,B,C,D,X × ∗ ▣ Υ (DTR)(LRI)(HRA₁)
- Park Shore Resort –156R– 600 Neapolitan Way,,33940 [4 min drive to beach] .... (813)263.2222
  Fax: (813)263.0946 Tx: 8811 42 Newport Ⓔ SB $72-170 •10% CC A,B,X × ∗ ▣ 🛄 Υ ➡◖ (FTS₁)
- Port of the Islands Resort & Marina –175R– 25000 Tamiami Trail E. 33961 .... (813)394.3101
  Fax: (813)394.4335 Ⓒ SB $65-95. TB 65-100 •10% CC A,B,C,D,X × ∗ ▣ Υ ➡◖ ⌁ ♿ TV (FLO₁)
- Quality Inn Golf & Country Club –204R– 4100 Golden Gate Pkwy, 33999 .... (813)455.1010
  Fax: (813)455.4038 Ⓒ SB $45-190, TB 45-190 •10% CC A,B,C,D,J,X × ∗ ▣ 🛄 Υ ➡◖ •◖ (CCQ)
- Quality Inn Gulfcoast –114R– 2555 N Tamiami Trail, 33940 .... (813)261.6046
  Fax: (813)261.5742 Ⓒ SB $45-100, TB 55-100 •10% CC A,B,C,D,E,X × ∗ ▣ Υ ➡◖ ⌁ (CCQ)(ARS₁)
- **The REGISTRY RESORT NAPLES –474R– 475 Seagate Dr, 33940** .... **(813)597.3232**
  Fax: (813)566.7919 Tx: 9102400335 Ⓔ SB $110-250 •10% CC A,B,C,D,X × ∗ ▣ 🛄 Υ ➡◖ ⌁ ♿ TV
  See advertisement on page 233 and map pg 232; reservations: (UI)(ARS₁)
- **The RITZ-CARLTON NAPLES –463R– 280 Vanderbilt Beach Rd, 33963** .... **(813)598.3300**
  Fax: (813)598.6690 Ⓔ $295-450, TB 295-450, •10% ♦ CC A,B,C,D,E,X × ∗ ▣ 🛄 Υ ➡◖ ⌁
  See advertisement on page 233 and map pg 232; reservations: (AMR₃)(RCH₁.₃)
- Spinnaker Inn –111R– 6600 Dudley Dr, 33999 [Off 1-75 Exit 16] .... (813)434.0444
  Fax: (813)434.0414 Ⓔ SB $38-60, TB 42-65 •10% CC A,B,X × ∗ ▣ Υ ➡◖ ⌁ ♿ TV
- Super 8 Motel Naples –104R– Exit 15 at 1-75, 33942 [Alligator Alley] .... (813)455.0808
  Fax: (813)455.7124 Ⓒ SB $43, TB 53 •10% CC A,B,C,D,X × ∗ ▣ Υ ⊛ 🚗 🅿 (SUP)
- Tennis Village at Windstar –48R– 4500 Bayshore Dr. 33962 .... (813)775.1400
  Ⓔ SB $110-135, TB 110-135 •10% CC A,B × ∗ ▣ Υ ➡◖ ⌁ ♿ TV
- The Tides Motor Inn –27R– 1801 Gulf Shore Blvd N. 33940 [On Gulf of Mexico] .... (813)262.6196
  Fax: (813)262.3055 Ⓔ SB $62-107 •7% CC A,B,X × TV 🚗 🅿
- **TRAILS END MOTEL –50R– 309 S. Tamiami Trail, 33940 [dwntn]** .... **(813)262.6336**
  Fax: (813)262.3381 Ⓒ SB $33-110 •10% ♦ CC A,B,D,X × 🅿 ⌁ TV ⊛ 🚗 🅿 🔄 ●
  See advertisement on this page and map pg 232
- Tropics Inn –60R– 312 Eighth Ave S, 33940 [2 blocks from beach] .... (813)262.5194
  Fax: (813)262.4876 Ⓒ SB $36-78 •10% CC A,B,D,X × ∗ ▣ Υ ➡◖ ⌁ ♿ TV
- Vanderbilt Beach Motel –66R– 9225 Gulf Shore Dr N, 33963 [On Gulf of Mexico] .... (813)597.3144
  Fax: (813)597.2199 Ⓔ TB $60-127 •10% CC A,B,X × ∗ ▣ Υ ➡◖ ⌁ ♿ TV
- **VANDERBILT INN ON THE GULF –150R– 11000 Gulfshore Dr, 33963 [At US 41]** .... **(813)597.3151**
  Fax: (813)597.3099 ♦ CC A,B,C,D,X × ∗ ▣ Υ ➡◖ ⌁ ♿ TV ⊛ 🚗 🅿 ●
  See advertisement on adjacent page and map pg 232
- Wellesley Inn –105R– 1555 Fifth Ave S, 33942 [Exit 15 off 1-75: 1 mi from dntn] .... (813)793.4646
  Fax: (813)793.5248 Ⓒ SB $39-79 •10% CC A,B,C,D,X × ∗ ▣ Υ ➡◖ ⌁ ♿ (HOW)
- World Tennis Center & Resort –124R– 4800 Airport Rd, 33942 [5 min from beach] .... (813)263.1900
  Fax: (813)649.7055 Ⓔ SB $75-130 •15% CC A,B,X × ∗ ▣ Υ ➡◖ ⌁ ♿ TV (VRS₂.₃)

Map panel:

NAPLES

Scheduled flight time from
Miami-3/4 hr   Tampa-1 hr
Other flights to Naples Municipal Airport
Connect in Miami or Tampa

Airport Transfers
Naples Municipal Airport to
city center -2 miles

Weather
Daily average hi/lo
Dec-Feb 77/53   Jun-Aug 91/71
Mar-May 85/61   Sep-nov 87/67

Hotel Location	Map Area
1 Best Western Naples Inn & Stes	H2
2 Cove Inn	J3
3 Days Inn & Lodge of Naples	J3
4 La Playa Beach Resort	A1
5 Registry Resort	E2
6 The Ritz-Carlton, Naples	B1
8 Vanderbilt Inn on the Gulf	A1

© by Reed Travel Group, a division of
Reed Elsevier inc.

Figure 3.9 Extract from *ABC and Hotel Travel Index*

- airlines' reservations systems
- central reservations systems (CRS).

Checking details

Prior to making accommodation reservations the travel agent should be very clear about the main details of the requested booking. These details would include

- dates
- expected time of arrival and departure
- preferred type of room
- names of persons in the party.

During the booking the following details should be checked

- the tariff and whether or not it includes tax and service charge
- supplements
- possible cancellation charges
- meal basis
- means of payment
- the amount of commission to be paid.

Central reservations systems

Utell International is the largest independent hotel sales representative organisation with its own central reservation system. Utell does not own any hotels but it represents over 6,500 hotels worldwide. Through Utell's Paycom and Paytell programs the travel agent can pay deposits and receive commission immediately. In the UK the brand name for Utell's reservation system is *Hotelspace* and it is accessible through the global CRSs such as GALILEO, SABRE and AMADEUS.

Hotel vouchers

Where a hotel is not available on a CRS the travel agent can use a standard hotel voucher which will indicate to the hotel the name of the client, details of arrival and departure, and means of payment. Commission is normally paid to the travel agent after the client has completed the stay at the hotel.

Revision Questions

Primary level

1 What do you understand by the terms 'Modified American Plan' and 'American Plan'?

2 Briefly describe THREE facilities which you would expect to find in an executive room as opposed to a standard twin room.

3 Name FOUR basic requirements for a hotel to be listed as a 2 star AA hotel.

4 Name FOUR minimum requirements for a guest house to be listed under the UK tourist boards' scheme.

5 If a client wished to have a direct dial telephone guaranteed in the bedroom, what is the MINIMUM UK tourist board classification of hotel which you should recommend?

6 If a client wished to have a hair drier guaranteed in the bedroom, what is the MINIMUM UK tourist board classification of hotel which you should recommend?

7 Name FOUR minimum requirements for self-catering apartments to be awarded a key rating under the UK National Tourist Boards' scheme.

8 If a client wished to have a dishwasher guaranteed in the self-catering apartment, what is the MINIMUM UK tourist board classification of accommodation which you should recommend?

9 What is the difference between a double room and a twin room?

10 In relation to accommodation, what do you understand by a gîte?

Advanced level

1 A client wishes to book a self-catering apartment which has cooker, fridge, iron and colour TV as well as the usual crockery, cutlery, etc. There are two establishments available – a highly commended four crown and an approved five crown. Which would you recommend? Why?

2 If a client was particularly concerned with the quality of food in a hotel, rather than the extent of the facilities, what aspect of the tourist board quality assurance scheme should you concentrate on when choosing the hotel: grading or classification?

3 List FIVE features which you would expect to find in a Holiday Centre or Village which may not be available in an average caravan park in the UK.

4 Define rack rate and corporate rate.

5 Name ONE hotel reservation system which could be used by a travel agent to book accommodation in Japan for a client.

6 Using the extract from the *ABC Hotel and Travel Index* in Fig. 3.9 give the names and telephone numbers of five hotels in the Naples area of Florida which offer both a golf course and a swimming pool.

7 Using the same Fig. 3.9, recommend a hotel which is listed as being close to the beach with a golf course and swimming pool and also close to the Olde Naples shopping area.

8 In classifying hotels which symbols are used by the following organisations

- English Tourist Board
- AA
- Thomson Holidays
- Jersey Tourist Board
- Greek Tourist Board
- Q Scheme for Scottish Holiday Parks.

9 In which areas could clients enjoy the following (match the letters with the numbers)

a flotilla holidays   1 Greece
b boating   2 Holland
c tavernas   3 Turkey
d gîtes   4 Norfolk Broads
e Center Parcs   5 France

10 Name three CRSs which can be used to book both accommodation and flights.

4) *Travel services*

Traditionally travel agents in the UK have provided advice to clients on a variety of issues. The EC Directive on Package Travel, Package Holidays and Package Tours which was adopted on 13 June 1990 requires member states to oblige travel agents to give correct information on matters such as visas and health regulations when booking overnight stays for groups. This EC Directive came into force in the UK on 31 December 1992. In this chapter we consider the ancillary services about which travel agents may give advice to tourists such as:

- insurance
- passports
- visas
- health regulations
- foreign exchange.

Insurance

Insurance is a means of providing financial compensation in the event of an accident or other misfortune, such as the delayed departure of a holiday. Holiday insurance is normally short term, for the duration of the holiday, although some insurance companies also offer annual insurance cover, particularly for individuals or groups who travel frequently. The person who takes out the insurance is called the insured and the insurance company is the insurer. Insurance is taken out in the names or names of the insured and is not transferable to anyone else. However, children under 3 years are normally covered free of charge through their parents' cover.

Risks

Holiday insurance is designed to cover the risks which are specific to a holiday such as:

- the client being unable to travel due to illness or redundancy
- the client being unable to travel due to death or injury to a close relative or business partner
- delayed departure
- lost or damaged luggage or property
- hospital bills while abroad
- the cost of returning a person to the UK in the case of serious illness or death.

Curtailment, which is when the holiday is cut short, is usually covered by insurance, although not when the holiday is interrupted by strikes, war, earthquakes or other natural phenomena which are called Acts of God or Force Majeur. Neither would clients be covered if their misfortune was a result of self-injury or wilful exposure to dangerous activities, drugs or alcohol. Insurers will pay only what clients have lost through no fault of their own, and this is called indemnity. Clients cannot for instance cut short their holiday because they do not like the hotel and expect the insurer to pay out!

Inclusive insurance

Inclusive holiday insurance which is designed for the package holiday market covers the following four basic categories:

- insurance of the person in case of sickness, injury or death
- insurance of the client's belongings in case they are lost or stolen
- insurance against unforeseen events
- personal liability insurance in case the client damages or injures another person or their property during the holiday.

Insurance policy

The document which provides details of the insurance cover is called a policy and this is a legally binding document. The details written into the policy are called the terms or conditions of the insurance. The travel agent should advise the client on the merits of one insurance cover against another, because not all insurance companies offer the same cover, and the client should read through the conditions and understand the extent of the cover. Where there are conditions such as the age of the person, certain medical conditions or pregnancy beyond six months which limit the extent of the cover, the client should inform the insurer of those special circumstances.

Insurance premiums

The money paid for insurance is called a premium and in the case of travel insurance the amount paid depends on

- the area to which the client is travelling
- the length of the holiday
- the age of the client at the time of departure, especially if clients are under 16 or over 65 years.

Figure 4.1 shows examples of areas used by insurance companies to structure premiums according to the distance travelled and the availability of medical care. Figure 4.2 shows net premiums charged by the insurance company. Travel agents are free to add their own percentage mark-up depending on their own market forces. The insurance premiums charged by an independent travel agent need to be competitive with both multiples' and tour operators' insurances. Very often the independent travel

Area 1	UK, Channel Islands, Isle of Man, Republic of Ireland
Area 2	Europe, visits to Israel or Egypt where the period on land does not exceed 24 hours
Area 3	Israel, Egypt, the Gambia
Area 4	Worldwide except USA, Canada, Caribbean
Area 5	USA, Canada, Caribbean

Figure 4.1
Insurance cover

NB The above areas are an example; each insurance company should be checked for their definition of areas covered

NET PREMIUMS										
Period up to	**Area 1**		**Area 2**		**Area 3**		**Area 4**		**Area 5**	
	Net	IPT	Net	IPT	Net	IPT	Net	IPT	Net	IPT
5 days	4.20	0.11	7.70	0.19	12.60	0.32	16.50	0.41	18.70	0.47
8 days	4.80	0.12	10.96	0.27	15.80	0.40	23.80	0.60	26.50	0.66
18 days	5.80	0.15	12.40	0.31	18.90	0.47	27.90	0.70	30.90	0.77
32 days	7.00	0.18	15.50	0.39	22.90	0.57	36.90	0.92	40.70	1.02

IPT = Insurance Premium Tax @ 2.5%

Infants under the age of 3 at date of departure – free, provided accompanied by an adult whose name appears on the same Policy

Children under the age of 16 at date of departure – 50% of above premiums

Persons aged over 65 at the date of departure at double premium in excess of 17 days in Area 2, and all durations in Areas 3, 4 and 5, but no loading for Area 1

Excess Waiver available at £2.70 Net, all areas, all Insured Persons

Winter Sports – double premium
Scuba Diving – down to 30ft (9 metres) – normal premium
down to 100ft (30 metres) – double premium
over 100ft (30 metres) – cannot be insured under this policy

Figure 4.2
Insurance premiums

agent uses 'free insurance' as an incentive for clients and in this case the travel agent simply pays the net figure to the insurance company.

For example, a travel agent who decided to put a mark-up of 30% on the premiums would charge clients the net figure in Fig. 4.2 plus 30%, plus a further 2.5% insurance premium tax (IPT). Therefore if a client planned to travel for fourteen days for a holiday in the USA the insurance premium would be

net	£30.90
plus 30%	9.27
	40.17
plus IPT @ 2.5%	1.00
premium	£41.17

If a family of two adults and two children aged 14 and 17 require insurance for a seven day skiing holiday in Switzerland, assuming a 30% mark-up, the premiums charged would be

two adults net @ 10.96	£21.92
child aged 14	5.48
child aged 17	10.96
	38.36
double premium for skiing	38.36
plus 30% mark-up	23.02
	99.74
plus IPT @ 2.5%	2.49
premium	102.23

Insurance claims

In the event of a claim, sometimes the client is expected to pay the first part of the costs: this is called an excess. For example if the client loses a watch, the client might be expected to meet the first £35 of the replacement cost. Figure 4.2 shows how the client can be offered an excess waiver for an additional fee. This charge per person would be added to the cost of the premiums. However, in other cases, such as if the client is delayed on departure by more than twelve hours, the insurance company will normally pay a set amount of compensation. Exclusions are those items, such as contact lenses, which are not normally covered by the insurance company.

Where the insurance is arranged by the travel agent and the client has a problem, the agent should assist the client in completing a claim form if necessary and ensure that all receipts and reports are sent to the insurer. Insurance claims can take a long time to process and cheques in settlement are normally sent direct to the client.

Passports

All clients travelling abroad on holiday or on business must be in possession of a valid passport. Until 31 December 1995 there were two types of British passports:

- British visitor's passport (VP)
- standard or full British passport.

British visitor's passport

This was valid for one year only from the date of issue of the passport and could be obtained from a Post Office. All applicants, including children, had to apply in person. The visitor's passport could be used only for holidays or unpaid business trips up to three months to the countries of Western Europe listed on the Form VP. Such countries include Germany, France and Norway.

A British visitor's passport could not be used to obtain visas of any kind and the passport could not be altered once it had been issued, even if for instance the client wished to add the names of children. Children under the age of 8 years could not hold a VP in their own name and once children reached the age of 16 they had to have their own passport. Visitor's passports could not be post-dated or issued in a future married name for use immediately after a marriage.

The visitor's passport was withdrawn on 31 December 1995, thus some clients may still wish to use them up until 31 December 1996.

Standard British passport

The standard British passport is valid for ten years for adults and five years for children under 16 holding their own passport and can be used worldwide. The standard passport can be obtained from designated passport offices and is issued only to UK citizens, whether or not they are resident in the UK. Until 1999 there will be some family or joint passports in use and these are valid until they expire. Joint passports, which were discontinued in 1989, were issued to husbands and wives who travelled together. However, the passport cannot be used by the wife alone as her name was simply added to the husband's passport. The names of children may be added to one or both parents' individual passports or that of a close relative at any time, although children over the age of 16 must have their own passport. Children under 16 may have their own passport but the photograph must be renewed after five years. It should be noted that even babies need to have or be included in a passport to be able to travel.

Clients must have a valid standard British passport if

- they are planning to stay over three months in any country listed on Form VP
- they are planning to visit any country not included in the VP list
- they are planning to visit any country which requires them to be in possession of a current visa.

Application forms for the standard British passport can be obtained from main post offices and clients should be advised to follow the detailed notes which accompany the forms. Applications should be made at least one month in advance of the trip and at peak times between February and August this could rise to three months. The application should be accompanied by:

- two photographs, one of which has to be countersigned on the back confirming that it is a true likeness
- original birth, marriage, naturalisation or registration documents
- the appropriate fee as detailed in the application form.

The passport application forms are:

Form A application for a standard British passport with either 32 or 94 pages, for applicants over the age of 16

Form B application for a standard British passport for a child under 16 years

Form C application to add children or make changes to a standard British passport

Form D application to extend a five year child's passport for a further five years with new photographs

Form R application to renew a standard ten year British passport for applicants over 16 years.

Travel agents should not assume that everyone who books a holiday through them holds a British passport. Persons who hold other nationalities are not subject to the same rules and regulations as regards visa and entry requirements. To exercise their role of giving sound advice, the travel agent should ask whether clients hold a British passport, especially if they wish to book a visit to a country which has particular restrictions. These details can be found in reference manuals such as the *ABC Guide to International Travel*.

Visas

A visa is a stamp in a passport giving the holder permission to enter or leave a country. It is granted by the authorities of that country, usually through a consulate and should be obtained prior to travel. However, the granting of a visa does not guarantee the holder permission to enter the country concerned. Permission to land is, in many cases, at the discretion of the immigration official at the port of entry.

Entry visas are the most usual, although some countries, for example China, require visitors to have an exit visa; some countries, for example India, require those who have stayed over a certain length of time to have clearance with regard to tax liability. Most travel agencies keep a stock of standard visa application forms such as for Australia, and some use an agency to obtain more unusual visas for potential clients. It is also possible sometimes to obtain visas through the services of a national airline. Prior to assisting a client in applying for a visa the travel agent should ensure that the client has:

- a full standard passport with at least six months to run
- necessary health documents if these apply
- an official invitation or company letter if the purpose of the visit is for business.

Business travellers

Where an official invitation is required for a business traveller the following symbol is used in the *ABC Guide to International Travel* under the business visa column

Y ■   business or company letter must be supplied

British passport holders

Tourist and business visas must be obtained for British passport holders who intend to travel to the following countries:

Algeria, Australia, Bangladesh, Bulgaria, China, Congo, Egypt, India, Iran, Turkey, Jordan, Mexico, Pakistan, Romania, Turkey and the Russian Federation.

Tourist visas, but not business visas, are required to visit Israel, the Maldives and the Seychelles. However, visas can normally be issued on arrival at these countries so long as the British passport is a standard one valid for at least six months.

In addition to a visa, certain countries such as Spain and South Africa may demand that the visitor shows proof of sufficient means of support and funds to maintain themselves while in the country. The intention to leave the country after the expiration of the visa should also be evident and this is normally given through evidence of a confirmed return flight.

Details of visa requirements can be found in the *ABC Guide to International Travel* and its *Quick Reference* insert is a useful guide for the holders of British passports.

Foreign passport holders

Travel agents should remember that the Quick Reference cannot be used when dealing with foreign passport holders. Some unexpected exceptions include the fact that although British and Canadian visitors staying in France for less than three months do not need a visa, entry is denied to Australians without a visa. Holders of Israeli passports are denied entry into several countries including Algeria, Bahrain, Indonesia, Morocco, Iran, Kuwait, Malaysia, Pakistan and Saudi Arabia.

Previous visits to Israel

Holders of passports of any nationality which contain visas or endorsements for Israel are refused entry into Bahrain, Kuwait and Saudi Arabia. Visitors to such countries should be advised by their travel agent to take two passports with them, keeping the references to Israel in one passport only.

Other restrictions

There are other restrictions which are placed on persons entering certain countries such as the stipulation in both Morocco and Thailand that persons 'not complying with general standards of appearance and dress' will be refused entry. In Costa Rica not only persons of 'unkempt appearance' will be refused entry but also gypsies of 'any nationality'.

Health regulations

E111

Travellers to member countries of the European Union (EU) should be advised to take a completed form E111 which is obtainable at offices of the Department of Social Services or the Department of Health. Countries in the EU are

- Belgium
- Denmark
- France
- Germany
- Gibraltar
- Greece
- Republic of Ireland
- Italy
- Luxembourg
- Netherlands
- Portugal
- Spain
- United Kingdom

An E111 can be used to obtain emergency treatment while the client is in an EU country although the treatment is not always free. Each country has its own rules, and details can be obtained in a Department of Health leaflet. The E111 does not cover reduced-cost medical treatment if that is the purpose of the visit, and it never covers the cost of bringing a person back to the UK in the event of illness or death.

Vaccination certificates

International travellers arriving in some countries outside Europe may be required by the local health authorities to produce valid vaccination certificates against cholera, yellow fever or both. The same restrictions may apply to a person arriving in an EU country directly from an infected area outside Europe. Airlines may refuse to carry passengers who do not have appropriate vaccination certificates and immigration control will also refuse entry where the certificates are not valid.

Tourists travelling abroad from the United Kingdom to infected areas must receive an appropriate international certificate of vaccination against yellow fever but they may also be advised for their own safety to obtain protection as well against cholera, malaria, hepatitis and typhoid. Requirements for particular holidays or journeys can be checked for clients in the *ABC Guide to International Travel* or information can be obtained through leaflets from the Department of Health. Areas where diseases are constantly found are known as endemic zones. Where there is the likelihood of a specific outbreak of disease or an epidemic in a particular destination, information is issued by the Foreign and Commonwealth Office to doctors. Brief information is also announced on Viewdata systems, including CEEFAX.

All certificates of vaccination and immunisation should be recorded on the approved forms of the World Health Organisation and signed by a doctor, but the client should be aware that there will be a charge for this. In all cases clients should be referred to their own doctor who can advise on specific vaccinations and the effects they could have with any medication being taken by the client.

Incubation periods

It should be pointed out that vaccination often involves an incubation period after the injection has been given before which the vaccine will not take effect. If clients arrive in a country with an invalid certificate because it is too early for the vaccination to have taken effect, they may be quarantined by the authorities of the countries concerned.

ABC Guide to International Travel

The Quick Reference insert for British passport holders in the *ABC Guide to International Travel* contains information about various diseases.

Yellow fever

Yellow fever is caught from the bite of an infected mosquito, and is endemic in the central countries of Africa such as the Gambia, Sierra Leone and Kenya, and in the northern South American countries of Colombia, Venezuela, Guyana, Peru, Bolivia and parts of Brazil. Many countries such as Australia, China and Egypt require certain travellers to have evidence of vaccination against yellow fever. Yellow fever certificates are valid from ten days after vaccination to a maximum of ten years.

Cholera

Cholera is caught from contaminated food and water, and is common in most parts of Central and South America, West and Central Africa, India, Pakistan and some tropical islands in the Far East. Cholera certificates are valid from six days after vaccination to a maximum of six months but the vaccine gives very little protection. No country now requires cholera vaccination as a condition of entry. However, it is recommended for travellers to cholera areas who may cross borders, especially overland, and may be asked for a certificate by checkpoint staff acting unofficially.

Typhoid

Typhoid fever is caught from contaminated food and water, and is common in Asia, Africa and many tropical islands. In particular, British tourists are recommended to have immunisation against typhoid before travelling to the Bahamas, Barbados, Brazil, Egypt and India. Protection against typhoid is often given as part of the cholera/typhoid injection but no certificate is issued for typhoid immunisation alone. Two injections are given four to six weeks apart and last for three years; after that a single injection is sufficient to boost immunity. Scrupulous care over food and water should be emphasised for those clients who travel to areas where sanitation is primitive.

Malaria

Malaria can be caught from the bite of an infected mosquito, and is common in the northern countries of South America, most of Central Africa, India, southern China and the islands of the Far East. In some countries, while the risk is not prevalent everywhere, British travellers are recommended to have protection. Such countries more commonly visited by British tourists include Brazil, China and Egypt. There is no certificate issued in the case of malaria because protection is given by means of anti-malarial medicines, not vaccination. However, clients should be advised to start taking anti-malarial tablets at least one week before departure. Further advice to clients would be to

- use insecticide repellent
- sleep in properly screened rooms
- use a mosquito net around the bed at night.

It should also be noted that no precautions give absolute protection against some virulent forms of malaria. Any fever developed abroad or up to one month after returning should be reported to a doctor.

Hepatitis

Hepatitis is a danger for visitors who do not observe normal standards of hygiene in many of the countries listed above. Hepatitis A is a particular concern in areas of Brazil, China, Egypt and India. The disease is usually caught by consuming contaminated food or water but it can also spread from person to person where sanitation is primitive. Hepatitis B is present worldwide and is spread through intimate contact in a similar manner to HIV, the virus which causes AIDS.

Poliomyelitis

Poliomyelitis is a danger to everyone travelling outside North America, Australia, New Zealand and northern Europe. Clients previously not vaccinated should be advised to receive a full course of three doses, and those previously vaccinated more than ten years ago should have a booster dose.

ABC Guide symbols

The *ABC Guide to International Travel* uses symbols to indicate the requirements with regard to health regulations for British passport holders (Fig. 4.3).

Specific advice

If travel agents need to give more detailed advice they should refer to the text of the *ABC Guide to International Travel* as for example with reference to Egypt there is an extensive list of countries regarded as infected from which the Egyptian authorities would require a compulsory vaccination. For the British traveller immunisation is recommended against hepatitis A, malaria, polio, tetanus and typhoid and the text goes on to say that risk from malaria is greatest from June to October in certain rural areas of the El Faiyum area, the oases and part of Upper Egypt (Fig. 4.4). Precautions recommended are to boil milk, cook food well and avoid bathing in fresh water.

U	Although immunisation is not compulsory, a certificate may be requested unofficially at immigration
U▲	Cholera immunisation required if arriving from an infected area
R	Risk of infection from Hepatitis A, typhoid, yellow fever or malaria, immunisation recommended
R●	Risk of malaria is not prevalent in all places at all times
M	Yellow fever certificate mandatory
Y▲	Yellow fever certificate required for certain travellers
Y†	Yellow fever certificate recommended and may be a requirement for certain travellers
R#	Yellow fever immunisation recommended for certain endemic areas only

Figure 4.3 Symbols used in the *ABC Guide to International Travel Quick Reference* insert to indicate requirements with regard to health regulations

Figure 4.4 The Sphinx in Egypt (*Photograph: Caroline Allen*)

Foreign exchange

Some travel agencies offer a full service handling foreign exchange and selling traveller's cheques and both are a source of commission. Where the turnover does not justify an inhouse foreign exchange facility, clients can be advised to use the services of a bank or building society. Tourists and business travellers have a choice of the ways in which they take enough money abroad for their trip:

- currency
- traveller's cheques
- credit or debit cards.

Currency

Money can be taken as sterling or in the currency of the country or countries of destination (Fig. 4.5). Currency seems the easiest form in which to take money but it can be easily lost or stolen and only a limited amount will be covered by the holiday insurance.

Rates of exchange

Currencies do not have the same value and in fact the values of currencies against each other vary almost every day. Rates of exchange are published in banks, building societies and financial sections of newspapers. To change sterling into foreign currency, always multiply the rate by the number of pounds. For example, if there are 2556 Italian lira to the pound on a certain day a tourist changing £100 would receive

2556 × 100 = 255,600 Italian lira, less commission

Sometimes the exchange rates are awkward amounts, so a calculator should be used. For example, if there are 2.153 Canadian dollars to the pound on a certain day a tourist changing £150 would receive:

Australia	Australian dollar
Austria	Schilling
Bahamas	Bahamian dollar
Barbados	Barbados dollar
Belgium	Belgian franc
Bermuda	Bermudian dollar
Bulgaria	Lev
Canada	Canadian dollar
Canary Islands	Spanish peseta
China	Renminbi
Cyprus	Cyprus pound
Denmark	Danish krone
Egypt	Egyptian pound
France	French franc
Germany	German mark
Greece	Drachma
Hungary	Forint
India	Rupee
Ireland	Irish pound (punt)
Israel	New shekel
Italy	Italian lira
Kenya	Kenyan shilling
Malta	Maltese lira
Morocco	Dirham
Netherlands	Guilder
Portugal	Escudo
Russian Federation	Rouble
South Africa	Rand
Spain	Peseta
Switzerland	Swiss franc
Thailand	Baht
Tunisia	Dinar
Turkey	Turkish lira
United States of America	US dollar

Figure 4.5 Foreign currencies most commonly used by British travellers

2.153 × 150 = 322 Canadian dollars, less commission

To change foreign currency back into sterling, always divide the amount of foreign currency by the rate. So for example, if a client returned from holiday in Spain with 5,000 pesetas when the exchange rate was 202, the client would receive

$$\frac{5,000}{202} = £24.75, \text{ less commission}$$

Traveller's cheques

Traveller's cheques are a safer way of taking money abroad because if they are lost or stolen the client can be recompensed during the holiday. Traveller's cheques can be obtained in sterling or units of foreign currency and rates of exchange will apply when the cheques are cashed or at the time they are used for a purchase (Fig. 4.6).

Country	Recommended currency of traveller's cheques	Local currency
Australia	Australian dollar	Australian dollar
Austria	Sterling/German mark	Austrian schilling
Belgium	Sterling	Belgian franc
Canada	Canadian dollar	Canadian dollar
Caribbean/West Indies	US dollar	Various
France	French franc	French franc
Germany	German mark	German mark
Greece	Sterling	Drachma
India	US dollar	Rupee
Morocco	Sterling	Dirham
Portugal	Sterling	Escudo
Russia	US dollar	Rouble
Spain/Canary Islands	Peseta	Peseta
Thailand	US dollar	Baht
Turkey	Sterling	Turkish lira
USA	US dollar	US dollar

Figure 4.6 Taking traveller's cheques abroad

Commission of about 1% is usually charged for buying traveller's cheques and further commission may be charged for cashing them. When clients are travelling to the USA they should be advised to take dollar cheques in relatively small units because many Americans frequently use traveller's cheques like currency. Clients should be advised not to take sterling cheques to the USA.

When traveller's cheques are issued they are signed in the presence of the issuing clerk and when they are cashed they are countersigned a second time. Without the first signature traveller's cheques are not insured. Clients should be advised to keep the list of serial numbers of the cheques separate from the actual cheques in case of theft. Normally replacement cheques can be supplied within 48 hours of a reported theft.

Credit or debit cards

A third alternative for cash on a holiday or trip is for the client to use a credit card or debit card abroad. Wherever the main Mastercard or Visa signs are displayed British travellers can use their cards at banks and cash machines in the same way as in the UK. The availability of this facility does of course depend on the frequency of the supply of banks and cash machines in the foreign country. Credit cards have limited acceptance in some countries such as Ghana, the Gambia and Tanzania. Purchases can also be made using cards abroad and the rate of exchange will apply at the time when the purchase is credited to the card in the UK.

Figure 4.7 summarises the methods of making payments abroad.

Commission

Commission as a percentage, or sometimes as a standard fee, is charged for exchanging foreign currency whether as cash, traveller's cheques or a card transaction and this is added to the cost for the client. If a client wished to buy £500 worth of traveller's cheques and the commission was 1% the actual cost to the client would be

value of traveller's cheques	£500.00
1% commission	5.00
total to pay	£505.00

Suppose a travel agency charged 1% on traveller's cheques and 2% on cash transactions when changing sterling into foreign currency, and a client wished to have 500 dollars in traveller's cheques and 150 dollars in US banknotes. If the exchange rate on that day were $1.56 to the £, the client would pay:

for the traveller's cheques

$$\frac{500}{1.56} = \text{£320.50}$$

plus 1% commision	+3.20
Total	£323.70

for the dollar notes

$$\frac{150}{1.56} = \text{£96.15}$$

plus 2% commission	+1.92
Total	£98.07

The client would pay in total £323.70 plus £98.07, that is £421.77.

Normally both a selling and a buying rate are published in foreign exchange bureaux in either travel agencies or banks. The rate is more favourable to the banks when they are selling foreign currency than for buying it back after the trip. Tourists can gain or lose by the change of rates and the timing of the purchase of currency (Fig. 4.8).

	ADVANTAGES	DISADVANTAGES
Sterling	• no commission to pay on unspent money	• limited acceptance • limited insurance if lost or stolen
Foreign currency	• unlimited acceptance in the specific country	• limited insurance if lost or stolen • may have to carry large sums of cash • may be left with currency at the end of the trip
Traveller's cheques	• insured for lost or stolen cheques • can be replaced within 48 hours • do not need to carry large sums of cash • can be used on later trips if necessary	
Credit and debit cards	• familiar use • do not need to carry large sums of cash	• may be limited availability of banks and cash machines in some areas and countries

Figure 4.7 Making payments while abroad

Traveller's Cheques BUY	COUNTRY	Currency SELL	BUY
2.2359	CANADA	2.153	2.313
8.0122	FRANCE	7.65	8.30 no less than 20s
2583	ITALY	2556	2672
199.12	SPAIN	189	202 no less than 1000s
1.6227	USA	1.56	1.6960
Commission			
Currency	2%, maximum £20.00		
Traveller's Cheques	SELL 1.5%, maximum £20.00		
	BUY 2%, minimum £3.00		

Figure 4.8 Sample bank charges for foreign currency exchange

100 French francs changed back into sterling

100/8.30 = £12.05 less 1% commission of 12p the client would receive £11.93 for 100 francs	100/8.30 = £12.05 less 2% commission of 24p the client would receive £11.81 for 100 francs	100/8.30 = £12.05 less £2.00 fee the client would receive £10.05 for 100 francs

2,000 French francs changed back into sterling

2000/8.30 = £240.96 less 1% commission of £2.41 the client would receive £238.55 for 2,000 francs	2000/8.30 = £240.96 less 2% commission of £4.82 the client would receive £236.14 for 2,000 francs	2000/8.30 = £240.96 less £2.00 fee the client would receive £238.96 for 2,000 francs

Figure 4.9 Comparison of agency charges for changing money

For example, a client may return from a holiday in France with 100 francs and wish to change them back into sterling. Figure 4.9 shows the difference in the amount the client would receive if the travel agency charged 1% commission, or 2% commission, or a £2.00 standard fee.

It is easy to see why many banks and bureaux de change charge a standard fee for changing small amounts of currency.

Currency restrictions

Some countries impose currency restrictions as to how much money may be either brought into or taken out of the country. Many countries stipulate that visitors may not take out more currency than they brought into the country. Details of these regulations can be found in the *ABC Guide to International Travel*, for example:

- local currency may neither be taken into nor brought out from Albania, India, Morocco or Poland
- in Cyprus there is limit of 50 Cyprus pounds for either import or export
- in Kenya no local currency may be brought out of the country although up to 200 Kenyan shillings may be taken in by visitors.

It is therefore important for tourists to be advised to retain receipts for money or traveller's cheques taken into such countries.

Revision Questions

Primary level

1 State the currency used in each of the following countries

(a) Spain   (b) Cyprus
(c) Greece   (d) Turkey
(e) France   (f) Morocco

2 Explain the meaning of the following insurance terms:

(a) excess   (b) exclusions

3 Explain the meaning of the following insurance terms:

(a) curtailment   (b) personal liability

4 A client wishes to settle the hotel bill of 27,602 drachma in sterling. Using the exchange rate of £1.00 = GRD 353.00 calculate the equivalent sterling amount.

5 A client's ten year old passport has expired; should the client be advised to ask at the Post Office for Form A, D or R?

6 Is it possible to add the name of a child to the passport of the following?

(a) father   (b) mother
(c) close family   (d) 17-year-old brother
   friend

7 State FIVE diseases or health risks against which people intending to travel abroad from the UK must or ought to protect themselves when recommended as necessary.

8 State the purpose of Form E111 with regard to health.

9 Give ONE example of a country which requires tourists to have an exit visa.

10 Suggest THREE pieces of advice a travel agent might give to a client who needs to apply for a visa.

Advanced level

1 When converting foreign currency to sterling, an agent charges a fee of £3.00 or 1.5% of the sterling value, whichever is the greater. Assuming an exchange rate of 1.56US$ to the UK£, how much, to the nearest penny, would a client actually receive from the agent in exchange for US$455?

2 A client who holds an Australian passport plans to visit Belgium, France and Spain. For which, if any, of these countries would the client need a visa?

3 (a) Under international regulations, an international certificate of vaccination is required for protection against only ONE disease; name that disease.

(b) Apart from your answer in (a), name THREE other diseases against which travellers should be advised to protect themselves when visiting a tropical country.

4 Match up the following diseases with the source from which they could be caught

a malaria   1 contaminated food
b typhoid   2 bite of a mosquito
c cholera   3 poor sanitation
d hepatitis A   4 contaminated water
e yellow fever 5 intimate contact
f hepatitis B   6 infected mosquitoes

5 Which denomination of traveller's cheques would you recommend a client to take to the following countries?

(a) Canada   (b) Thailand
(c) Austria   (d) Russia
(e) Greece   (f) Portugal

6 Using Figs 4.1 and 4.2 on pages 50 and 51, calculate the insurance premiums to be charged to a family of two adults (both aged 45), a grandparent aged 69, and two children aged 13 and 17, travelling to Egypt for a seven night holiday. Assume a travel agency mark-up of 35%.

7 What special restrictions would apply to a British client who had business in Saudi Arabia but had visited Israel in the past few months?

8 State the major difference in the way that a client's claim is settled in the case of flight delay insurance, as opposed to an insurance for loss of, or damage to, luggage.

9 A 20-year-old woman and her fiancée are booking their honeymoon in the Seychelles. The woman's standard British passport is currently two years old.

(a) Is it possible for her to have her married name placed in the passport prior to travelling?

(b) If so which passport form should she be advised to complete?

10 State THREE regulations which apply to children and British passports.

Travel destinations

The holiday scene

Types of holidays

Fast cheap travel and the development of the tourist trade have made holiday destinations all over the world accessible to British tourists. Figure 5.1 shows the location of physical features such as oceans and mountains and Fig. 5.2 is a simple guide to world climate zones. It should be remembered that many areas, particularly in the tropics, are subject to seasonal rains which can be torrential. Countries south of the equator have seasons in reverse of those in UK with New Zealand for example having a very similar climate to UK but with winter in August and summer at Christmas time.

British tourists are attracted to a wide variety of holidays, some of which are listed in Fig. 5.3.

Holidays range from the sport and activity, city breaks and mass tourist holidays which are open to everyone, to the age orientated 'teens and 20s' and 'over 55' markets. Business and conference travellers are a lucrative source of income for the travel trade, and incentive travel, offered as prizes in competitions or targets in sales and industry, usually require the same excellent standards as the business market. Pilgrims of the world religions of Christianity, Buddhism and Islam have travelled to various shrines throughout the centuries. 'Elite' travellers are those who have both the time and money to pursue exotic and unusual destinations, which very often become in later years the 'new' resorts of the mass tourist industry.

Ease of access to destinations can vary from mass charter transport, which keeps the cost down for 'teens and 20s', to excellent business-class travel for delegates to conferences or the elite, independent travellers. Once at their destination, tourists' requirements with regard to scenery and climate will depend on their reason for travelling. Not everyone goes on holiday for the sun; in fact snow, sea and wind may be far more important for a sporting holiday, while the scenery and weather would be unimportant to a group of enthusiastic amateur historians visiting museums and art galleries during a city break.

Amenities and accommodation requirements also vary, with groups needing good facilities in a larger hotel, families possibly requiring self-catering or good entertainment, and pilgrims being satisfied with basic to good facilities which offer some degree of comfort. The length of stay can vary, depending on the time and money available and also on the distance travelled to reach the destination.

According to the 1992 statistics of the World Tourism Organisation, 80% of British tourists take their holidays in Europe; 11% go to North or South America; 5% go to the Far East; 2% go to Africa and the remaining 2% go to the Middle East or South Asia (Fig. 5.4).

Package holidays

Sometimes British tourists make independent travel and accommodation arrangements but many still prefer to book a package holiday from a brochure.

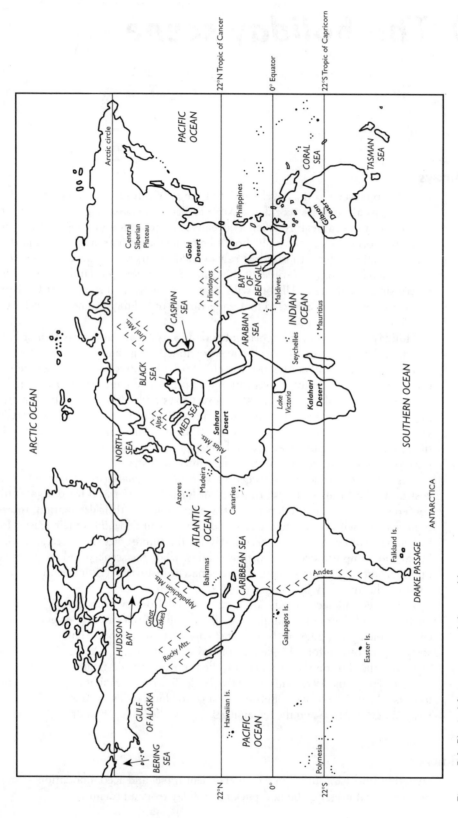

Figure 5.1 Physical features around the world

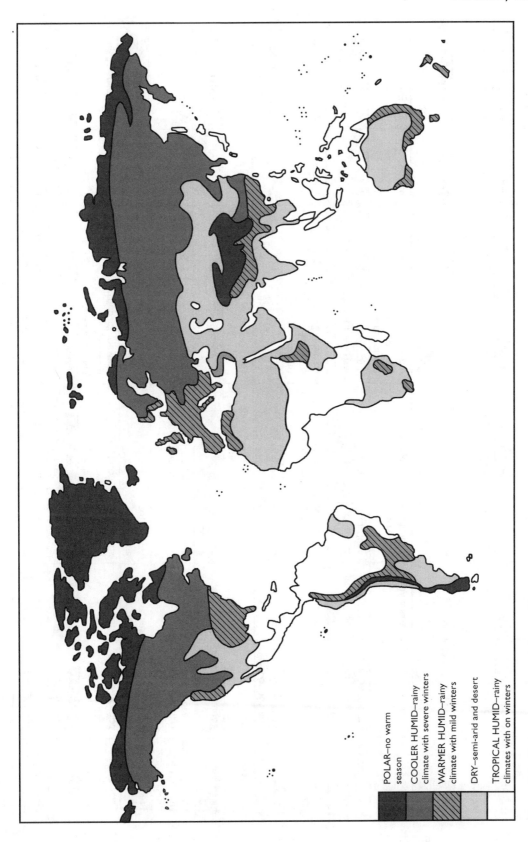

Figure 5.2 Climatic zones around the world

POLAR–no warm
season

COOLER HUMID–rainy
climate with severe winters

WARMER HUMID–rainy
climate with mild winters

DRY–semi-arid and desert

TROPICAL HUMID–rainy
climates with on winters

Types of tourist	Requirements							
	access	natural resources	climate	amenities and accommodation	cultural facilities	possible size of party	usual length of stay	possible destinations
Pilgrims	good	any	any	basic to good	religious	1–30	3–7 days	Lourdes, France
Sport / Activity	good and reliable	snow, sea, wind as appropriate	appropriate to season	sporting facilities	none	2–6	7–14 days	The Alps, Austria
City breaks	good and quick	any	any	basic to excellent	museums, theatres, theme parks	2	2–4 days	Paris, France
Elite	excellent	attractive	appropriate to season	excellent	museums, festivals, theatres, architecture	2–6	month	Far East
Independent tourist	scheduled but off the beaten track	attractive and unusual	appropriate to season	basic to good	museums, festivals, theatres, architecture	1–4	3–4 weeks	self-drive through Tuscany, Italy
Group travel	good and reliable	attractive	appropriate to season	good group accommodation	festivals, gardens, theatres, theme parks	12–20	1 week	The Netherlands
Business	quick, easy and comfortable	any	any	excellent	any	1–3	2–5 days	New York, USA
Conferences	excellent	any	any	excellent group accommodation	any	12–60	2–5 days	Malta
Incentives	good to excellent	attractive	appropriate to season	good to excellent	as appropriate	2	1 week	Caribbean
Visiting Friends and Relatives (VFR)	cheap and reliable	any	any	local entertainment	local	1–6	2–10 weeks	Australia
Teens and 20s	cheap mass charter	sun and sand	sunny, hot and dry	basic to good	organised entertainment	1–20	1–2 weeks	Magaluf, Majorca
Over 55	good and reliable	attractive	sunny and warm	good	festivals, gardens, theatres, entertainment	1–2	2–12 weeks	Benidorm, Spain
Families	good, cheap and reliable	sun and sand	sunny and warm	basic to good, often self catering	theme parks, water parks	4–10	1–2 weeks	Florida, USA
Mass tourist	cheap, mass charter	sun, sand and scenery	sunny and dry	basic to good	festivals, theme parks	plane or coach load	1–2 weeks	Corfu, Greece

Figure 5.3 Types of holidays

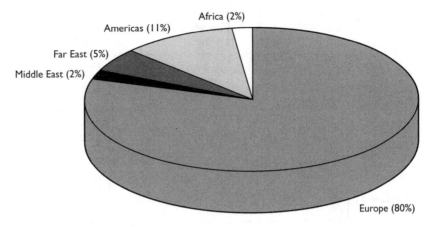

Figure 5.4 British tourists' destinations

Package holidays can be

- short haul
- medium haul
- long haul.

Short haul
Short haul holidays are often taken for a weekend or short break for a variety of reasons:

- the clients may have little money to spend and so may be able to afford only a short break
- the clients may be older and prefer not to travel too far from home
- the clients may be affluent and the break may be additional to their traditional one or two weeks abroad.

Short haul breaks abroad are often taken in one of the European capitals within a couple of hours' flight from the UK.

Medium haul
Medium haul holidays are usually one or two week packages to a European country, possibly bordering the Mediterranean, such as Spain, Greece or Italy. Generally speaking these will be the main holiday especially for groups of young people, families and older clients. Most European countries are within two or four hours' flight from the UK.

Long haul
Long haul holidays are to destinations beyond Europe, which require a flight of more than eight hours from the UK. The most popular long haul destinations for British tourists are

- USA
- Canada
- Australia
- the Far East
- some African countries.

Most of these long haul destinations are English speaking which reflects the fact that most British tourists like to feel comfortable abroad. Many long haul British tourists also

	hours of flying time	possible destinations	usual length of stay
short haul	1–2 hours	Paris Belgium The Netherlands	few days to a week
medium haul	2–4 hours	Spain Greece Italy	1–2 weeks
long haul	8–30+ hours	USA Far East Australia	3–6 weeks

Figure 5.5 Holiday journey times

try to combine a visit to friends and family abroad with having a holiday which satisfies their desire to see different scenery and cultures. For example, a holiday to Australia may include stopovers in Singapore, Malaysia or Thailand to experience for a few days a culture which is totally different from the British in scenery, customs, dress and food.

Figures 5.5 and 5.6 summarise information with regard to international destinations, flying times involved and usual length of holidays taken.

Independent holidays

As British people become more accustomed to travelling abroad so many now opt to travel independently rather than on a package holiday. Chapter 16 deals with tailor-made holidays but at this stage we should note that independent travellers will most probably request the travel agent to provide some elements of their holiday such as

- airline or ferry booking
- accommodation
- theatre tickets
- airport transfers
- car hire
- insurance
- information about passport, visa and health regulations
- itinerary
- information about time differences.

Transport and accommodation bookings were dealt with in Chapters 2 and 3, and insurance, passport, visa and health regulations in Chapter 4. Here we consider itineraries and time differences.

Itineraries

In order to produce itineraries the travel agent needs to know

- the time and place of departure
- the distances to be travelled
- the speed at which the journey will take place or the scheduled times of the chosen transport
- places to be visited
- overnight stops where appropriate
- the desired time and place of destination.

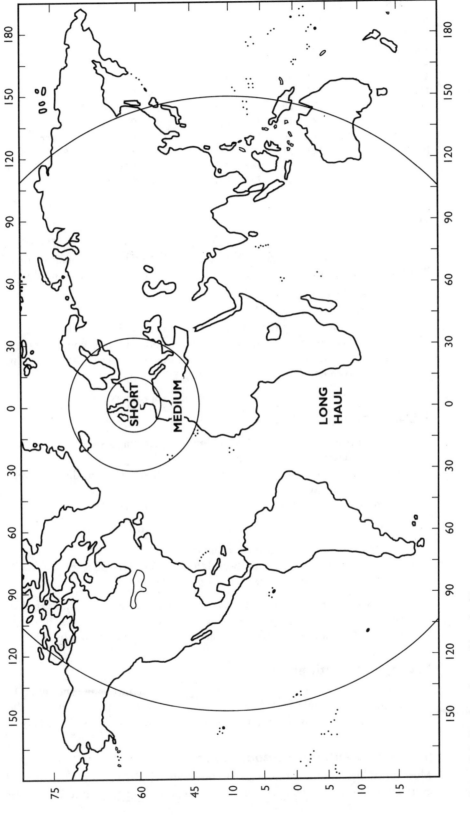

Figure 5.6 Short, medium and long haul journeys

	Aberdeen	Birmingham	Cambridge	Dover	Exeter	Glasgow	Hull	Leicester	Manchester	Oxford	Perth	York	London
Aberdeen													
Birmingham	420												
Cambridge	471	100											
Dover	588	182	125										
Exeter	569	162	249	242									
Glasgow	142	287	350	480	449								
Hull	364	124	123	256	309	245							
Leicester	412	39	68	169	191	299	102						
Manchester	329	79	154	276	235	211	93	87					
Oxford	483	64	80	141	156	350	192	69	142				
Perth	81	329	371	484	484	61	265	322	254	390			
York	319	127	151	282	289	207	38	103	64	172	228		
London	517	110	54	72	181	392	184	98	184	57	417	207	

Figure 5.7
Distance chart

Distances

Maps and charts are used to find out the distances between places. The time taken to cover the distance will then depend on the speed at which the person is travelling. When calculating the times involved for a journey the travel agent should

- estimate the distance
- estimate the average speed
- divide the distance by the average speed, remembering that if using a calculator, any numbers after the point should be multiplied by 6 to convert them to minutes.
- suggest a break in the journey every two hours or every 100 miles, whichever is more convenient.

Figure 5.7 shows a simple distance chart which appears as a triangle.

To find the appropriate distance

- find the place the client is leaving down the left hand side
- find the destination on the slope
- use a ruler to trace across the line from left hand name to directly under the destination name
- the number reached is the distance between the two places.

For example, to find the distance from Manchester to Hull

- locate Manchester down the left hand side
- move across reading the numbers 329, 79, 154, 276, 235, 211
- stop under Hull, where the distance reads 93.

Some charts give the distances in kilometres and some give both kilometres and miles. It is useful to remember that eight kilometres are equal to five miles. If a client asks for kilometres to be changed to miles this can be done by multiplying by 5/8.

Setting out an itinerary

In setting out an itinerary the guidelines shown on the next page should be followed. Similar guidelines should be followed for itineraries abroad although care should be taken with local times when different times zones are crossed, as described below.

Timetables and the 24-hour clock

Most timetables use the 24-hour clock, but many clients use the 12-hour clock in everyday use so the travel agent should be prepared if requested to convert times for a

---

Itineraries always show LOCAL TIMES

<u>Day 1</u>

time	depart from AAA
time	coffee stop at BBB for 15 minutes
time	arrive at CCC staying at the Hotel Grand, aaa Street, bbbtown,
Tel	visits will be arranged to
	◡ ddd castle
	◡ the new shopping centre

<u>Day 2</u>

time	depart from CCC
time	coffee stop at DDD
time	arrive at EEE
etc	

---

client. For example the travel agent may be asked to plan an itinerary for a senior citizen who is travelling to London to meet her son for a holiday abroad together. However, she has difficulty in understanding the British Rail timetable which says

Birmingham New Street	d. 22.15
London Euston	a. 00.18

The travel agent should explain that the train will leave Birmingham New Street station at a quarter past ten at night and will arrive in London just before twenty minutes past midnight, the journey taking about two hours.

It should be noted that midnight or 00.00 never appears on timetables. This is because it is not precise enough since there could be confusion as to which day is being used when the time is given in isolation from the rest of the timetable. If it is necessary to show midnight it will be shown as 23.59 or 00.01.

On international air routes, taking into account time zones, it is possible to arrive the previous calendar day or up to three days later than the date of departure. The internationally recognised symbols for these time differences are

¶ for arrival on the previous day
* for arrival the following day
\# for arrival on the third day
§ for arrival on the fourth day

International timetables use numbers for the days of the week so that

1 = Monday, 2 = Tuesday, etc.

and so:

1 3 6 indicates a service on Mondays, Wednesdays and Saturdays

The number of stops during an international flight are indicated by numbers which appear in the right hand column of timetables:

0 means a non-stop flight
1 means one stop, 2 means two stops, etc.
M indicates more than eight stops.

Each major city and airport around the world has a three letter code which identifies it uniquely for air travel. Some codes are easily recognisable such as LPL for Liverpool or

AMS for Amsterdam but others seem to bear no relation to the actual name. Examples of these are the Canadian cities of Vancouver and Montreal which are YVR and YUL and O'Hare airport in Chicago, USA, which is ORD. A list of all city and airport codes can be found in the *ABC World Airways Guide*.

Figure 5.8 shows the three traffic conference areas of the International Air Traffic Association (IATA).

- Area 1 covers North and South America and Greenland
- Area 2 covers Europe, the Middle East and Africa
- Area 3 covers Asia, the Indian Ocean islands, Australia and New Zealand.

Time differences

Greenwich Mean Time

To measure the passage of time people used to use sundials which marked the time according to the position of the sun in the sky. This measurement is a continually changing scale according to where you are on earth. For instance, the sundial time in London is about ten minutes ahead of the time in Bristol and five minutes behind the time in Norwich. Nowadays we require time to be standardised over a particular area. Various types of clocks are used to measure time and these use the average of the sundial days throughout the year. The time used by clocks is called mean time.

In 1884 an international agreement was reached to use Greenwich in London as a base time for all times around the world. From then on, each area of the world took a time which was so many hours behind or ahead of Greenwich Mean Time (GMT). For example, Chicago time is six hours behind Greenwich Mean Time and we refer to the time in Chicago as GMT–6. Hong Kong is on GMT+8 because it is eight hours ahead of Greenwich Mean Time.

The term GMT was replaced in 1979 by Universal Time Co-ordinate (UTC), although the times are the same and it is still known as GMT in the UK and USA. UTC is used throughout the world for marine and airline navigation.

Time zones

Time zones, which indicate the number of hours behind or ahead of GMT, are worked out according to the distance from London. The lines of longitude of the world join at the north and south poles, forming 360° around the point of the pole. The earth travels around the sun at the rate of one turn in every 24 hours. If we divide 360 by 24 we get 15. Therefore every 15° longitude is used as a basis for time zones indicating hourly time changes throughout a 24-hour period around the world.

Some lines have been changed to accommodate the countries over which they pass. The Republic of Ireland, for example, should strictly speaking have two time zones but it is easier for the country to adopt only one time zone. Some countries such as the USA and Australia are so large that they need more than one time zone. Figure 5.9 shows the time zones as agreed around the world.

Greenwich Mean Time is on the 0° line of longitude; on the other side of the world there is the half-way point or the 180° line of longitude. This line bends and twists so that it does not pass over any country because on the 180° line the date changes and it is known as the International Date Line. For example, the Fiji Islands (GMT+12) are west of the International Date Line but the Samoan Islands (GMT 11) are to the east. When it is 3 pm on Tuesday in the Fiji Islands it is still 4 pm on Monday in the Samoan Islands, even though the distance between the groups of islands is no more than 800 miles (Fig. 5.10).

International time calculators such as that published in the *ABC World Airways Guide* in Fig. 5.11 make the calculation of time changes a little easier. For example, for the above time changes for Fiji and Samoa

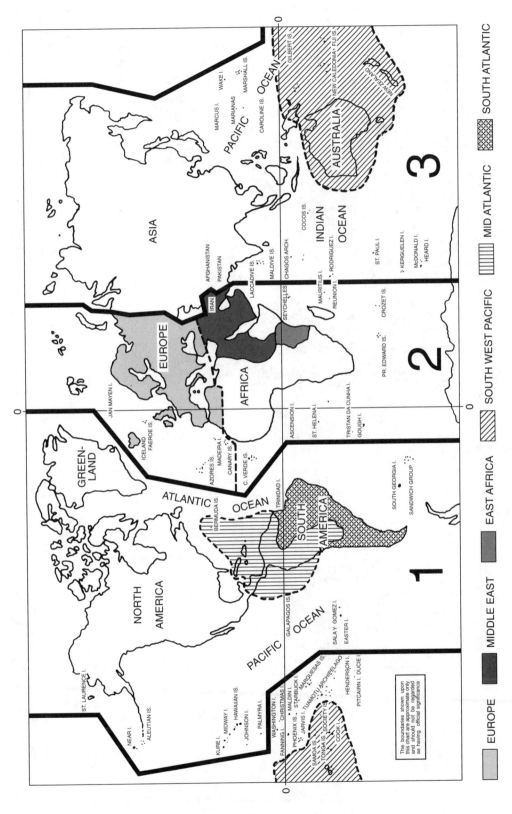

Figure 5.8 IATA traffic conference areas. Source: *ABC World Airways Guide*

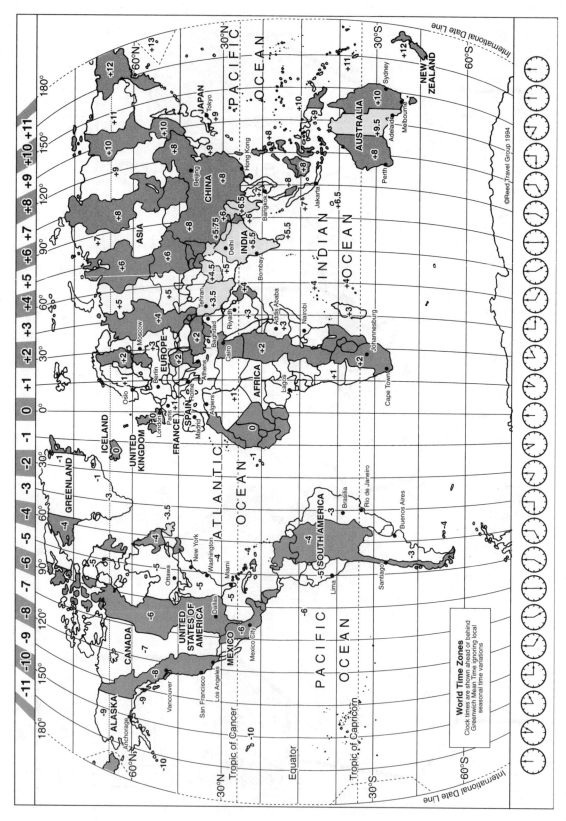

Figure 5.9 Time zones around the world. *Source: ABC World Airways Guide*

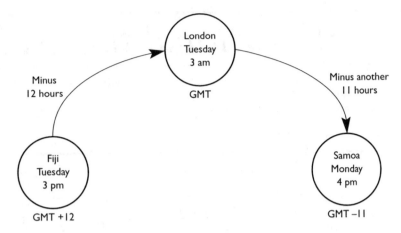

Figure 5.10 International Date Line example

- Fiji is listed as GMT+12
- if the time in Fiji is 3 pm Tuesday, then GMT is 3 pm less 12 hours, i.e. 3 am Tuesday
- Samoa is listed as GMT-11
- that means that the time in Samoa is 3 am Tuesday (GMT) minus 11, i.e. 4 pm Monday

The international time calculator as shown in Fig. 5.11 gives a column showing any changes of time during the year, such as British Summer Time. Internationally this change is known as Daylight Saving Time (DST). The third column shows the dates on which the DST applies. For example, a business client may wish to make telephone calls during a stay in Bahrain. If the date were 3 November and the time 9.30 am, the time in London would be 6.30 am. This is reached by

- Bahrain is listed as GMT +3
- the time in Bahrain is 9.30 am, so GMT is 9.30 less three hours, i.e. 6.30 am.

Another client may wish to make a telephone call while in Bermuda on 25 October at 6 pm.

- Bermuda is listed as GMT-3 in the DST column for 25 October
- GMT is therefore 18.00 (6 pm) plus 3, i.e. GMT is 21.00
- check UK and find that GMT applies (UK is not on DST on that date)
- the time in London will therefore be 9 pm (21.00).

It is of course possible that both London and the foreign destination will be on Daylight Saving Time. This makes the calculation more complicated but if all calculations are made through GMT then the problem should be minimised. For example the business client may wish to make a telephone call from Bermuda at 16.30 on 1 June.

- Bermuda is listed as GMT-3 in the DST column for 1 June
- GMT is therefore 16.30 plus 3, i.e. 19.30
- check UK and find GMT+1 in the DST column for 1 June
- the time in London will therefore be 19.30 (GMT) plus 1, i.e. 20.30 on 1 June.

All of these examples have been worked from abroad to London, but it may also be necessary to calculate the other way. For example if the travel agent wishes to contact a hotel in Turkey on 22 July at 4 pm:

International time calculator

Standard Clock Time is shown in hours and minutes fast (+) or slow (–) of GMT (Greenwich Mean time). Many countries also have a period of Daylight Saving Time (DST). This is shown together with the period it is effective.

Countries with more than one time zone are marked **.

To establish the local time for a particular city, refer to its entry in *Worldwide city-to-city* schedules.

E = Estimated

Country/area	Standard Clock Time	Daylight Saving Time	DST effective period
Afghanistan	+4.30		
Albania	+1	+2	27 Mar 94–24 Sep 94 E
Algeria	+1		
Andaman Is.	+5.30		
Andorra	+1	+2	27 Mar 94–24 Sep 94 E
Angola	+1		
Anguilla	–4		
Antigua and Barbuda	–4		
Argentina	–3		
Armenia	+3	+4	27 Mar 94–24 Sep 94
Aruba	–4		
Ascension Is.	GMT		
Austalia **			
Western Australia	+8		
South Australia	+9.30	+10.30	30 Oct 94–04 Mar 95
Northern Territory	+9.30		
Capital Territory	+10	+11	30 Oct 94–04 Mar 95
New South Wales	+10	+11	30 Oct 94–04 Mar 95
Queensland	+10		
Whitsunday Islands	+10	+11	30 Oct 94–04 Mar 95
Tasmania	+10	+11	02 Oct 94–04 Mar 95
Victoria	+10	+11	30 Oct 94–25 Mar 95
Lord Howe Island	+10.30	+11	30 Oct 94–04 Mar 95
Austria	+1	+2	27 Mar 94–24 Sep 94
Azerbaijan	+4		
Azores	–1		GMT 27 Mar 94–24 Sep 94
Bahamas	–5	–4	03 Apr 94–29 Oct 94 E
Bahrain	+3		
Bangladesh	+6		
Barbados	–4		
Belarus	+2	+3	27 Mar 94–24 Sep 94 E
Belgium	+1	+2	27 Mar 94–24 Sep 94
Belize	–6		
Benin	+1		
Bermuda	–4	–3	03 Apr 94–29 Oct 94 E
Bhutan	+6		
Bolivia	–4		
Bosnia and Herzegovina	+1	+2	27 Mar 94–24 Sep 94 E
Botswana	+2		
Brazil **			
Fernando do Noronha	–2		
S.E. Coast, inc. Bahia, Goias and Brasilia	–3	–2	23 Oct 94–28 Jan 95
N.E. Coastal States, and E of Para	–3		
Central and N.W. States, and W of Para	–4		
Amazonas, Mato Grosso and Mato Grosso do Sul	–4	–3	23 Oct 94–28 Jan 95
Teritory of Acre	–5		
British Virgin Is.	–4		

Country/area	Standard Clock Time	Daylight Saving Time	DST effective period
Brunei Darussalam	+8		
Bulgaria	+2	+3	27 Mar 94–24 Sep 94 E
Burkina Faso	GMT		
Burundi	+2		
Cambodia	+7		
Cameroon	+1		
Taiwan	+8		
Tajikistan	+5		
Tanzania	+3		
Thailand	+7		
Togo	GMT		
Tonga	+13		
Trinidad and Tobago	–4		
Tuamotu Is.	–10		
Tubuai Is.	–10		
Tunisia	+1		
Turkey	+2	+3	20 Mar 94–24 Sep 94
Turkmenistan	+5		
Turks and Caicos Is.	–5	–4	03 Apr 94–29 Oct 94 E
Tuvalu	+12		
Uganda	+3		
Ukraine **			
Simferopol	+3	+4	27 Mar 94–24 Sep 94 E
General	+2	+3	27 Mar 94–24 Sep 94 E
United Arab Emirates	+4		
United Kingdom	GMT	+1	27 Mar 94–22 Oct 94
U.S.A. **			
Eastern Time	–5	–4	03 Apr 94–29 Oct 94
Indiana (East)	–5		
Central Time	–6	–5	03 Apr 94–29 Oct 94
Mountain Time	–7	–6	03 Apr 94–29 Oct 94
Arizona	–7		
Pacific Time	–8	–7	03 Apr 94–29 Oct 94
Alaska – All locations (except Aleutian Islands West of 169.30 deg W)	–9	–8	03 Apr 94–29 Oct 94
Alaska – Aleutian Islands (West of 169.30 deg W)	–10	–9	03 Apr 94–29 Oct 94
Hawaiian Islands	–10		
U.S. Virgin Is.	–4		
Uruguay	–3		
Uzbekistan	+5		
Vanuatu	+11		
Venezuela	–4		
Viet Nam	+7		
Wake Is.	+12		
Wallis and Futuna Is.	+12		
Windward Is.	–4		
Yemen	+3		
Zaire **			
Kinshasa, Mbandaka	+1		
Haut–Zaire, Kasai, Kivu and Shaba	+2		
Zambia	+2		
Zimbabwe	+2		

Figure 5.11 International time calculator *Source: ABC World Airways Guide*

- UK is listed as GMT+1 in the DST column for 22 July
- GMT is therefore 16.00 (4 pm) minus 1, i.e. 15.00
- check Turkey and find GMT+3 in DST column for 22 July
- the time in Turkey will therefore be 15.00 (GMT) plus 3, i.e. 18.00 or 6 pm.

International journey times

When calculating journey times across the world, time zone changes must be taken into account because timetables are always given in local time. For example if a ferry leaves England during August at 11.30 and arrives in France at 17.35 the following calculation needs to be done to calculate the journey time. Assume that England is GMT+1 and France is GMT +2.

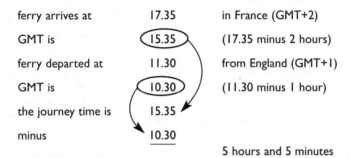

ferry arrives at	17.35	in France (GMT+2)
GMT is	15.35	(17.35 minus 2 hours)
ferry departed at	11.30	from England (GMT+1)
GMT is	10.30	(11.30 minus 1 hour)
the journey time is	15.35	
minus	10.30	
	5 hours and 5 minutes	

In doing such calculations always work with both times in GMT.

Revision Questions

Primary level

1 It is GMT+1 in the UK and GMT-4 in Venezuela. What local time is it in Venezuela when it is midday in Britain?

2 With respect to dates and times, name the 180th parallel of longitude and explain the effect of travelling across this parallel from East to West.

3 A client comes into your office to book a P&O European ferry crossing from Portsmouth to Le Havre. If the ferry leaves Portsmouth at 08.30 and the journey takes 5 hours 35 minutes, at what time will the ferry arrive at Le Havre, given that France is GMT+2 and England GMT+1?

4 A client is flying from London to Hong Kong departing Heathrow at 11.00 and arriving into Hong Kong International at 09.10 the following day, local time.
   Calculate the client's actual flying time given that Hong Kong is GMT+8 and London is GMT.

5 You are required to visit two different locations in the same day. The shorter journey between the two locations will take 2 hours 15 minutes on a busy route at an average speed of 28 miles per hour. However, by taking a route that is 14 miles longer you could save time because your average speed would reach 44 miles per hour.
Using the information above calculate
(a) the distance in miles between the two locations by the shorter route
(b) the distance in miles between the two locations by the longer route
(c) the time saved in minutes by taking the longer route.

6 The customers shown in Fig. 5.12 wish to book their holiday through your travel agency. From the list of holidays provided, select the most suitable for EACH customer type. Indicate your choice by matching up the letters and numbers.

7 Give ONE example for EACH of the following of a destination popular with British tourists
short haul   medium haul   long haul.

8 Apart from travel and accommodation, list FIVE services which could be offered by a travel agent to an independent traveller.

a	a group of five young women wanting plenty of nightlife	1	Pontins Holiday Centre, Southport
b	two widows who are keen Scrabble players and want a UK break in the winter	2	two weeks in Ibiza with The Club
c	a couple who have won £200,000 on the lottery and want to book their first long haul holiday	3	two weeks flotilla holiday off the coast of Turkey
d	a young couple wanting a winter sports holiday on a budget	4	Saga activity holiday in Bournmouth with dancing and Scrabble competitions
e	a family with two young children who want a UK holiday with plenty of entertainment	5	one week skiing at Les Arcs, France
f	a group of five young men who want a sailing holiday in the sun	6	three weeks with Bales Tours in China and the Far East

Figure 5.12
Holiday customers

9 Name THREE destinations which lie in IATA Area 3 which are popular with British tourists.

10 In which IATA Area do the Seychelles lie?

Advanced level

1 A client is flying from London to St Lucia, departing Gatwick at 11.45 and arriving into St Lucia at 16.05 the same day. Calculate the actual flying time given that St Lucia is GMT-4 and London is GMT+1.

2 A US city is shown in the manuals as GMT-8. State the time and day in that US city, when it is Tuesday 07.00 GMT in Britain. On which coast of the USA is this city situated?

3 Mr and Mrs Bolton would like to celebrate their silver wedding anniversary by booking a tailor-made holiday to Florida and the Caribbean staying in the double room at the Granada Hotel, Kissimmee, for the first week. You have managed to book them on AA flights from Manchester to Orlando, departing 13.30 on Saturday 5 February and returning into Manchester on Sunday 20 February at 07.00. The transatlantic flights each way will be via New York and will take nine hours. The second week will be spent on a Caribbean cruise aboard *SS Windswept* sailing from Fort Lauderdale at 14.00 on Saturday 12 February and will return the following Saturday at 08.00. They have booked an Alamo car rental for the first week which they can pick up at the airport and return at Fort Lauderdale. You have arranged for a limousine transfer to Orlando airport on their return from the cruise.

Design an itinerary for the Boltons showing the bookings you have made so far. Assume a two hour check-in for both the flights and cruise and that England is on GMT and Florida GMT-6. You may use an atlas or distance charts to calculate any mileages you need.

Use the three letter codes and an international time calculator from a current ABC World Airways Guide to name the airports for the connecting flights in questions 4–6 and say how long it will take to travel from Liverpool to the final destination on the date given. Hint: for the journey time you need consider only the time of departure from Liverpool and time of arrival at the final destination.

4 0700 LPL   0755 LHR
  1200 LHR   2325 AUH   on 24 January

5 1530 LPL   1630 LHR
  1800 LHR   2000 AMS   on 22 July

6 1830 LPL   1930 LHR
  2100 LHR   *1025 BOM   on 5 May

7 On Fig. 5.13 identify the physical features indicated by letters and the cities/airports indicated by numbers.

8 Name TWO specifications which a conference venue would need to offer over and above the facilities normally found in a package holiday resort.

9 Name THREE features which often distinguish a 'teens to 20s' holiday from a family package holiday.

10 Explain the following symbols as used in international airline timetables
  3   #   *   M

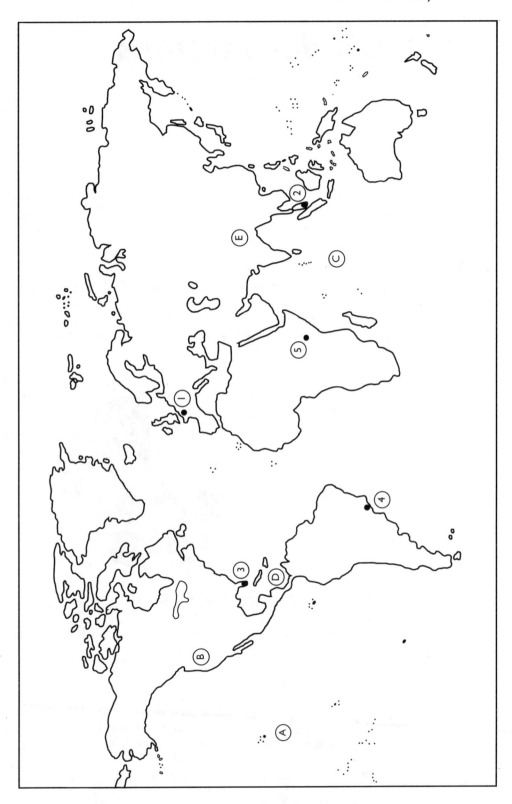

Figure 5.13
World map

6) UK destinations

This chapter and the next two are concerned with destinations and attractions which appeal to British tourists. It is impossible to cover all aspects in these chapters but they will serve as indicators to the principal places of interest for British tourists.

UK domestic tourism

During 1993 UK tourism was worth £33,670 million to the national economy with 65% of this income coming from domestic tourists on overnight breaks and day trips. The UK residents taking overnight breaks spent £9,489 million (28%) and those on day trips spent £12,430 million (37%). Figure 6.1 shows how important this spending was to UK tourism in 1993.

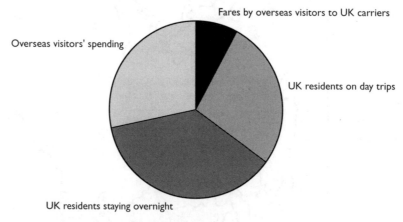

Figure 6.1 Value of tourism to the UK in 1993

The main reasons given in 1993 by UK tourists for their overnight trips were:

- holiday
- business
- visiting friends and relatives (VFR).

The relative importance of each of these reasons is shown in Fig. 6.2.

A quarter of the domestic trips made by UK residents in 1993 were made during July and August, but otherwise there was a fairly even spread of visits throughout the year (Fig. 6.3).

In general, spending on the trips went on:

- accommodation
- eating out
- shopping
- travel
- entertainment.

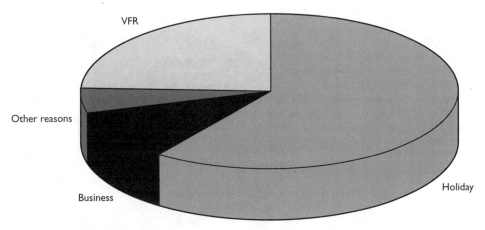

Figure 6.2 Reasons given by UK residents for overnight trips in 1993

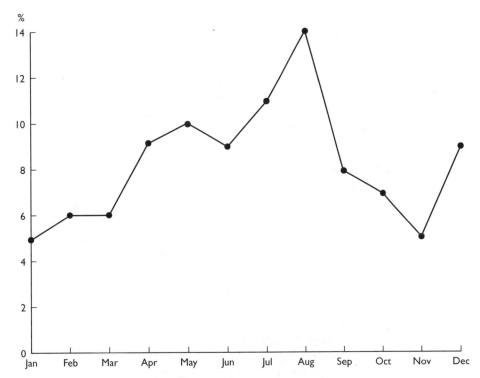

Figure 6.3 The spread of trips by UK residents throughout 1993
Source: National facts of Tourism, BTA, April 1995

Most of the overnight trips by UK residents in 1993 were taken in England, followed by Scotland, Wales and Northern Ireland. However, the likelihood of a permanent peace in Northern Ireland meant that in 1994 a record 1.29 million visitors went there, of whom 276,000 were holiday visitors (Fig. 6.4).

There are eleven regional tourist boards in England, as shown in Fig. 6.5; thirty-five regional tourist boards in Scotland; and three regional tourist boards in Wales. In 1993 the most popular areas with UK residents were as follows:

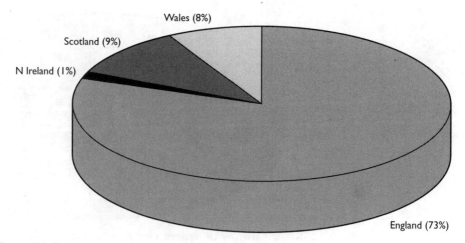

Figure 6.4 Destinations of domestic trips for UK residents in 1993

- The West Country attracted 13 million visitors (18%)
- Southern region attracted 8.9 million visitors (12%)
- East Anglia attracted 8.4 million visitors (5%)
- London attracted 7.2 million visitors (10%)

British tourists' weekend and short breaks in the UK can be to seaside resorts, towns, cities, or inland holiday centres (Fig. 6.6). During these breaks, tourists may choose to visit natural attractions, such as lakes and mountains, or man-made attractions, such as museums and theme parks.

Tourist attractions in the UK

The main types of attractions monitored by the tourist boards in the UK are historic houses, museums and art galleries, gardens, wildlife, and other attractions, which include parklands and theme parks. Figure 6.7 shows the relative appeal of 5,000 UK attractions which were monitored by the national tourist boards in 1990.

According to the British Tourist Authority (BTA) the top ten tourist attractions charging admission in 1993 were:

1 Alton Towers, Staffordshire
2 Madame Tussaud's, London
3 Tower of London
4 St Paul's Cathedral, London
5 Natural History Museum, London
6 Chessington World of Adventures
7 Thorpe Park, Surrey
8 Science Museum, London
9 Blackpool Tower
10 Drayton Manor Park, Staffordshire.

Free attractions with 2 million or more visitors in 1993 included:

- Blackpool Pleasure Beach
- British Museum, London
- National Gallery, London

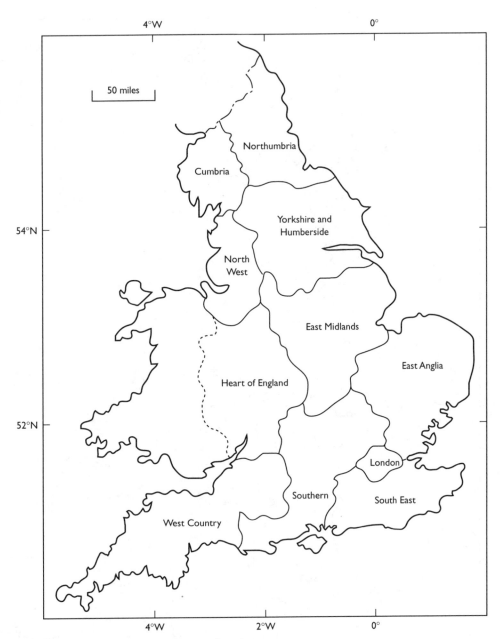

Figure 6.5 The 11 English regional tourist boards

- Palace Pier, Brighton
- Pleasure Beach, Great Yarmouth
- Pleasureland Amusement Park, Southport
- River Lee Country Park, Waltham Abbey
- Strathclyde Country Park.

The statistics for this league table are based on the number of visitors to the centres in a year. Attractions which are not listed are areas of natural beauty such as the Lake District, the New Forest and the Highlands of Scotland. These are missing from the

Figure 6.6 Cities, resorts and gateways in the UK

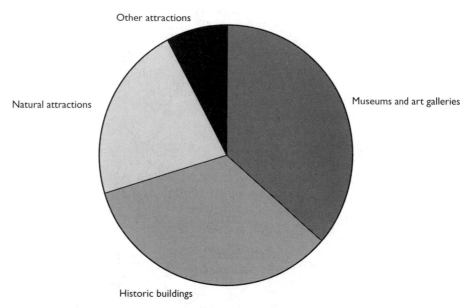

Other attractions

Natural attractions

Museums and art galleries

Historic buildings

Figure 6.7 Relative appeal of UK attractions to UK residents
Source: 5,000 UK attractions monitored by the National Trust Boards in 1990

lists because of the nature of the statistics, which are collected as people enter by turnstiles, especially at the human-made attractions. Many areas of natural beauty around the country are freely open to anyone; some of them are actively preserved as national parks and others through the work of the National Trust.

Natural attractions

The most popular outdoor activities in the UK include:

- walking
- fishing
- horse riding
- climbing
- bird-watching
- cycling
- camping
- sailing
- potholing
- air sports.

The increasing popularity of leisure activities on water was considered in Chapter 3. The Wildfowl and Wetlands Trust, which was founded in 1946 by the late Sir Peter Scott, provides eight centres around the UK, six of them with collections of thousands of exotic wildfowl from all over the world. Special promotions are organised throughout the year to attract visitors to the centres. Figure 6.8 shows the location of the centres in England, Scotland and Northern Ireland.

According to the BTA, in 1993 the top ten UK country parks which attracted visitors were:

1 Strathclyde Country Park, Motherwell
2 Bradgate Park, Leicestershire
3 Clumber Park, Worksop
4 Dunstable Downs Country Park, Bedfordshire
5 River Lee Country Park, Waltham Abbey
6 Sandwell Valley Country Park, West Bromwich
7 Sherwood Forest Country Park, Notts
8 Thetford Forest Park, Norfolk

Figure 6.8 Wildfowl and Wetland Centres in the UK

9 Temple Newsam Country Park, Leeds
10 Moors Valley Country, Ringwood.

Countryside Commission

The Countryside Commission was established in 1968 as an advisory body with responsibility for conservation of natural beauty in England and Wales and with a mandate to encourage facilities for recreation in the countryside. In 1967 the Countryside Commission for Scotland was set up but it merged with the Scottish National Heritage in 1991. The Countryside Commission has powers to designate:

- National parks
- Areas of outstanding natural beauty (AONB)
- Long distance footpaths or national trails.

National parks

The ten national parks of England and Wales were designated in the 1950s to conserve and enhance their natural beauty, and to provide opportunities for everyone to enjoy them. The parks, which cover 9% of England and Wales, are neither nationally owned nor are they 'parks' in the usual sense of the word. They are living and working environments but they are protected from exploitation, and encouragement is given for quiet pursuits such as walking and climbing. Two 'equivalent areas', which are similarly protected, have also been identified, namely the Norfolk Broads and the New Forest. In Scotland the corresponding designated areas, which cover about 13% of the country, are called national scenic areas. Figure 6.9 shows the national parks of England and Wales.

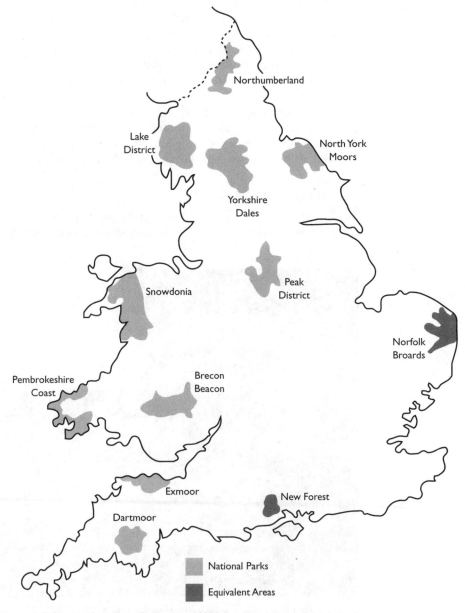

Figure 6.9 National parks in England and Wales

The national parks are good places to start if a client wishes to see an area which is renowned for its natural beauty. The parks offer walks through varied scenery which changes with the seasons. The North York Moors and the hills of the Derbyshire Peak District are covered with a mass of purple heather in late summer, whereas wild moorland dominates the Dartmoor National Park, where most of the land is over 1,000 ft with menacing granite tors rising out of the mist.

A ranger service can guide visitors through easy or medium walks in the national parks. For the more experienced walkers there are routes such as the Cleveland Way, which circles the northern edges of the North York Moors, or the 40-mile Lyke Wake Walk, which crosses the moors from Osmotherley to Ravenscar.

The Lake District (Fig. 6.10) and the Yorkshire Dales are also very popular with motorists and it is possible to buy touring books which suggest routes to see the scenery as well as some villages off the beaten track. Clients should be encouraged to explore these lesser known areas and not to spend their time in a traffic jam on the main roads through the parks.

In North Wales, Snowdonia National Park covers over 800 square miles and is dominated by Snowdon itself, which at 3,569 ft is the highest mountain in Wales. The scenery in the park offers a mixture of mountains, lakes and deep valleys and there are some noted beauty spots such as Betws-y-Coed.

In South Wales, the 167-mile footpath of the Pembrokeshire Coast preserves the wild nature of the landscape from Amroth to St Dogmaels, near to Cardigan, and there is an abundance of small villages offering bed and breakfast to visitors.

Areas of outstanding natural beauty

The Countryside Commission has designated many places as areas of outstanding national beauty (AONB). These areas vary in size and include mountain, fell and dale,

Figure 6.10 Lake Windermere, in the Lake District National Park, Cumbria

cliffs, sand dunes and tidal flats as well as woods and areas preserved for wildlife. Figure 6.11 shows the AONB in England and Wales and the heritage coasts, which cover some 730 miles of coastline and preserve areas of particular beauty ranging from magnificent cliffs to flat sand dunes.

Most of the coast of the island of Anglesey is protected as an AONB for its unspoiled beaches and bird colonies. The Cotswolds, Britain's second largest AONB, is an area of limestone hill country with attractive Cotswold-stone towns and villages. Chichester Harbour with its sea creeks and tidal flats is a paradise for people with yachts. The Norfolk Coast, which is also preserved as a Heritage Coastline, is a unique

Figure 6.11 AONB and heritage coasts in England and Wales

area of sand dunes, shingle ridges, mud flats and saltings. A 60-mile stretch of the Kent Downs and extensive areas of Dorset and Hampshire include magnificent scenery as well as some attractive villages.

The Lochs and Highlands of Scotland have scenery and beauty which it would be hard to match in any part of the world. Loch Lomond in Strathclyde is the largest lake in the UK but is within easy reach of Glasgow or Edinburgh. Inverness has long been regarded as the 'capital of the highlands' and is the gateway to the Cairngorms, the tragic battlefield of Culloden and Loch Ness with its stories of monsters dating back to the seventh century. Figure 6.12 shows the areas of outstanding natural beauty and forest parks of Scotland.

The Northern Ireland Tourist Board produces motorists' tours taking in the winding coastline, the beautiful mountains of Mourne and the Fermanagh lakes. Northern Ireland offers holidays in unspoilt scenery which was for many years ignored by visitors from the British mainland during the unsettled political period.

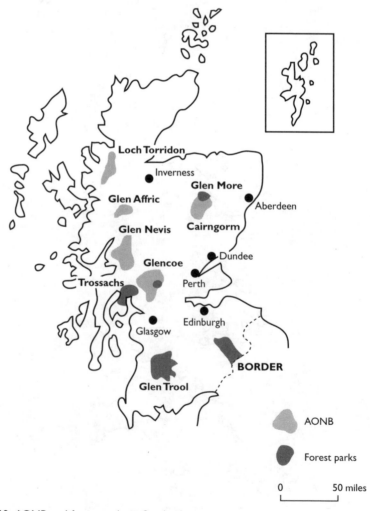

Figure 6.12 AONB and forest parks in Scotland

Long distance footpaths or national trails

Long distance footpaths and bridleways are designated by the Countryside Commission so that it is possible to enjoy these beautiful areas avoiding as far as possible major towns and roads.

Figure 6.13 shows nine of the routes approved by the Secretary of State for the Environment or for Wales.

- The Pennine Way, the first long distance footpath to be designated, links three national parks and stretches from Derbyshire to the Scottish border. It can be walked in fourteen days, or even less by exceptionally fit people.

Figure 6.13 Long-distance footpaths and bridle-ways in England and Wales

- The South West Peninsula Coast Path, the longest footpath, follows the old coastguards' paths through North Devon, Cornwall, South Devon and Dorset.
- The South Downs Way, which stretches from Eastbourne to South Harting, near Petersfield, is the only long distance bridleway, which means that horse-riders and cyclists as well as walkers can enjoy the path following the ridge of the South Downs in an AONB.

National Trust

The National Trust is the country's largest private landowner. Its properties include farms, woodland, nature reserves, 50 villages and hamlets and many stretches of coastline. The Trust has a special campaign called Enterprise Neptune devoted to acquiring and preserving coastline property and currently it protects 500 miles of coastline in England, Wales and Northern Ireland. There is an independent National Trust for Scotland with concern for conservation. The National Trust controls access to their land and makes every effort to screen car parks and service buildings from view by tree planting.

Man-made attractions

With the uncertain weather of Britain, man-made attractions are very popular. Almost every town has its museum or art gallery, some have zoos, others have castles, ancient abbeys or stately homes within an hour's drive. Since the late 1980s indoor attractions have sprung up around the country. The success of theme parks such as Alton Towers and Thorpe Park depends on some of their facilities being available regardless of the weather. Exhibitions and displays connected with industrial heritage have been brought to life, with living museums such as Wigan Pier and the Ironbridge Museum. Leisure complexes, both municipal and private, can offer all day entertainment in tropical heat under cover.

Historical buildings and country houses

It is estimated that 70 million visits were made to historic properties in 1994, of which almost half were to cathedrals and churches. Of the 56 historic properties which attracted over 200,000 visitors, 28 charged admission and 28 were free. St Paul's Cathedral is the most heavily visited historic property in England and is estimated to have attracted 2.6 million visits in 1994. The Tower of London attracted by far the highest number of paid admissions and visits to royal properties were also popular, with Windsor Castle and the State Apartments at Buckingham Palace attracting nearly 2 million visitors between them.

According to the BTA, the top ten historic houses and monuments in 1994 were:

1 Tower of London
2 Windsor Castle, Berkshire
3 Edinburgh Castle
4 Roman Baths and Pump Room, Bath
5 Warwick Castle
6 Stonehenge, Wiltshire
7 Shakespeare's Birthplace, Stratford
8 Hampton Court Palace
9 Leeds Castle, Kent
10 Blenheim Palace, Oxfordshire.

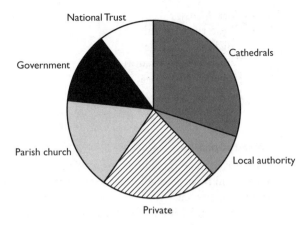

Figure 6.14 Visits to historic properties in England in 1994

Figure 6.14 shows the proportion of visits in England during 1994 to cathedrals and churches, private historic properties, National Trust properties, and local authority and government properties.

In Wales there are castles dating from the earliest times to the series of castles built or strengthened by Edward I in the fourteenth century. The beautiful Caernarfon Castle was the scene for the investiture of the Prince of Wales in 1969 and is one of Britain's best known historical sites. Chepstow Castle, which stands in a superb setting above the Wye river, was probably the first stone castle in Britain. It was added to right up to the English Civil War in the mid-seventeenth century and so illustrates different periods of castle building.

Edinburgh boasts not only the Castle, site of the annual Military Tattoo in August, but also the Palace of Holyroodhouse, official residence of the Queen in Scotland, and New Town, one of the best preserved Georgian areas in the UK.

During 1995 London (121) and Kent (114) had the largest number of historic properties regularly open to the public, followed by Cumbria (102), Devon (91) and North Yorkshire (90).

Church properties

It has been estimated that there are about 8,000 listed Anglican churches which can be visited in England and, according to an English Tourist Board (ETB) survey of visits to churches in August 1993, the most visited parish churches in England were:

- Bath Abbey
- St Martin-in-the-Fields, London
- St Mary the Virgin, Oxford.

The number of visits to cathedrals and churches is difficult to monitor but various methods are used such as distributing leaflets, using counting devices and estimating numbers from visitors' books. According to the BTA, the top ten cathedrals and churches in 1994 were:

1 St Paul's Cathedral
2 Canterbury Cathedral
3 Westminster Abbey

4   York Minster
5   Chester Cathedral
6   Salisbury Cathedral
7   Winchester Cathedral
8   Norwich Cathedral
9   Buckfast Abbey
10 Exeter Cathedral.

Private properties

Britain is rich in country houses which not only are furnished in their period but also have been lived in by the same family for generations. Indeed in some of the smaller properties it is possible to chat with the owners. Privately owned homes sometimes specialise in topics which are of interest to their owner. Arley Hall in Cheshire has spectacular gardens and also encourages local craft workers to demonstrate their skills for visitors.

Many stately home owners have realised that they need to entertain children while parents enjoy the historical treasures and so adventure playgrounds have been introduced. The Earl of Shelburne at Bowood in Wiltshire has a paradise of treetop cabins, rope bridges, trampolines and a life-size pirate galleon to delight any child.

Private owners have banded together to form the Historic Houses Association which at April 1995, had 1,416 full members of whom 393 had properties regularly open to the public. Other private properties have formed an association as the Treasure Houses of England and these include the following:

- Beaulieu in Hampshire, owned by Lord Beaulieu, has the National Motor Museum as well as the house, abbey and gardens open to the public.
- Blenheim Palace near Woodstock in Oxfordshire, owned by the Duke of Marlborough, and birthplace of Winston Churchill; is set in extensive parkland originally laid out by Capability Brown.
- Broadlands in Hampshire, owned by Lord Romsey, was previously the home of the late Lord Mountbatten and the country home of Lord Palmerston, the Victorian prime minister.
- Castle Howard in North Yorkshire, owned by the Howard family, was chosen by Evelyn Waugh as the setting for his novel *Brideshead Revisited* and used as the principal location for the television series.
- Harewood House in West Yorkshire, owned by the Earl of Harewood, cousin of the Queen, has fine ceilings and furniture, a bird garden and tropical houses simulating rain forest, river banks and waterfalls.
- Warwick Castle in Warwickshire, owned by the Tussauds Group, is marketed as 'the finest medieval castle in England'. Madam Tussaud waxwork figures are used to enhance the furnishings and décor in the former Private Apartments.
- Woburn Abbey in Bedfordshire, owned by the Marquess of Tavistock and home of the Dukes of Bedford for over 300 years, contains one of the most important private collections of furniture, porcelain, silver and Canaletto paintings.
- Chatsworth in Derbyshire, owned by the Duke of Devonshire, is a beautiful house and gardens which is home in early September each year to the two-day Chatsworth Country Fair (Fig. 6.15).

National trust properties

The National Trust cares for a wide variety of buildings of architectural and historical interest. These range from humble cottages, which may be rented to tenants, to larger houses of country families, including the following:

Figure 6.15 September Country Fair, Chatsworth, Derbyshire

- The home of the Browne family at Townend, Troutbeck, in the Lake District, dates from the seventeenth century and contains much of the Brownes' personal furniture and belongings.
- Sizergh Castle in Cumbria was in the Strickland family from the thirteenth century until it was handed into the care of the National Trust in 1950.
- Little Moreton Hall in Cheshire is a fine example of a traditional timber-frame black and white construction.

The National Trust manages 140 country houses, some of which, like Hardwick Hall in Derbyshire, Petworth House in West Sussex and Blickling Hall in Norfolk, have great collections of art and furniture. The gardens of many of these houses are also of interest. The guidebook of Blickling Hall takes the visitor through the gardens with every detail of shrubs and trees. A fifth of the National Trust properties are in the West Country, 18 of them in Devon and 11 in Cornwall.

English Heritage properties

The Department of the Environment, under the banner of English Heritage, operates many historic properties. Fountains Abbey near Ripon in Yorkshire is said to be one of the finest examples in Europe of a medieval monastery (Fig. 6.16). Much of it is now in ruins but it is still possible to trace the life of the community. Several English Heritage properties are brought to life for visitors with an extensive programme each year of events and activities.

Local authority properties

Of the 2,000 historic buildings and monuments regularly open to the public in 1995, 25% were owned by local authorities. National Trust and private properties tend to be

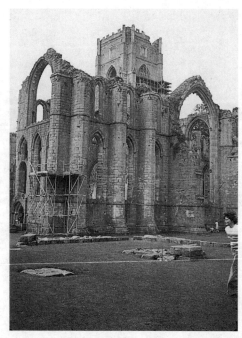

Figure 6.16 Fountains Abbey, near Ripon, Yorkshire

found in rural locations in the south of England, but government and local authority properties are more evenly distributed between the north and south. Many local authority properties, particularly in the large Northern and Midland cities, are museum conversions. For example in Greater Manchester, thirteen out of the twenty historic buildings open to the public are owned by the local authority.

An initiative to open historic buildings to the public started in 1994 when the Department of National Heritage funded the Civic Trust to organise Heritage Open Days over a weekend in September. In its first year over 250,000 visits were made to about 900 historic buildings, many of which would not normally be open to the public.

Town trails have been drawn up in many cities to guide the public to appreciate historic and church buildings, many of which have impressive façades. Without the trails many such buildings might stand unnoticed in the midst of undistinguished architecture.

Heritage trails are used in some areas to link together different towns, villages and buildings through a single unifying theme. Such trails are particularly successful in Scotland, for example:

- The Whisky Trail is a 70 mile trip around the whisky distilleries of Speyside, including Glenfiddich, Glen Grant and Cardhu.
- The Scottish Quality Trail not only includes the Glenfiddich distillery but also takes visitors to Baxter's where they can see the Victorian kitchen where the famous soups were first made.
- The Castle Trail takes visitors to nine castles to the west of Aberdeen.

Museums and art galleries

Throughout the UK there is a wide network of museums, many of which are free to the public. From the British Museum, with its worldwide reputation, to small local collections, most museums have changed their image in recent years and the dour curator has become the friend and confidant of children as they enter a new environment.

In the Liverpool Museum, children queue to be the first into the natural history section during afternoons in the school holidays when there are countless activities and exhibits for them to use. The Science Museum in Kensington could keep anyone, child or adult, occupied for days. On the five floors of the museum visitors can explore space, engineering, chemistry, oceanography and medicine.

Several museums have introduced drama to help interpret their collections. The National Museum of Photography at Bradford has a team of dancers who interpret both recent photographic history and modern photographic collections in a unique art form. The Museum of the Moving Image on the South Bank of the Thames in London uses actors both to interpret their displays for visitors and to act as security staff in all areas of the museums.

During 1994, according to the BTA, the ten most visited UK museums and art galleries were:

1	British Museum, London	F
2	National Gallery, London	F
3	Tate Gallery, London	F
4	Natural History Museum, London	
5	Victoria and Albert Museum, London	F
6	Science Museum, London	
7	National Portrait Gallery, London	F
8	Royal Academy, London	
9	Glasgow Art Gallery and Museum	F
10	National Museum of Photography, Bradford	F

Those museums marked with an F offered free admission to visitors.

One of the more unusual museums in the UK must be the National Railway Museum, a part of the Science Museum, which is based in York. Here are housed some of the earliest locomotives; Victorian royal carriages; an enormous engine weighing over 190 tons which was built in 1935 for the Chinese National Railways; and many more, including Mallard, which holds the world speed record for steam locomotives.

York also has the country's largest folk museum in the Castle Museum (Fig. 6.17). This collection was started by a country doctor at the end of the nineteenth century as he made his round of visits and saw a traditional way of life that was still unaffected by the modern world. He began to collect items of interest, many of which other people regarded as mere rubbish. His collection extended from truncheons, bicycles and musical boxes to fireplaces, redundant farm equipment and even shop fronts. Today it is possible to walk down cobbled streets within the museum, to enter shops which have the sights and smells of Victorian days, and even, bringing heritage nearer to modern times, to see a fully fitted sitting room and kitchen of the 1950s.

Glasgow's Burrell Collection of over 8,000 items from the ancient world to nineteenth-century French paintings is world famous. The entire collection was a gift to the city in 1944 and it is housed in a specially designed gallery which was opened by the Queen in 1983. The McLellan Galleries were also opened by the Queen and the beautifully restored setting is host to touring and temporary art exhibitions.

Figure 6.17 Castle Museum, York

Industrial heritage and modern museums

In recent years industrial heritage has become a popular subject for tourism. Buildings dating from the Industrial Revolution have been restored and tools and implements associated with local trades are displayed in an attractive and informative manner.

At the Wrekin Heritage in Staffordshire it is possible, within a ten mile radius, to visit the Aerospace Museum at RAF Cosford, the Ironbridge Gorge Museum and the Midland Motor Museum as well as the Severn Valley Railway. Ironbridge, which claims to be the birthplace of the Industrial Revolution, has a total of six museum sites for the visitor.

Around the country, open air living museums of industrial heritage have been developed at:

- Beamish Open Air Museum, Co Durham
- The Black Country Museum, Dudley
- Blists Hill, Ironbridge
- Morwellham Quay, Devon
- Weald and Downland Museum, near Chichester.

Beamish Open Air Museum

At many of these industrial heritage sites interpreters are dressed in period costume to enhance the experience of the past for visitors. Artefacts and period buildings are used at Beamish to recreate 1913 (Fig. 6.18). Visitors can be served in the local co-op, can visit the dentist where instruments and smells recall the past vividly for older guests, or can even go down the confined passages of a drift mine, escorted by retired miners in period dress who bring the working conditions of the past to life.

Figure 6.18 Beamish Open Air Museum, Co. Durham

Wigan Pier

Wigan in Lancashire has capitalised on an old music-hall joke and created Wigan Pier, a unique complex of restored canalside warehouses and mill buildings. However, this is no dry museum for within its walls is the living world of cloggers, tinsmiths and boltmakers. Tourists can become children again in a real live Victorian schoolroom, complete with the strictest of teachers; they can even pay their respects in a bereaved home where they are welcomed through the kitchen by the son of the house.

Jorvik Museum

The accidental discovery of Viking remains on the building site for a supermarket led eventually to the fascinating Jorvik Museum in York. At Jorvik visitors travel backwards in a time carriage and wander through the main street of Viking York, complete with realistic sights, sounds and even smells. At the end of the tour, for the Viking enthusiast, there is a museum of actual treasure found on the site during the excavations. The prize exhibit is the Coppergate Helmet, which is not Viking but in fact a unique example of the kind of helmet probably worn by royal or noble Anglo-Saxons in Northumbria at about the time of the first Viking attacks. The same company which created this unusual museum has gone on to create equally fascinating historical exhibits at Canterbury, Dover and Oxford.

Theme parks

Theme parks hold great attraction for all ages in all parts of the country. These parks usually have fairground rides for children, teenagers and adults alike, many have beautiful gardens and all aim to provide enough under cover entertainment to keep visitors happy for at least one full day.

Alton Towers

Alton Towers, in Staffordshire, is centrally located for visitors from many parts of England and Wales and its popularity testifies to this. Not only does it contain a fairground to rival any other for youngsters, but also its gardens are a pleasure for more sedate guests.

Thorpe Park

Thorpe Park in Surrey just off the M 25 is accessible to many people in the Greater London area and each summer has over a million visitors. The organisers claim that there are up to four hours of entertainment completely under cover should the weather be bad (Fig. 6.19).

Other theme parks

The American Adventure in Derbyshire and the Magical Kingdom of Camelot in Lancashire, while not on the same scale as the other parks, nevertheless offer great days out, with under cover entertainment and thrilling and daring rides. Granada Studios in Manchester is a new style of theme park which takes the visitor into the magical world of television where everything is not what it seems. Visitors can walk

Figure 6.19 Thorpe park, Surrey (*Photograph: Thorpe park*)

Figure 6.20 Granada Studios, Manchester

down famous streets, drink in well-known bars, become children in a giant's world or chat with the housekeeper of Sherlock Holmes in his private study (Fig. 6.20).

Theme parks also have an eye to the business world with each one offering conference or business entertaining facilities. During 1994, according to the BTA, the top ten leisure parks and piers were

1	Blackpool Pleasure Beach	*	F
2	Palace Pier, Brighton	*	F
3	Alton Towers, Staffordshire		
4	Funland and Laserbowl, Trocadero, London	*	F
5	Pleasure Beach, Great Yarmouth	*	F
6	Pleasureland, Southport	*	F
7	Chessington World of Adventures		
8	Blackpool Tower		
9	Frontierland, Morecambe	*	F
10	Hornsea Pottery, Hornsea	*	F

Those listed with * gave estimated visitor numbers and those listed with F offered free admission.

Leisure complexes and holiday villages

Leisure and sports facilities are becoming very popular with today's emphasis on fitness and health. Some local authorities have opened their own facilities, such as the dry ski slope at Southampton and the Waves Water Fun Centre at Blackburn. The management in most of the larger hotels throughout the country realise the attraction of these complexes and it is not uncommon to find a hotel offering not only a small swimming pool but also a jaccuzi, sauna and sunbeds together with mini-gym. Such facilities add to the potential of the hotel for staging conferences and business entertainment.

Holiday Villages may offer self-catering or full board in accommodation which ranges from the most basic to luxurious fully equipped cabins. Three of the main companies offering holiday complexes in the UK are Center Parcs, Butlins and Pontins.

Center Parcs

Center Parcs, in Nottinghamshire, was one of the first complexes in the UK to be built with a central dome over the swimming area creating a subtropical paradise. Other parcs have been built in East Anglia and at Longleat in Wiltshire. Accommodation is in modern purpose-built cabins and on-site facilities include cycling, walking, adventure trails and evening entertainment.

Butlins

Butlins holiday camps were totally updated during the 1980s. Five of the original camps have been renamed Holiday Worlds and the brochure also offers holidays in five hotels. The Holiday Worlds offer self-catering, half or full board accommodation. Entertainment facilities include fairgrounds, fully equipped theatres, fun pools with slides and flume rides and clubs to occupy children of all ages.

Pontins

Fred Pontin started his holiday camps in the late 1940s and today's brochure offers a choice of twenty Holiday Centres around England and Wales, as well as Plemont Bay on Jersey. Five of the mainland centres are Chalet Hotels with full table service as well as all the entertainment offered in the other centres. Five of Pontins holiday centres offer holidays for adults only. These are very popular with older people, particularly during the summer months of the school holidays.

These leisure and holiday centres offer holidays which are very often enjoyed by three generations of a family. Some of the centres which have been built on flat land near to the sea are also particularly suitable for holidays for disabled people.

London

Many of the top attractions are in London and all travel agents, wherever they live in the UK, need a special awareness and knowledge of the capital. Many clients will want to visit London for short breaks and others will have occasion to travel through the capital. In either case the travel agent needs enough information to be able to advise them about routes, accommodation and places of interest (Fig. 6.21).

Famous landmarks

Royal Albert Hall, Kensington
Palace of Westminister, Houses of Parliament
Westminster Abbey
St Paul's Cathedral, City of London
Tower of London
Tower Bridge
Bank of England, Threadneedle Street, City of London

Famous streets

Whitehall
Trafalgar Square
Downing Street
Strand
Piccadilly Circus
Leicester Square
Shaftesbury Avenue
Oxford Street

Royal London

Buckingham Palace, The Mall
Hampton Court Palace, Kingston-upon-Thames
Royal Parks
  Hyde Park
  Kensington Gardens
  Richmond Park
  Green Park
  Regent's Park
  St James's Park

River Thames

Westminster Pier
Cleopatra's Needle
South Bank Complex
HMS *Belfast*
Tower Bridge
Tower of London
St Katherine's Dock
Isle of Dogs
Greenwich

Markets and shopping areas

Petticoat Lane Market, Middlesex Street
Portobello Road Market, Nottting Hill
Harrods, Brompton Road

Figure 6.21 Summary of London attractions

Oxford Street, Regent Street, Bond Street

Museums, art galleries and theatres

British Museum, Great Russell Street
Science Museum, Kensington
Geological Museum, Kensington
Natural History Museum, Kensington
Victoria and Albert Museum, Kensington
National Gallery, Trafalgar Square
National Portrait Gallery, Trafalgar Square
Tate Gallery, Millbank
West End theatres
Barbican, City of London
Museum of London, London Wall
Museum of the Moving Image, South Bank

Modern attractions

Wembley Stadium
Earls Court
Madame Tussaud's
London Planetarium
Rock Circus
Guinness World of Records
London Dungeon
Tower Hill Pageant

London festivals and ceremonies

March	Harness Horse Parade, Regent's Park
	Oxford and Cambridge Boat Race, Putney to Mortlake
April	London Marathon
May	Chelsea Flower Show
June	Trooping the Colour, Horse Guards Parade, Whitehall
	Lawn Tennis Championships, Wimbledon
August	Notting Hill Carnival
October	State Opening of Parliament, Westminster
November	RAC London to Brighton Veteran Car Run, Hyde Park
	Lord Mayor's Show, City of London
	Remembrance Day Service, The Cenotaph, Whitehall
December	Christmas Tree, Trafalgar Square
	Illuminated Decorations, Regent Street and Oxford Street

Revision Questions

Primary level

1 Name the COUNTY in which you would find each of the following resorts

Southport
Torquay
New Quay
Oban
Brighton
Newquay
Saltcoats
Scarborough
Great Yarmouth
Rhyl

2 Name THREE English national parks.

3 Name THREE airports in the London area.

4 Name the motorways linking the following

Preston to Birmingham
Birmingham to Exeter
London to Bristol
Sheffield to London
London to Dover

5 Name FOUR UK attractions which are linked to the Royal Family.

6 Name the longest long distance footpath in the UK.

7 What is the name of the UK's largest private landowner which protects both countryside and coastline?

8 Name FOUR outdoor activities which are popular with tourists in the UK.

9 Name FOUR open air museums which preserve industrial heritage in the UK.

10 Name TWO theme parks in the north west of England which would appeal to young children.

Advanced level

1 Name THREE officially designated areas of outstanding natural beauty and explain how to reach them from your home town.

2 Name ONE example of EACH of the following which may be visited within a 50 mile radius of Birmingham:

an historical site
a living museum
a theme park
a holiday village.

3 Name the nearest town or city to the following attractions:

Jorvik Viking Centre
Stonehenge
Chatsworth
Blenheim Palace
Granada Studios
Alton Towers
Fountains Abbey
Ironbridge Gorge

4 Name the city in which you would find each of the following attractions:

Palace of Holyroodhouse
Castle Museum
National Museum of Photography, Film and Television
Science Museum
National Railway Museum

5 Name TWO national organisations dedicated to the preservation of coastline and countryside in England.

6 Name TWO national parks in Wales.

7 Which agency is responsible for designating national parks, areas of outstanding natural beauty and long distance footpaths in England and Wales?

8 Give ONE example of a heritage trail and explain briefly the marketing value of such initiatives.

9 Describe TWO features which distinguish industrial heritage sites from regular museums.

10 Describe FOUR features which contribute to the appeal of holiday villages such as Center Parcs, Butlins and Pontins to the family market.

7) *European destinations*

In this chapter we consider some of the most popular destinations for British tourists in Europe. There are new markets opening up all the time and an awareness of current trends can be maintained through the travel trade press and daily newspapers. With the Single European Market (see Fig. 7.1) British tourists have increased opportunities for travel in other EU countries.

According to the data from the International Passenger Survey, the most popular European destinations for UK tourists in the 1990s are

- France
- Spain
- Greece
- Italy
- Alpine areas.

France, Spain, Greece and Italy are considered in some detail in this chapter and the Alpine ski resorts will be considered in Chapter 11.

Eastern Europe

The greatest increase in interest in other areas of Europe in the 1990s has been to Eastern European countries such as Poland and Hungary, where the number of British tourists has gone up dramatically. These countries were relatively inaccessible during the Cold War but once the Berlin Wall was demolished in 1989 and the Iron Curtain raised, the former communist countries of Eastern Europe became very desirable destinations for their curiosity value and the wealth of cultural and architectural interest.

The political changes in Eastern Europe have meant that some borders have been redrawn, resulting for example in a reunited Germany and a divided Czechoslovakia. Yugoslavia, torn by internal war, became in the mid-1990s an undesirable tourist destination, in spite of its high degree of popularity with British tourists in the 1980s. In 1990, 385,000 British tourists visited Yugoslavia, but only 31,000, mainly in the first quarter, made the trip in 1991, which represented a loss of 79 per cent of tourist trade. Numbers have steadily declined throughout the 1990s and in 1995 Yugotours, the national tour operator, ceased trading.

Information sources

The national tourist offices, many of which are based in London, are excellent sources of material for creating a European file of information. World Travel Market (WTM) is an invaluable source of information and material. WTM is an exhibition held at Earls Court in London at the end of November each year. This is the largest travel trade show in the world and European countries such as France, Spain, Portugal, Switzerland and Austria are always well represented. The World Travel Market affords an opportunity to talk to nationals from the countries, as well as being able to obtain information, maps and posters.

Figure 7.1 shows the European countries most popular with British tourists, including most capital cities, and the darker shading indicates those which are winter-sun destinations.

Figure 7.2 indicates the wide variety of physical features in Europe from the flat landscape of the Netherlands to the mountains of the Swiss Alps or the high plateau of Spain.

Capital cities

Capital cities tend to be all-year destinations for those clients who have an interest in culture and heritage. They are also important business destinations and are very often the gateway airport to a country.

Country	Capital	Country	Capital
Albania	Tirana	Macedonia	Skopje
Austria	Vienna	Malta	Valetta
Belgium	Brussels	Moldavia	Kishinev
Belorussia	Minsk	Netherlands	Amsterdam
Bosnia	Sarajevo	Norway	Oslo
Bulgaria	Sofia	Poland	Warsaw
Croatia	Zagreb	Portugal	Lisbon
Denmark	Copenhagen	Republic of Ireland	Dublin
Estonia	Tallinn	Romania	Bucharest
Finland	Helsinki	Russia	Moscow
France	Paris	Serbia	Belgrade
Germany	Berlin	Slovenia	Ljubljana
Greece	Athens	Spain	Madrid
Hungary	Budapest	Sweden	Stockholm
Iceland	Reykjavik	Switzerland	Bern
Italy	Rome	Turkey	Ankara
Latvia	Riga	Ukraine	Kiev
Lithuania	Vilnius		

Independent travellers have long appreciated Europe but many brochures are more concerned with the mass tourist market of package holidays by air to 'sun and sand' destinations in Spain, Greece or Italy. The larger tour operators produce these brochures but more specialist tour operators offer smaller brochures which sometimes give the client the opportunity to put together a more personalised holiday. These brochures usually offer a modularised package with a choice as regards

- the means of travel
- the route to be taken
- the length of stay
- the type of accommodation.

Individualised tours are increasing in popularity as British tourists, who have gained confidence through the package industry, seek experiences other than sand, sea and lager. Reflecting demographic trends, the teens and 20s market is growing and during the 1990s high growth rates of about 30 per cent are expected for seat-only sales, winter sports and the over-55 markets. Hobby based and special interest holidays are also expected to grow at about 10 per cent. In other European countries there is a tendency to sell modularised packages and it is thought that such holidays will become more popular with British tourists from 1995 onwards.

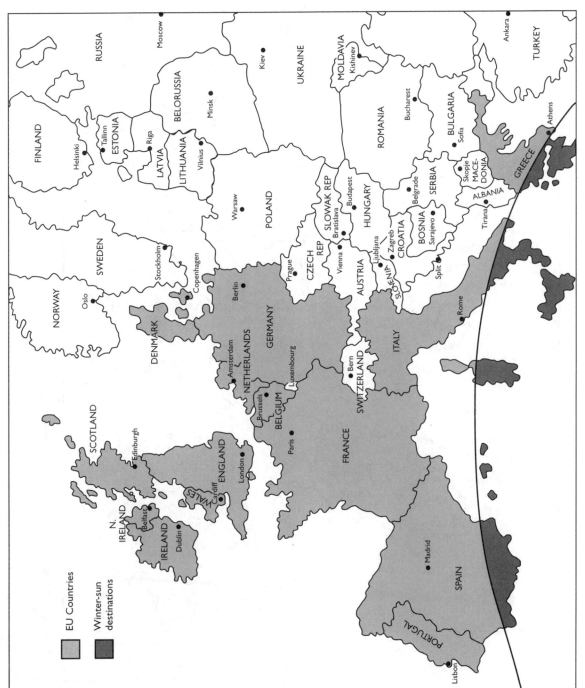

Figure 7.1 European capital cities

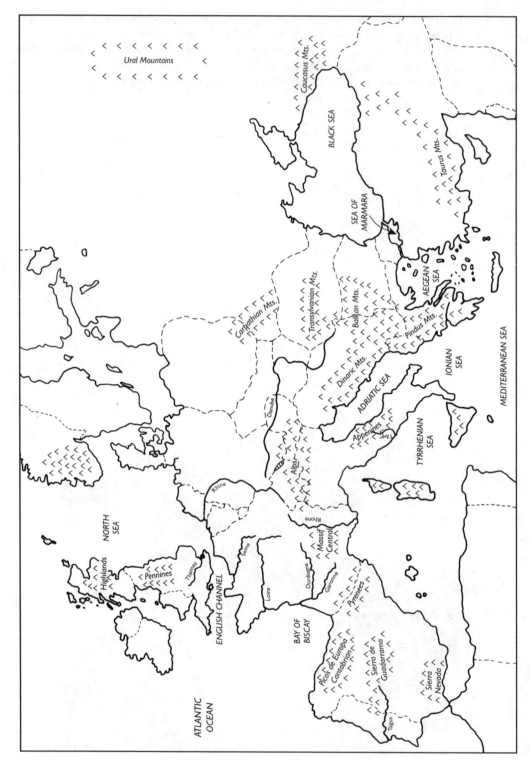

Figure 7.2 Physical features around Europe

France

France is mainly popular as a destination for British tourists who prefer to drive their own car, camping or caravanning or using some of the excellent and varied accommodation which is available in France. Ferry crossings can take from one hour on the short Dover to Calais route to eight hours on the longer overnight routes. The Channel Tunnel services were considered in Chapter 2.

Figure 7.3 outlines some of the areas of France which are popular with British tourists.

Figure 7.4 gives an indication of travelling times from the French ports to some of the popular areas of France. These timings are based on the car travelling at 40 miles per hour, without stops and using major roads. The timings are given only as a guideline. Tolls apply on motorways in France with an average cost of £35 for about 600 miles (960 kilometres). Toll booths do not accept traveller's cheques but some take credit cards.

Paris

Paris, the capital of France, has that international atmosphere which makes it special to people the world over. There are many guide books as well as specialist brochures available but the attractions of Paris, both in the city and within a day's excursion trip, which are included in most itineraries are:

- The Eiffel Tower, at a height of 1,000 feet (308 metres), dominates the Seine; from it there is a magnificent view of Paris. Probably the best place from which to view the Eiffel Tower itself is across the Seine on the Trocadero, a raised marble piazza which is surrounded by museums and galleries (Fig. 7.5).
- The Champs Elysées is an elegant avenue of shops and galleries.
- The Arc de Triomphe, at the west end of the Champs Elysées, is a memorial to France's heroes in which the eternal flame burns.
- The Place de La Concorde, at the other end of the Champs Elysées, has an Egyptian obelisk and 365 lamps, one for each day of the year.
- The Louvre, with its numerous exhibits in the traditional palace, is entered through a controversial pyramid of 666 panes of glass placed in the square. The Tuileries gardens in front of the Louvre will be restored to their former classic glory during the 1990s.
- The church of Notre Dame dominates the Ile de la Cité, a small island in the Seine which was the first settlement in Celtic times.
- Sacre Coeur is a beautiful white church situated high on the hill of Montmartre with terraced gardens giving uninterrupted views of Paris.
- The Ile de France is a wooded area surrounding Paris in which tourists can visit the magnificent chateaux of Versailles and Fontainebleau.

The list of buildings alone is endless but Paris is also famous for fashionable stores and numerous night clubs and shows.

Disneyland, Paris

In 1992 EuroDisney, which was renamed Disneyland, Paris in 1995, opened its doors on a site one-fifth the size of Paris and only 20 miles (32 kilometres) east of the city

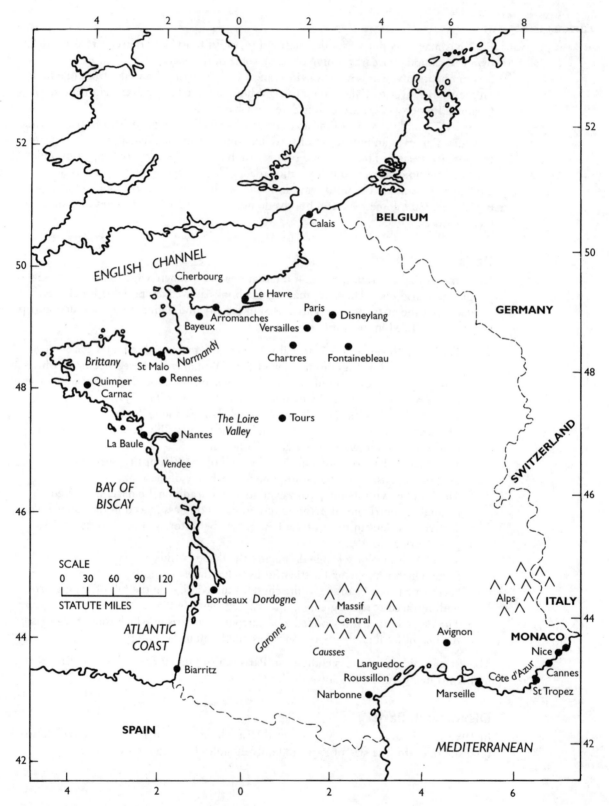

Figure 7.3 Areas in France popular with British tourists

From To	Calais Boulogne Dunkirk	Dieppe	Cherbourg	Le Havre	Caen	St Malo	Roscoff
Normandy	5–7 hrs	3–4 hrs	1–2 hrs	2–3 hrs	1–2 hrs	1–2 hrs	3–5 hrs
Brittany	8–11 hrs	6–8 hrs	3–6 hrs	5–6 hrs	3–6 hrs	1–4 hrs	1–5 hrs
Loire Valley	8 hrs	5 hrs	5 hrs	4 hrs	4 hrs	5 hrs	7 hrs
The Causses	14 hrs	11 hrs	11 hrs	10 hrs	9 hrs	10 hrs	12 hrs
Atlantic Coast	16 hrs	12 hrs	12 hrs	13 hrs	12 hrs	10 hrs	12 hrs
Côte d' Azur	18 hrs	18 hrs	17 hrs	17 hrs	19 hrs	17 hrs	20 hrs

Figure 7.4 Travelling times from French ports

Figure 7.5 Eiffel Tower, Paris

centre. The American-style theme park is just off the A4 highway from Paris to Nancy/Metz in Marne-la-Vallée. There is car parking for 12,000 cars or alternatively the journey takes about 45 minutes on the Regional Express Metro Network (RER).

Like its counterparts in Florida (Disney World) and California (Disneyland) Paris's Magic Kingdom has the five lands of Main Street USA, Adventureland, Fantasyland, Frontierland and Discoveryland. The complex also has a golf course and Festival Disney with themed restaurants, shops and entertainment in the evening. Disney hotels on the site range from luxurious to budget accommodation, and the local hotels of the Climat, Fimotel and Novotel chains offer economical accommodation in the vicinity. Disneyland, Paris has probably extended the range of British tourists visiting Paris because families and small groups, as well as business, independent and city break tourists are now attracted to the area.

Brittany

Brittany is the peninsula in northern France which juts out into the Atlantic and where the sea is never more than 50 miles away. The area has a Celtic culture distinct from the rest of France and more akin to the Celtic areas of Britain such as Cornwall, Wales and Scotland (Fig. 7.6).

Figure 7.6 Redon, Brittany, France

The many scattered fishing ports of Brittany offer quaint and interesting backdrops for the tourist, as well as being centres for yachting. The light in this northern part of France makes the ports ideal subjects for artists. Inland there are many villages dating from the Middle Ages which have narrow winding streets of brown and cream half-timbered houses. Most villages can boast a market and some have interesting prehistoric remains, such as the ancient Standing Stones at Carnac.

Quimper on the River Odet is particularly attractive to tourists during the Cornouaille Festival in July when all the local villages are represented in a fantastic parade celebrating the culture of the Breton people. The people of each village dress in their traditionally embroidered black velvet costumes and carry flowers, fishing baskets, or dogs, indeed anything that could be regarded as typical of their village. The black and white Breton flag is in great evidence and traditional instruments such as the bagpipes are played as the procession marches past.

Normandy

Normandy has a rugged coastline in the north similar to Cornwall while inland there is beautiful woodland scenery. The coastline has associations with battles in both the First and Second World Wars and the area round Arromanches, the site of the D-Day landings in 1944, is particularly interesting to ex-soldiers and historians. The much earlier invasion in 1066 is commemorated in the Bayeux tapestry in a small town about 20 miles from the coast.

Loire Valley

The Loire Valley is a beautiful area with its gentle, soft landscape, chosen by aristocrats over the centuries for their country houses. Today it is a popular area for tourists and rose nurseries, flower gardens and fruit trees make it particularly beautiful in the spring.

La Baule at the mouth of the River Loire is a summer resort with a long sandy beach, traditional promenade, hotels, restaurants and a casino. Inland both Chartres and Tours have beautiful thirteenth-century cathedrals and throughout the region there are numerous châteaux open to the public, some of them offering accommodation as well.

The Causses

The Causses in the southern part of the Massif Central has spectacular limestone plateaux and gorges, and daily living is cheap for those who are prepared to live as the French. This is not the ideal holiday for those who expect to find coca cola and hamburgers at every corner.

Dordogne

Further west the Dordogne river flows through an area which has several other beautiful and interesting rivers and finally meets the River Garonne north of Bordeaux before emptying into the Bay of Biscay. This Atlantic coast of France has many smaller resorts, as yet unspoilt by mass tourism.

French Alps

The French Alps provide one of the most important skiing areas in Europe. With the height of the Alps reaching to over 6,000 feet, snow can be guaranteed even in the mildest winter. The purpose-built resorts in the Alps offer good accommodation at reasonable prices and ski runs which would test even the most proficient skier. More details about skiing holidays can be found in Chapter 11.

Côte d'Azur

The Côte d'Azur or French Riviera on the south eastern coast of France is long established as a tourist area. Here are the world famous Nice, Cannes and further east the principality of Monaco with its casino in Monte Carlo.

On the Côte d'Azur the beautiful, rich and famous parade themselves on their yachts and in the gambling clubs, or hide from view in their closely guarded homes. The lure and attraction of such an area is inevitable and, alongside the rich and famous, there are countless tent and caravan sites for the not so rich.

Corsica

Corsica, the French island in the Mediterranean, is a mountainous island with vast forested areas rich in cork oaks, chestnuts and olives. Ajaccio its capital is famous as the birthplace of Napoleon and Bastia in the north is an historic citadel which has preserved its medieval street pattern while encouraging a modern commercial port.

Summary of France

Capital:	Paris
Currency:	French franc (FF) with one franc =100 centimes. Some hotels will change money but the most convenient places are the Crédit Mutuel and the Crédit Agricole
Getting there:	**By air:** there are airports in Paris (Charles de Gaulle and Orly), Bordeaux, Lille, Lyon, Marseille, Nice and Toulouse.
	By sea: English Channel ferry ports include Dunkirk, Calais, Boulogne, Dieppe, Le Havre, Caen, Cherbourg, St Malo and Roscoff. The south of France can be accessed by sea through the ports of Marseille, Toulon and Nice.
	By rail: there are connections, including Channel Tunnel and ferry crossing, from London using British Rail and the French Railway (SNCF).
Main interests for British tourists include:	the sights of Paris, Disneyland, the tranquillity of Brittany and Normandy, the sunshine of the south of France, the pleasure of touring, and skiing in the Alps.
Banking hours:	09.00–12.00 and 14.00–16.00 Monday to Friday. Some banks close all day Saturday, others close all day Monday.
Shopping hours:	09.00–18.30 Monday to Saturday in the larger stores, but many stores outside Paris close for a two hour lunch break. Hypermarkets are usually open until 21.00. Small bakeries will often open on a Sunday, but may be closed on Mondays.
Special note:	In the months of July and August, when the French take their holidays, the city attractions are quieter while the coastal resorts are more crowded.

Spain

Madrid

Madrid, the capital of Spain, does not have the international jet-setting image of Paris, but nevertheless it is a fascinating city and is important as a business destination. In winter Madrid, which is on the high plateau, is very cold but in summer it is so hot that the Spanish government moves north to San Sebastian on the Atlantic coast.

Madrid has many interesting museums, the largest of which is the Prado which houses paintings by artists of the Spanish, Italian and Venetian schools as well as works of classical sculpture. The Plaza Mayor is a magnificent large square enclosed by some of the most beautiful buildings in Europe.

The countryside surrounding Madrid is filled with castles and ancient cities including:

- Segovia with its Alcazar, the fortress built by the Moors, and the long viaduct which the Romans constructed across the city
- Toledo, a former capital of Spain, which was world famous at one time for its swords and jewellery
- the dramatic walled city of Avila, a well preserved medieval city with many historical connections.

The 'costas'

Most British tourists who travel to Spain on a package holiday go for the sun and sand of the 'costas'. These are the areas along the Mediterranean coastline, stretching from the Costa Brava near the French border, through Barcelona and the Costa Dorada, to Benidorm and the Costa Blanca, down to the Costa de Almeria and finally the Costa del Sol on the south coast. Figure 7.7 shows the outline of these areas in Spain.

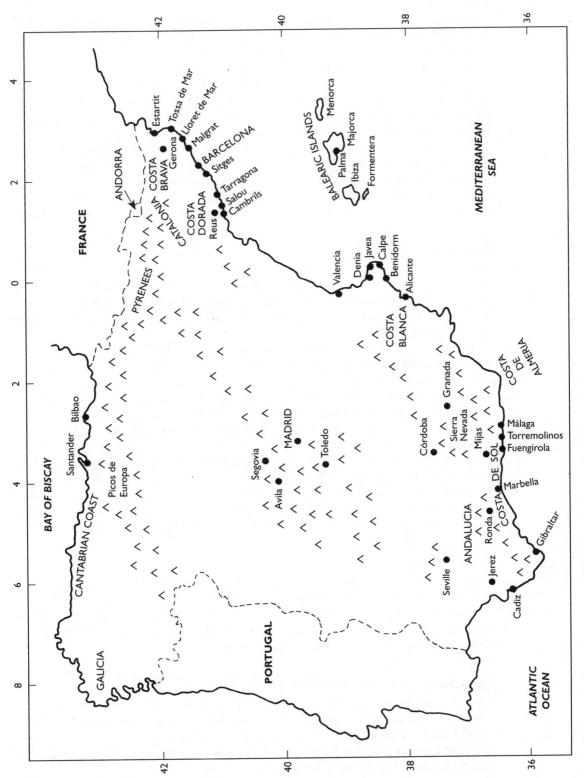

Figure 7.7 Areas in Spain popular with British tourists

Costa Brava

The Costa Brava, the 'wild rugged coast', was the first area to open up to tourists in large numbers, with many resorts along the coastline of Catalonia. The Costa Brava is accessible to British tourists through the airport at Gerona.

Most of the resorts of the Costa Brava are either small fishing villages which have been taken over by tourists, or resorts such as Malgrat which are a cluster of hotels and apartments lying along the coast and the main railway line to Barcelona. Much of the accommodation in this area is now becoming dated but it still provides holidays at the best value for money for the average tourist who wants two weeks in the sun.

The largest resort in the area is Lloret de Mar which has English pubs and clubs, funny hats and rock and is overrun by tourists throughout the summer. Quieter resorts are also to be found along the Costa Brava and, for those who are prepared to make their own way, there are some delightful, unspoilt villages in this friendly area of Catalonia which preserves a language and heritage distinct from that of the rest of Spain.

Barcelona

Barcelona, the capital of Catalonia, is a fascinating city in both summer and winter. On the harbour front is the statue of Columbus who returned from his transatlantic trip to the port of Barcelona. Beside the statue is moored a replica of his ship, the *Santa Maria*, and further along the quay is the Maritime Museum which has nautical exhibits from all over the world.

Inland from the harbour is the famous Ramblas, a tree-lined street with a central promenade. In summer, market stalls display their wares and in December the area, both here and outside the medieval cathedral, is a wonderland of Christmas novelties. Wandering through the old Gothic quarter near to the cathedral, visitors can enter coffee shops which take them back through time with their décor and old world charm. At the end of the Ramblas is the fashionable shopping area with El Corte Ingles, a national department store chain.

Overlooking the city is the hillside of Montjuic with the Olympic stadium and the Pueblo Espanhol or Spanish Village which has numerous shops and cafés set within its façades designed to represent the various architectures to be found throughout Spain.

All of this, together with many churches, a bullring, the football stadium and countless museums, go to make Barcelona a city of varied and ever changing interest.

Costa Dorada

The Costa Dorada, the 'golden coast', south of Barcelona, has quieter resorts than those to be found to the north. The Costa Dorada is accessible through the airport at Reus.

Sitges has steep winding streets and a long tree-lined promenade, while Salou, which is a little brasher, still maintains a genteel air with the height of buildings limited and a wide rambla-type promenade stretching for miles (Fig. 7.8).

Costa Blanca

Further south the skyline of Benidorm on the Costa Blanca, the 'white coast', is dominated by high-rise apartments and hotels, often reaching to over 30 storeys. The Costa Blanca is accessible through the airport of Alicante.

Benidorm is a resort which might be said to have a split personality. In summer it is the throbbing destination for millions of families and teenagers so that in July or August it is difficult to put a foot between the bodies on the beach. However, in the

Figure 7.8 Salou, Costa Dorada, Spain

winter it is a paradise for those who can afford the time to take a break from the winter weather in UK. The beaches are empty and spotless, making a beautiful sight with their clusters of palm trees; the weather is calm and warm, rivalling the average British summer; the discos and bars on the seafront resound to the music of tea dances; and the British pensioner reigns supreme in a resort where English is becoming as common as Spanish. Once the summer season returns, the entertainment, restaurants and hotels adapt themselves so that the busiest resort on the Mediterranean can once again offer its clients everything in the way of sand, sea and fun (Fig. 7.9).

Only a few miles out of Benidorm are the villas and apartments of those who prefer to buy their own property and some of these are in fishing ports such as Calpe, while others like those in Javea, feature prestigious, landscaped holiday developments. Some brochures offer self-catering accommodation in the villages outside Benidorm but it is worth noting that car hire would be essential if holidaymakers are not to be stranded in these villages.

Costa de Almeria

The southern coast of Spain has a series of resorts catering for the British market, from the Costa de Almeria to Gibraltar. The Costa de Almeria was opened up, to a great extent, by Horizon, a company which now forms part of the Thomson Holidays group, who even have a street named after them. The accommodation on the Costa de Almeria is generally in very modern but Moorish-style hotels and apartments complete with every amenity. The sun is hot almost every week of the year, as can be testified by the desert-like surroundings in which many a Spaghetti Western was filmed. For those who want guaranteed sun and sand, without being concerned about experiencing Spanish culture, there really could not be a better choice.

Figure 7.9 Benidorm, Costa Blanca, Spain

Costa del Sol

Further west is the Costa del Sol, the 'sun coast', with the traditional resorts of Torremolinos, Fuengirola and Marbella along the coastline of Andalucia. The Costa del Sol is accessed through the airport at Malaga.

Each resort on the Costa del Sol has its own distinct atmosphere, with Torremolinos appealing to the younger end of the market and Marbella shedding its up-market image in order to appeal to the average tourist. The more expensive life-style can be experienced at Puerto Banus where the yachts of the wealthy are moored and it is well worth a visit.

Outside the towns it is quite easy to travel into the hills and encounter the true spirit of Andalucia with its white-washed cottages and brightly coloured flowers. Mijas is such a town which, while being commercialised to the extent that it offers a donkey taxi for the tourist as well as numerous gift shops, still retains the charm of a mountain village.

Gibraltar

From all of the resorts of southern Spain it is possible to take a trip to Gibraltar. For some it is a nostalgic trip with memories of days in the Services, for others it is simply one more opportunity for duty free goods.

Northern Spain

Apart from the main holiday areas for the mass tourist market, Spain has much more to offer. Both Brittany Ferries and P&O Ferries take clients direct from Britain to Spain, landing at Santander or Bilbao in the north. Although the summer weather is cooler than in the south, the Cantabrian coast in the north has beautiful, unspoilt beaches and coves while further west, the green and beautiful Galicia hides behind the mountains revealing its secrets to very few foreign tourists.

Mountainous Spain

To the east are the mountains of the Pyrenees, with the independent principality of Andorra. Trips are arranged to this area from the Costa Brava in the summer, and skiing is becoming very popular in the winter. Skiing is also to be found in the Sierra Nevada in the south where it is possible to experience a combined winter and summer holiday during spring when the mountains are cold, but the warm beaches are only a short drive away. The Sierra Nevada mountains also lead to the historical Andalucian cities of Granada, with its Moorish palaces, Córdoba with its fantastic mosque and Seville and Jerez, the centre of the sherry industry.

Spanish Islands

Spain has the Balearic islands in the Mediterranean and the Canary islands in the Atlantic.

Balearic islands

- Majorca is the largest of this group of islands and has a variety of resorts on the eastern and southern coasts with the main concentration in the south around the capital Palma. The west coast can be reached on a special train to Puerto Soller and the north is the least developed of the 186 mile (300 kilometre) coastline. The centre of the island is very rural and tends to attract independent travellers as opposed to the mass tourists who flock to the coast.
- Menorca, the second largest island, has a concentration of accommodation around Mahon the capital and Cuidadela the former capital.
- Ibiza is a very popular destination which retains some of its traditional atmosphere and many parts of the island are still densely wooded.
- Formentera, which is separated from Ibiza by an hourly boat service in the summer, is the smallest of the Balearic islands and the pace of life is generally more relaxing than on the other islands

Canary islands

- Tenerife is volcanic in origin and has a subtropical, dry and warm climate with a dramatic landscape including Mount Teide with its 12 mile (19 kilometre) wide crater.
- Grand Canary is the third largest of the group of islands and is the most beautiful with splendid beaches and a profusion of flowering plants. The high season for visits to Grand Canary is the winter and spring.
- Lanzarote is a dry fairly flat island which has an eerie, volcanic landscape. The most popular excursions are on camel to the volcanic areas of the island

Summary of Spain

Capital: Madrid

Currency: Peseta (Pta). Money can be changed in any bank, most hotels and in the small bureaux de change which are located in most resorts.

Getting there: *By air:* the main airports are Gerona, Barcelona (del Prat), Reus, Alicante (Altet), Valencia (Manises), Almeria, Malaga, Seville, Madrid (Barajas) and Bilbao.

By sea: many British tourists use the routes from Plymouth to Santander or Portsmouth to Bilbao. Ferries also go to the Balearic islands from Barcelona, and to north Africa from the ports of Alicante, Almeria, Malaga and Algeciras.

By rail: there are direct trains from Lisbon, Paris and Geneva.

Main interests for British tourists include: the sun and sand of the 'costas' and the islands, the historical attractions of Granada, Córdoba and Seville and the tourist and business interests of Madrid.

Banking hours: 09.00–14.00 Monday to Friday, 09.00–13.00 Saturday.

Shopping hours: vary; shops are generally open from 09.00 to 20.00 Monday to Saturday, but they close for a long break in the middle of the day from 13.00 to 16.00. Larger department stores in the cities may not close in the afternoon.

Special note: Tourists who take their own cars to Spain are strongly advised to take out a bail bond. This is because, if anyone injures another person in an accident in Spain, they may be jailed while the accident is being investigated. The bail bond means that the person can afford to be bailed out of jail by putting up the necessary money which will be covered by the bond, almost like an insurance.

Greece

Greece is the most popular European destination after Spain for British package tours. Greece enjoys a warm Mediterranean climate with dry hot days in summer relieved by breezes on the islands. Possibly the greatest attraction for many UK tourists who repeatedly visit Greece is the friendly charm of the Greek people and the relaxed way of life.

The mainland offers a wealth of culture and history but most UK package holidays are located on one of the many islands. Corfu and Rhodes have enjoyed most popularity over the years.

Athens

Athens the capital has many museums, art galleries and archaeological sites. The Acropolis, situated on a limestone plateau above the city, was originally a royal fortress, and later the stronghold of the gods. Its crowning glory is the ruins of the Parthenon, which was destroyed by a Venetian grenade attack in 1687. Further destruction however is continuing at an alarming pace, due to twentieth-century pollution and 3 million tourists tramping across the Acropolis each year. From Piraeus, the port of Athens, regular ferries can be taken to the larger Greek islands.

Approximate journey times from mainland Greece

Corfu	2 hrs
Crete	12 hrs
Kos	15 hrs
Mykonos	6 hrs
Naxos	8 hrs
Rhodes	19 hrs
Zakynthos	1 hr 15 mins

Corfu

Corfu with its lush green countryside is in the Ionian chain of islands just off the west coast of the Greek mainland. In Corfu town, cricket is still played on the Central Square, recalling memories of British rule from 1815 to 1864. Most resorts are along the eastern coastline from Ipsos in the north to Kavos in the south. Benitses, the oldest resort, is trying to shed its brash image. Noisy bars have been toned down, fresh sand is imported

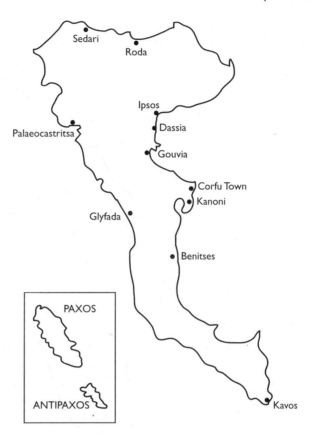

Figure 7.10 Corfu

each year to clean the beach and a bypass takes traffic away from the original fishing village. Kavos in the south of Corfu was at one time a haven of rest and tranquillity with little in the way of organised entertainment. However, since the construction of a new road from the airport, the image of Kavos has changed completely to become the liveliest resort on the island, appealing mainly to the 18–30 market (Fig. 7.10).

Rhodes

Rhodes, the largest of the twelve Dodecanese islands, is just off the coast of Turkey and has a great concentration of holiday accommodation on its northern tip around the main town, also called Rhodes. The presence of a casino probably contributes to the international image which Rhodes has over other Greek islands. The main resorts are Faliraki with lively nightlife and Lindos with its ancient acropolis and the nearby Valley of the Butterflies (Fig. 7.11).

Crete

Crete is the largest and most southerly of the Greek islands and it has its loyal admirers who return year after year. The north of the island has more sophisticated resorts whilst the south coast has some beautiful, peaceful areas for those who want to get away to tranquillity. Historically Crete is famous for its ruins of the Minoan era which lasted from 2800 to 1150 BC. The people of Crete retain a spirit of independence, regarding themselves as different from other Greeks, and the national costume of baggily cut trousers and knee-high boots is still frequently worn in mountain villages (Fig. 7.12).

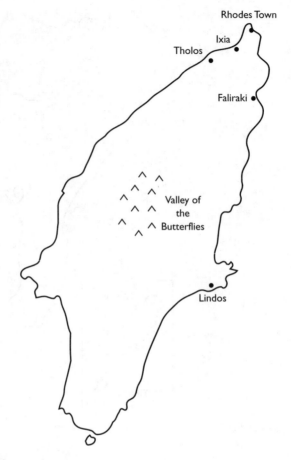

Figure 7.11 Rhodes

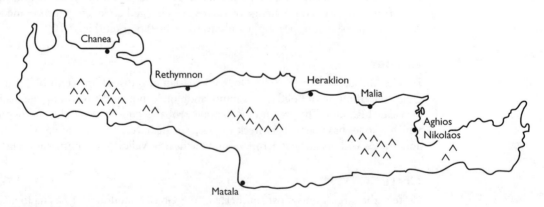

Figure 7.12 Crete

Island groups

The islands of the Cyclades, the Saronic and the Sporades chains have resorts to suit every taste, from the jet-setting Mykonos, with its varied nightlife to isolated, sometimes volcanic islands, where tourists can just relax in the sun and the warmth of the local welcome. It is interesting to remember that the Greek word 'Xenos' means both stranger and friend.

Cyclades islands

The Cyclades are a group of 56 islands in the Aegean Sea which take their name from the circle (kyklos) which they form around the little island of Delos, said to be the birthplace of Apollo. Mykonos, a rather barren hilly island, is the most cosmopolitan island and over the years it has been popular with the gay community. Santorini has black beaches as the result of an earlier volcanic eruption. Paros by contrast is a richly cultivated island which has a popular wine and fish festival in the summer months. Naxos is the largest of this group and the most fertile.

Saronic islands

The Saronic Gulf islands are popular with Athenians in the summer months because of their proximity to the capital. Spetses is the most popular with British tourists who are attracted by its tavernas and old houses clustered around the harbour. The almost total absence of cars and the use of bicycles and horse-drawn carriages add to the special charm for tourists.

Sporades Islands

The Sporades, which means the 'scattered' islands, include the Dodecanese islands of which Rhodes is one. Euboea or Evia is the second largest Greek island after Crete. There is plenty of variety on the island from beaches to mountain climbing, from peaceful villages to busy towns. Skiathos is popular for its peace and quiet, beautiful scenery and safe sandy beaches backed by pine trees.

Summary of Greece

Capital:	Athens
Currency:	Drachma (Dr) with one drachma = 100 lepta. Traveller's cheques and currency can be changed at banks and exchange counters. Exchange rates can vary between one bank and another.
Getting there:	**By air:** to the mainland airports of Athens or Thessalonika or direct to the islands of Crete, Corfu or Rhodes.
	By sea: to the main port of Piraeus or on any of the multitude of ferries which connect the islands.
	By rail: there is the Athens Express direct connection from London, via Paris, Milan and Belgrade.
Main interests for British tourists include:	the casual way of life to be experienced with Greek hosts who always make their visitors welcome; the historical sites and the variety of scenery and coastline on the many islands.
Banking hours:	08.00–14.00 Monday to Friday, although banks in some resorts offer currency exchange facilities in the afternoon as well. Banks are closed on Saturday, Sunday and public holidays.
Shopping hours:	vary a great deal but some shops will be open from 08.00 through to 20.30. Some take a long lunch break and others, especially corner kiosks, may stay open very late.

Italy

The climate in Italy varies greatly owing to the length of the country and the mountainous barriers of the Alps in the north and the Apennines down the spine. The south is drier and warmer but mountainous regions in the Alps and the Apennines are colder with heavy winter snowfalls.

Bearing in mind a fourteen-hour drive from Calais, British tourists on a one or two week package holiday to Italy generally fly to Rome, Milan, Naples, Venice or Palermo. Florence in the heart of Tuscany has only a ten-minute transfer time to the city centre, but it is not used by the large tour operators because it can only accommodate smaller aircraft. Independent travellers also use rail or car to Italy, while elite travellers may arrive in the sheer luxury of the Orient Express, a special train renovated to its original Victorian splendour. The main rail connections including motorail, are from London and Paris.

Figure 7.13 shows the main resort areas in Italy which are popular with British tourists. These can be regarded in four categories:

Figure 7.13 Areas in Italy popular with British tourists

- Rome and other cities such as Venice, Pisa, Naples and Florence, which are of historical and business interest as well as having pleasant countryside within easy reach
- the beautiful, tranquil lakes in the north
- the rivieras with their traditional seaside resorts
- the islands of Sardinia and Sicily.

Italian cities

Rome

Rome is the capital of Italy and appeals to a great variety of tourists because of its diverse interests and associations (Fig. 7.14). It was the capital of the ancient Roman world, it is a modern-day centre for high fashion and shopping and within its boundaries is the independent Vatican City, centre of Christianity and residence of the Pope, the leader of the Roman Catholic Church.

Florence

Florence, the old capital of Tuscany, is Italy's intellectual centre. Patronage of the arts over the centuries by families such as the Medici has resulted in an outstanding collection of sculpture and paintings in Florence. The most famous of the 40 museums in the city is the Uffizi Gallery, which has over 4,500 pictures, 700 of which are on display at any one time. Accommodation in picturesque Tuscan farmhouses does not come cheaply, but eating out in Tuscany is cheaper than in France. Excursions can be taken to:

Figure 7.14 St Peter's Basilica, Rome

- Viareggio, a seaside resort with a safe, sandy beach
- Pisa with its famous leaning bell tower
- Sienna, a beautiful medieval town, famous for its Palio horserace through the Piazza Campo during July and August
- Padua, home of St Anthony, which has unique works of art such as Giotto frescoes and Donatello's equestrian statue.

Venice

Venice, built on 118 small islands, with over 100 canals spanned by about 400 bridges, is a work of art in itself. The Grand Canal, the 'main street' of Venice, is lined with about 200 palaces built between the thirteenth and eighteenth centuries. Today most of these buildings house offices, hotels and museums. The Rialto Bridge links the two banks of the canal in the busiest shopping area where a daily outdoor market is situated. The bridge itself is also lined with a double row of shops. The Piazza, or St Mark's Square, filled with its famous pigeons, is the centre of the city's life. In the south-east corner stands the 99-metre high Campanile of St Mark's, which was rebuilt in 1902, having stood for 1,000 years.

Naples

Southern Italy has the city of Naples, overshadowed by Mount Vesuvius and the preserved cities of Pompeii and Herculaneum which were engulfed by lava from the erupting Mount Vesuvius in AD 79. The Neapolitan Riviera has drawn British poets, artists and tourists over the centuries. Capri, Amalfi and the resorts of Sorrento and Ischia are the most popular destinations for British tourists to the area.

Italian lakes

The Italian lakes and mountains are a popular summer destination for older clients who appreciate the scenery and serenity of the region. Glacial action has deepened the valleys in the Alps forming Lakes Maggiore and Como. The largest of the lakes is Lake Garda, which extends south into the great open plain of Lombardy, Italy's economic heartland. The lakes provide a beautiful setting for walks, with frequent ferry boats and picturesque villages adding to the charm of a holiday. The surrounding Alps give fine views of Mont Blanc on the French border and the Matterhorn on the Swiss border.

Italian seaside resorts

Adriatic resorts

The Adriatic resorts, with Rimini at their centre, are geared to the package holiday trade with basic hotels and regimented beaches. Lifeguard cover is excellent on popular Italian beaches but sunbeds and shades tend to be set out in an extremely orderly fashion and tourists are encouraged to stay in the area of the beach reserved for their hotel (Fig. 7.15). A favourite day trip from this area is to the independent principality of San Marino, set high in the mountains and 30 minutes drive from Rimini.

Neapolitan Riviera

The Neapolitan Riviera, centred around the city of Naples, has drawn British poets, artists and tourists over the centuries. Amalfi on the mainland has some of the oldest

Figure 7.15 A regimented beach in Italy

hotels in Italy and along with the resorts of Sorrento and Ischia it has possibly now reached its capacity for tourists. The most popular excursions in the area are to neighbouring resorts and to the cities of Pompeii and Herculaneum.

Italian islands

The Italian islands of Sardinia and Sicily market themselves with glossy brochures to the elite traveller. Both islands offer spectacular diverse scenery and a chance to observe the old rural culture of Italy. Sicily has the added attraction of Mount Etna, a volcano which has erupted in recent times. Both islands tend to be expensive destinations and generally appeal to the elite and independent travellers rather than to the package tourist market.

Summary of Italy

Capital: Rome

Currency: Italian lira (L) with notes in denominations from L500 to L100,000. Money can be exchanged in banks, airports and many railway stations.

Getting there: *By air:* the main airports are Rome (Leonardo da Vinci), Bologna (Borgo Panigale), Genoa (Cristoforo Colombo, Sestri), Milan (Enrico Forlanini and Malpensa), Naples (Capodichino), Pisa (Galileo Galilei), Turin (Caselle) and Venice (Marco Polo).

By sea: there are ferries to all the main islands as well as some links along the coasts.

By rail: there are main connections from London and Paris.

Main interests for British tourists include: the coastal resorts, the lakes and mountains, skiing, Venice and other historical cities and sites, and Rome. Vatican City, which holds great attraction for Roman Catholics and others, is a separate state in its own right.

Banking hours: vary in different parts of the country, but in general 08.30–13.30 and 15.30–16.30 Monday to Friday.

Shopping hours: 08.30 to 20.00 with a long lunch break from 13.00 to 16.00, except in the north where the break could be shorter. Food shops are often closed on Wednesday afternoons.

Special note: For tourists who take their own car to Italy there is a scheme to give reduced priced petrol by means of pre-paid petrol coupons. Coupons can be purchased in Britain through the AA or the RAC.

Eastern Europe

In 1989 when the Berlin Wall came down and largely peaceful revolutions changed the political face of Eastern Europe, inevitably the tourism scene was dramatically changed. Before 1989 the main Eastern European destinations for British tourists were Yugoslavia, Bulgaria and Romania. The latter offered cheap holidays and a taste of the unknown although many British tourists returned from Bulgaria and Romania complaining of less than basic facilities and food that left a lot to be desired.

Since 1989 all the former communist countries have their curiosity value for Western tourists in the short term but these countries also have a long-term tourism potential. The museums, art galleries and architecture of major cities such as Prague, Budapest, Moscow and St Petersburg are now available to the West (Fig. 7.16). The beaches of Bulgaria and Romania are untouched by modern commercialisation, while the lakes and mountains of Hungary and Poland are uncharted territory for many British tourists.

Figure 7.16 St Basil's Cathedral, Moscow

Turkey

Where East meets West, Turkey is the fastest growing destination for British tourists in Europe. The story of mass tourism in Turkey spans the 1980s. At the beginning of the decade, Turkey was the kind of destination which appealed to independent or elite travellers who possibly liked sailing or visiting unusual places, but almost certainly did not like to go away with a large crowd of noisy and conspicuous British holidaymakers. Then in the mid-1980s, some of the bigger tour operators realised the potential of this new unusual and cheap destination. By 1990, all the big tour operators included Turkey as a destination and several dedicated brochures were produced.

Aegean coast

The Aegean coastal resorts, with temperatures of 32°C (90°F) in the summer and beautiful white beaches backed by wooded mountain slopes, are a tourist brochure's dream come true. However each resort has its own characteristics and excursions, which dictate its appeal to different groups.

Kusadasi

Kusadasi is a busy harbour, although only 2 miles (3 kilometres) from the town centre is the beautiful Ladies Beach. The Grand Bazaar is a covered market which is very popular with British tourists and Pigeon Island, a fortified islet in the bay, adds atmosphere to the scenery. Probably the greatest attraction of this resort is its proximity to Ephesus, only 10 miles (17 kilometres) away, and formerly one of the most important cities in the Roman Empire. Substantial ruins remain standing to this day and during May each year drama, music and folklore events are staged in the Grand Theatre. This resort appeals especially to older clients without children.

Bodrum

Bodrum is the biggest and brightest resort on the Aegean coast and its yachting marina, numerous restaurants and lively nightlife make it a favourite with younger tourists. Excursions can be taken in sailing boats to quieter resorts such as Gumbet along the coast.

Marmaris

Marmaris is a resort with a wide appeal. The beach is good and the shopping has all the Turkish atmosphere one would expect. There are carpet centres in the area where tourists can see weaving techniques and understand the intricate patterns. Trips inland to the thermal baths at Denizil and the unusual calcified waterfall at Pamukkale, or the Cotton Castle as it is called, add to the interest of the resort for a variety of tourists.

Sailing holidays

Turkish sailing holidays can be taken in traditional boats called *gulets*, or sometimes *caiques*. These are small one or two-masted craft built of pine which can accommodate groups of eight to sixteen passengers. Cabins are usually double, with en suite facilities in the better boats, and a crew of captain, mate and cook who sail the boat and provide the meals. The advantages of such a holiday are a chance to experience the scenery and beaches of Turkey in remote locations, and to take trips to ancient sites near to shore, all in the company of other tourists and with ideal conditions for sunbathing. As the yachts take such a small number, frequently they are hired by large parties or groups of friends.

Revision Questions

Primary level

1 Which of the following is the most popular resort with British tourists BOTH in summer and winter?

- Lloret de Mar
- Magaluf
- Benidorm

2 State the CAPITAL of each of the following countries:

- Switzerland
- Denmark
- The Netherlands
- France
- Portugal

3 Give the departure and arrival ports for ONE car ferry route operated between the UK and the following countries:

- France
- Denmark
- Belgium
- Spain
- The Netherlands

4 Name THREE French resorts on the Côte d'Azur.

5 Name THREE Greek resorts on the island of Corfu.

6 Which statements are true?
The Alps can be found in

- Switzerland
- Italy
- Germany
- France
- Spain

7 Name THREE buildings of interest to British tourists in Paris.

8 Use an *ABC Airways Guide* to identify the following European airports and cities from their three-letter codes

(a)	ATH	(d)	FLR
(b)	BER	(e)	LIS
(c)	DUB	(f)	AMS

9 During the month of August which Mediterranean island would generally be hotter: Corfu or Majorca?

10 Name THREE of the lakes in northern Italy which are popular destinations for British tourists.

Advanced level

1 Name THREE European countries east of Berlin which feature in brochures for UK tourists.

2 Of which countries are the following the capitals?

- Madrid
- Reykjavik
- Oslo
- Stockholm
- Amsterdam

3 In which European cities would you find EACH of the following museums:

- Uffizi
- Prado
- Louvre

4 For EACH of the following areas of Spain, name the gateway airport and ONE resort which is popular with UK tourists:

- Costa del Sol
- Costa Dorada
- Costa Blanca
- Costa Brava

5 Suggest THREE day trips which could be made by a business traveller who had a few days for relaxation while visiting Madrid.

6 For EACH of the following name:
- the largest Spanish island in the Mediterranean
- the island whose capital is Valetta
- the island where Napoleon was born
- the island which has a volcano called Mount Etna
- the Greek island group to which Rhodes belongs
- the largest Greek island

7 Which area of France is associated with the 1944 D-Day Landings of the Allied Forces in the Second World War?

8 Use an *ABC Airways Guide* to identify the following European airports and cities from their three-letter codes:

(a) AGP   (d) EBJ

(b) BCN   (e) WAW

(c) CDG   (f) BRN

9 Name TWO European countries which are usually featured in brochures as Winter Sun destinations.

10 Name TWO different reasons for which a British tourist may wish to book a holiday in Rome.

In Chapters 6 and 7 we considered some UK and European destinations which appeal to British tourists. This chapter will highlight a few areas in the rest of the world which are popular with tourists from Britain. Holidays to destinations beyond Europe are known in the travel industry as long haul and the most popular long haul destinations for tourists from UK are

- United States of America
- Canada
- Australia
- Far East.

The fact that many of the places visited are English speaking probably stems as much from the fact that the British like to feel comfortable abroad, as from the desire to meet friends and relatives. Many try to combine a stay with friends with a holiday which satisfies the desire to see different scenery or other cultures. So, a holiday to Australia or New Zealand very often includes stopovers in Singapore, Malaysia or Thailand to experience a culture which is totally different from Britain and other European countries in scenery, customs, dress and food.

United States of America

The USA is popular with British holidaymakers for several reasons:

- many people visit relatives and friends
- films and TV shows stimulate interest in the USA
- there is a variety of spectacular scenery
- English is spoken
- in the 1990s USA appears cheap to British tourists, especially for food and clothes.

As one holidaymaker commented 'It is possible to cross the 21 miles between Dover and Calais and feel totally lost in a strange land, yet after crossing 3,000 miles to America the British tourist can feel totally at home.'

The United States Travel and Tourism Administration (USTTA) has, for the purpose of promoting tourism, divided US states into twelve areas with eighteen gateway airports. The areas most popular with British tourists are:

- Florida and the Southeast Sun Country
- California and the Golden West
- New York and the Eastern Gateway
- Historic Washington Country
- Boston and New England.

Florida and the Southeast Sun Country

If you were to ask people which destination comes to mind when you mention the USA, the majority would probably mention Florida as one of their first three choices.

Between 1986 and 1989 the market grew so quickly that from only 4 charters per week out of the UK to Florida in 1986, there were 51 per week only three years later. Since 70% of holidays booked were repeat holidays, this vouches for the fact that the clients had experienced a good quality holiday in a stable, friendly society.

There are three gateway airports to Florida (Fig. 8.1):

- Orlando
- Miami
- Tampa.

Orlando

Orlando in the centre of Florida has the greatest concentration of man-made attractions in the world. Within a hundred mile radius are:

- Walt Disney World
- Sea World of Florida

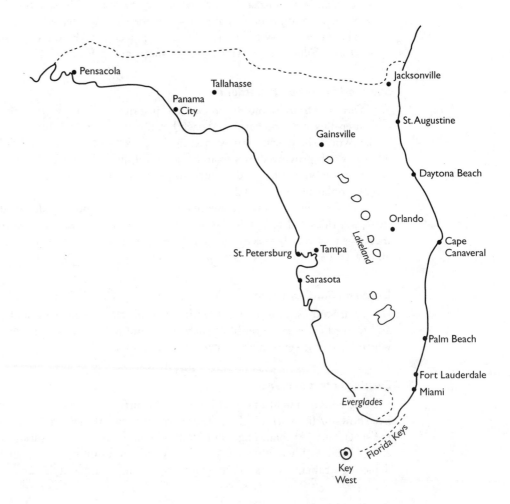

Figure 8.1
Florida, USA

- Wet and Wild
- Universal Studios, Florida
- Cypress Gardens
- Busch Gardens
- Kennedy Space Centre
- an extensive range of nightclubs and themed entertainment.

Walt Disney World

Walt Disney World is a complex of attractions and hotels covering an area of 40 square miles between Orlando and Kissimmee. The main attractions are as follows:

- Magic Kingdom has five themed areas with rides and shows for an all-in price.
- EPCOT has one area dedicated to the latest technological inventions and another, on the far side of an attractive lake, with rides and shows, each themed around the culture and traditions of a different country, from Britain to China.
- MGM Studios has exciting rides and film sets themed around various MGM films, the most spectacular being a live show depicting the filming of an Indiana Jones film.
- Extensive recreation facilities include golf courses and water rides, the most unusual being Blizzard Beach which has fantasy ski lifts, snow-capped peaks and slides with improbable names such as the slush gusher.
- There is a variety of hotels, self-catering accommodation and restaurants.
- Disney Village has a wide range of shops and cafés.

Sea World and Busch Gardens

Sea World in Orlando and Busch Gardens just outside Tampa are both owned by the Anhéuser–Busch theme parks and each has themed rides and shows for an all-in price.

Sea World the world's largest marine life park, is themed around dolphins and whales which provide shows from morning till night. There is also an emphasis on conservation with exhibits dedicated to penguins, the almost extinct manatee and most recently polar bears (Fig. 8.2).

Busch Gardens takes the theme of an African safari and includes exciting roller coaster rides, wet rides and several live shows. The ice skating show in the Moroccan Palace theatre is particularly spectacular, especially in the heat of summer. New for 1996 is an all new themed area, Egypt, which includes the largest ever 'hanging' roller coaster.

Universal Studios, Florida

Universal Studios, Florida, in Orlando has film sets of New York and San Francisco, and themed rides based on films such as *ET* and *King Kong*, all placed around a lake which forms the centrepiece of evening entertainment.

Evening entertainment

Evening entertainment in the Orlando area is provided in most of the theme parks with live shows or firework displays. There are also several themed dinner shows including the spectacular Arabian Nights in Orlando where up to 1,200 guests are served a three course meal with wine while watching a varied programme from over 50 horses depicting Arabian stories to the wild west in a large circus style ring.

Figure 8.2 Sea World, Florida, USA (*Photograph: © Sea World*)

Kennedy Space Center

Kennedy Space Center on the east coast is best observed from the official two hour guided coach trip which takes in a variety of locations on the site, including the launch pad for space travel and an original moon rocket.

Miami

Miami is Florida's mecca of glamour, romance, excitement, suntans, skyscrapers and nightlife. With high humidity in the summer months, the prices of accommodation drop in April and remain low until mid-December, when American tourists arrive for their winter vacations.

Tampa

Tampa on the Gulf of Mexico is a centre for quieter holidays in charming older resorts with a Spanish flavour. Nearby St Petersburg is considered the boating capital of the USA and the Pinellas Suncoast offers 28 miles of sandy beaches and 128 miles of coastline linking eight Gulf Coast resorts. During the summer months there is an abundance of accommodation on this coast both in hotels and self-catering apartments.

Georgia and the Carolinas

Florida is marketed as part of the Southeast Sun Country which includes North and South Carolina as well as Georgia. Many British tourists, who experienced the American way of life in Florida during the 1980s, are now trying new destinations in Georgia and South Carolina in the 1990s. The abundance of golf courses in these two states makes the area very attractive to many independent British tourists. Further north in North Carolina the breathtaking scenery of the Great Smokey and Blue Ridge Mountains is proving to be very popular.

California and the Golden West

California and Nevada are marketed as the Golden West with the emphasis on sunshine, glamour and adventure.

There are two gateway airports to California (Fig. 8.3):

- Los Angeles
- San Francisco.

Los Angeles

Los Angeles (LA) is a fast moving city, full of entertainment with the constant excitement of the possibility of meeting a star. The homes of the stars can be seen in Beverly Hills and memories of old movies can be relived on the back sets of Universal Studios.

Disneyland

Disneyland, the original and smaller version of Florida's Disney World, is in Anaheim just outside Los Angeles. Just as in Florida, the Magic Kingdom is divided into the five themed areas of Main St USA, Fantasyland, Tomorrowland, Adventureland and Frontierland, and visitors can experience exciting rides, musical parades and photo opportunities with Mickey Mouse or Donald Duck.

Figure 8.3 California, USA

San Diego

San Diego, California's oldest city, is several hours' drive to the south of Los Angeles, almost on the Mexican border. Here visitors can see the old town which has been restored as it was 150 years ago, take part in one of the fantastic shows at Sea World, or go to the beach where surfing is the most popular activity.

San Franciso

San Francisco's steep hilly streets and beautiful bay are only a few hours' flight to the north of Los Angeles. This is a truly cosmopolitan city, both in its people and restaurants. Chinatown has the largest community of its kind outside Asia and at Fisherman's Wharf visitors can taste freshly caught crab right out of a steaming cauldron. Inland is the marvellous Yosemite National Park with some of the highest waterfalls in the world as well as ancient trees dating back to 4,000 years ago.

Las Vegas

Las Vegas, the city that never sleeps, hides its bright lights in the deserts of Nevada to the east of Los Angeles. Here is a world of casinos, nightclubs and bars with many of the top stars and artists performing in some of the best hotels and theatres in the West (Fig. 8.4).

Figure 8.4 Las Vegas, Nevada, USA

Grand Canyon

The Grand Canyon is so magnificent that it is difficult to comprehend its beauty and size, and it is probably best viewed from an air tour out of Las Vegas.

New York and the Eastern Gateway

Marketed as the Eastern Gateway, New York with its noise, crime and slums still holds a fascination for many British people with its variety of entertainment, shopping and commerce, and constant, vibrant bustle and excitement.

Manhattan is the original city of New York and here visitors can see:

- the Statue of Liberty in the bay
- the Rockefeller Center, a complex of 21 buildings including a business centre, underground shops, the NBC Network, restaurants, an open-air ice rink, or cafe depending on the season, in the centre of the buildings as well as a fantastic view from the top
- Fifth Avenue, which once housed the wealthy of the last century and now has exclusive, expensive shops, or stores
- Central Park which offers breathing space and peace in the heart of the city
- Times Square and Broadway, the main area for theatres, cinemas and colourful nightlife
- the Empire State Building with its 1930s décor and the equally high twin towers of the World Trade Center
- South Street Seaport Museum, an open air museum and shopping complex, which includes the pier at which liners from Britain docked earlier in the twentieth century (Fig. 8.5)
- Wall Street Stock Exchange which has free guided tours for visitors.

Figure 8.5 Seaport Museum, Pier 17, New York, USA

Historic Washington Country

Washington DC, the capital of USA and its surrounding area, is marketed as Historic Washington Country and includes the states of West Virginia and Virginia, as well as the federal District of Columbia (DC).

Washington DC

Washington DC is a beautiful, southern city with magnificent state buildings, museums and monuments set in green parkland. Many of the main attractions in Washington are freely open to the public.

- The White House is the official residence of the President of the United States and home for every President since George Washington.
- The Capitol Building houses the Senate and the House of Representatives.
- The Smithsonian Institute includes the National Air and Space Museum, with some of the earliest aeroplanes right through to the spacecraft Friendship 7.
- There is a magnificent view from the top of the 555-feet (170 metre) Washington Monument, as well as the peace and tranquillity of the nearby Lincoln and Jefferson Memorials.
- In Arlington National Cemetery lie thousands of American soldiers who fought from the Revolutionary wars onwards. Here too is the eternal flame to President Kennedy who was assassinated in Dallas, Texas, in 1963.
- The Vietnam Veterans War Memorial is on Constitution Avenue.
- Potomac Park, bordering the river of the same name, offers many recreational activities.

Williamsburg

Williamsburg in Virginia to the south of Washington is increasing in popularity with British tourists. The weather in this part of USA is less humid than in the south and the attractions are wide ranging from historical to pure entertainment. At the centre of the historical attractions is the triangle made with Williamsburg by Yorktown and Jamestown (Fig. 8.6). The entire area has associations with both the War of Independence and the Civil War and living museums and tourist trails help the visitor to understand the area.

Lighter entertainment is also to be found in the area with seaside resorts, golf courses, Water Country USA and Busch Gardens Williamsburg. This Busch Gardens takes the theme of 'old Europe' and includes rides and live shows.

Boston and New England

New England

In the north east of the United States is New England, an area which is particularly popular with British tourists. It comprises six US states (Fig. 8.7).

There are two gateway airports to New England:

- Boston
- New York.

New England is already well established as a tourist destination for Americans and Canadians especially in autumn or the Fall, as it is called, when the profusion of trees turn a tremendous variety of colours. Although winters can be a bit sharp and cold in New England, summer and spring are very pleasant with only occasional humidity, unlike many other US destinations.

Figure 8.6 Jamestown Settlement, Williamsburg, Virginia, USA (*Photograph: Jamestown–Yorktown Foundation*)

Figure 8.7 New England, USA

New England includes some of the smallest US states, including Connecticut, Massachusetts and Rhode Island, which is not an island at all. The larger states of New Hampshire, Vermont and Maine to the north are beautiful mountainous areas, ablaze with colours in the autumn and a paradise of snow in the winter.

Boston

Boston, the capital of Massachusetts, is the cradle of American democracy for it was here that the Boston Tea Party sparked the independent spirit which led to the American Revolution and the Declaration of Independence in 1776. The Freedom Trail is a three kilometre walk around the city, marked by red stripes on the pavement, which traces places of historical interest connected with the period of the War of Independence. Boston is regarded as a capital of culture with theatres, museums, parks and two symphony orchestras.

Other attractions

The rest of New England also has many places of interest for British tourists, including the universities of Harvard and Yale; several living museums depicting life at the turn of the century; and, for yachting enthusiasts, numerous small ports along the indented coastline.

Summary of United States of America

Capital:	Washington DC
Currency:	US dollar (US$) with one dollar = 100 cents. The cent is sometimes called a nickel, the 10 cents piece is called a dime and the 25 cents piece is called a quarter. Money and traveller's cheques can be exchanged at banks. American Express traveller's cheques can be used virtually as currency, preferably in denominations of $10 and $20.
Getting there:	**By air** to any of the eighteen gateway airports. The most popular airports for British travellers are New York (JFK International) and Orlando. Visitors to the west coast use the airports of San Francisco or Los Angeles International. Baggage allowance is usually according to the number of pieces of luggage rather than the weight of the cases.
	By sea is more unusual nowadays, although the QE2 still does a number of trips each year.
Main interests for British tourists include:	visiting friends and relatives, shopping, Florida and Disney World, the natural wonders of the national parks in the west and the attractions of New York in the east.
Climate:	varies greatly but summers tend to be much hotter than in Europe. Some areas, such as Florida, can experience high humidity in summer, and other areas, such as the Mid-west, are extremely cold in winter.
Banking hours:	09.00–15.00 Monday to Friday
Shopping hours:	09.30–18.00 Monday to Saturday with many supermarkets staying open until later in the evening. Some states permit Sunday trading.
Special note:	• Visitors should be advised to carry at least one credit card because they are used for identification in the USA and, for example, it is almost impossible to hire a car without a credit card.
	• Cheap coach travel is available for non-nationals but passes should be purchased in the UK from either the Greyhound or the Trailways bus companies.
	• The USA has state as well as federal laws and this means, for example; that laws regarding age limits for alcohol consumption can vary from state to state.

Canada

Canada is a land of such vastness and variety that it is sometimes difficult for many Europeans to comprehend. Canada covers about 4 million square miles, the second largest country in the world, after Russia, yet it has only 23 million people, a mere tenth of the population of the United States. Most Canadians live just north of the border between Canada and USA, leaving tracts of untouched land to the north whose beauty is largely unspoilt by humans and where it is possible to retreat from the busy twentieth century, by fishing and camping in isolation (Fig. 8.8).

Spring is particularly beautiful in Canada with a profusion of blossom trees and, as in New England, autumn, or the Fall, brings a wealth of glorious colours. Winter turns the country into a skiing paradise and summer sees the Canadians take to the outdoor life with zest and enthusiasm.

Western Canada

Western Canada is dominated by the Rocky Mountains, and here national parks such as Banff and Jaspar preserve the beauty for visitors to enjoy in comparative comfort. The cities of Vancouver and Victoria offer all amenities but, in contrast, further north the Yukon and the Northern Territories are the last great frontiers and a haven for naturalists and those who seek adventure.

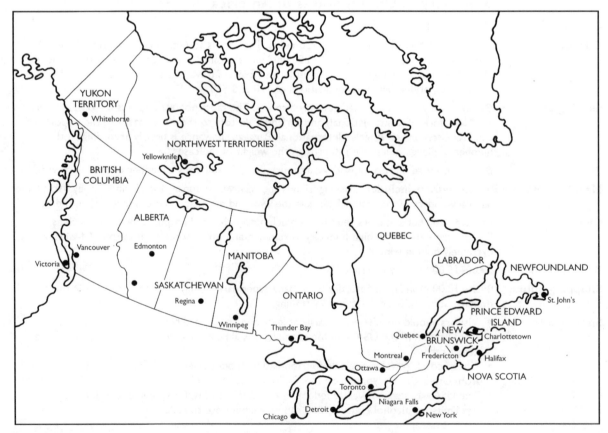

Figure 8.8 Canada

National parks

The national parks of Banff, Elk Island, Jasper, Waterton Lakes and Wood Buffalo attract British tourists. Banff was originally a spa of hot sulphur springs. Nowadays tourists are drawn in their thousands to the attractive alpine scenery and winter sports, the variety of wild animals and the beautiful tranquil Lake Louise. Hunting is forbidden in the national parks but fishing is very popular. Jasper National Park is 170 miles (290 kilometres) north of Banff and with its turbulent rivers and rushing waters is a paradise of both wildlife and sport. There is an international golf course and the area has numerous resorts offering winter downhill and cross-country skiing in a beautiful wilderness setting.

Calgary

Calgary is a great place to experience the thrills of the West, especially at the famous Calgary Stampede in July when the horsemanship and skills of the cowboys are tested to their limit in the Chuck Wagon Race.

The area around Calgary has other attractions:

- Heritage Park is a living museum where visitors can ride a steam railroad.
- In the Dinosaur Park on St George's Island prehistoric times are brought alive.
- The sports facilities were created for the Winter Olympics, which were held there in 1988.

Eastern Canada

Further east, Toronto and Montreal are great favourites with the British, and Quebec with its French culture and history is an unusual North American destination.

Toronto

Toronto is the provincial capital of Ontario and the largest Canadian city. The airport to the north of the city is a major gateway for British visitors to Canada. Although Canada is officially bilingual, with equal prominence given to French and English, the area around Toronto is predominantly English speaking. Sights to be seen in and around Toronto include the following (Fig. 8.9).

- The CN Tower at 1,815 feet (558 metres) is one of the world's tallest free-standing structures. CN stands for Canadian National, once the national railway, which now makes special trips with tourists out to the western states.
- the Ontario Science Centre and the Metro Zoo.
- Several modern recreational and shopping areas such as Ontario Place on the Harbourfront.
- Canada's Wonderland theme park 20 miles (32 kilometres) to the north-west has rides, roller coasters, entertainment and dolphin shows.
- A day's trip can be made from Toronto to the Niagara Falls 80 miles (128 kilometres) away where tourists can view the magnificent falls from the *Maid of the Mist* boat, through tunnels at the edge of the rapids or from the park laid out along the land overlooking the horseshoe falls. A red double decker bus provides transport through the park and an IMAX cinema gives visitors a history of the falls.
- Trips can also be made to the towns of London and Stratford, the centre for the Canadian Shakespearian Festival.
- Trips to the more remote regions such as Agawa Canyon in the north can be taken through the rail routes from Sault Ste Marie in the east at the centre of the Great Lakes.

Figure 8.9 The Niagara Falls (*Photograph: Pauline Gillett*)

Montréal

Montréal is in the French speaking state of Quebec, but about one-third of the city's population speak English as their first language. Montréal, the second largest city in Canada, is the business and commercial capital of the country, although the actual capital is Ottawa in Ontario. There is an unusual series of underground recreation and shopping complexes in Montréal, all linked by a metro system, with every station having a different decor. At the highest point of the city is the Mont Royal park affording a haven of peace and tranquillity in a modern, bustling city.

Quebec City

Quebec, the only walled city in North America, has a true French atmosphere with sidewalk cafés, religious shrines, carriage rides and a culture dating back to the French occupation of the area in the early seventeenth century. The city is dominated by the Château Frontenac, a massive hotel opened in 1893 which still welcomes visitors in opulent style. The heart of the city is the seventeenth-century Place Royale whose small town houses and cobbled streets have been designated by UNESCO as a world heritage treasure. Just outside the city is the Battlefields Park or Plains of Abraham, site of the last battle fought in the area between the British and French troops. The great St Lawrence River flows right through the region and at its mouth are some beautiful sights on the Gaspe Peninsular and at Percé Rock.

Summary of Canada

Capital: Ottawa

Currency: Canadian dollar (C$) with one dollar = 100 cents. As in USA the cent is also called a nickel, the 10 cents piece is called a dime and the 25 cents piece is called a quarter. Traveller's cheques are best bought in Canadian dollars which are widely negotiable.

Getting there: **By air** the airports most frequently used by British tourists are Toronto, Montréal, Calgary and Vancouver.

By sea Montréal is the only port for passenger liners from Europe.

By rail there are several connections with USA including New York to Montréal, Chicago to Toronto and Detroit to Ottawa.

Main interests for British tourists include visiting friends and relatives, sightseeing at Niagara Falls and visiting the national parks in the west.

Climate: varies in such a large country but generally the summers from May to September are warm, and the winters are very cold with snow. British Columbia in the west is the mildest state with very warm summers and relatively mild winters.

Banking hours: 10.00–15.00 Monday to Friday

Shopping hours: 09.00–18.00 Monday to Friday with late night shopping until 21.00 Thursday and Friday. Some shops also open Saturday.

Special note:
- Canada has two official languages – English and French. The French speaking areas are in the east of the country, mainly in the state of Quebec.
- Smoking has been banned in most public areas in Canada.

Australia

With the present trend for Australian programmes on British television channels, many Australians could possibly feel quite at home in the UK, but British tourists going to Australia find a totally new and different world. Australia is as large as the USA or the whole of Europe. From Sydney in the east to Perth in the west it is over 2,500 miles (4,000 kilometres), and from Adelaide in the south it is over 2,000 miles (3,200 kilometres) to Darwin in the north (Fig. 8.10).

The Australian climate varies from tropical, humid and wet in the north to hot, dry desert in the centre, and milder weather in the south, with skiing becoming popular along the border between the states of Victoria and New South Wales.

Many British tourists go to Australia either to experience a true adventure holiday in the outback or to visit friends and relatives, usually on the east or south coast.

Australian adventure holidays

Adventure holidays, camping or using small hotels can be taken by coach, rail or genuine 'jeep' type vehicles. Such holidays can be booked with several reputable specialist tour operators and may last from sixteen to forty days. The areas popularly used for adventure holidays include:

Figure 8.10 Australia

- Kimberley in the north-west with its spectacular scenery filled with gorges and enormous chasms
- coral islands of the Great Barrier Reef and crocodile farms in the north
- Tanami Desert with traces of old mining towns and even dinosaur tracks in the centre of the country.

Alice Springs and Ayers Rock

In the southern part of the Tanami Desert are the Macdonnell Ranges with the old telegraph station of Alice Springs. This remote town in the dry red centre of Australia is an ever more popular tourist destination and can even boast a casino. About half a day's drive away is the haunting Ayers Rock with its Aboriginal caves and paintings. The rock rises straight out of the desert and changes to fantastic colours especially in the sunset. It is easy to understand why it is a place of special significance for the Aboriginal population.

Australian city holidays

Most British emigrants to Australia settled around the cities of Sydney, Melbourne and Adelaide and each of these has places of interest for British visitors in the surrounding area.

Sydney

Sydney is an excellent centre from which to experience the variety of Australia in a comparatively small area.

- inland are the Blue Mountains, so called because of the fine blue mists given off by the many eucalyptus trees
- even further inland, adventurous tourists can experience the utter emptiness of the outback
- on the coast, there are beautiful beaches, including the famous Bondi Beach which is about 20 minutes by road south of the city
- to the north, frequent flights will take visitors to Brisbane or the coral beauty of the Barrier Reef in Queensland.

Sydney itself, with its famous Opera House in the harbour, can offer all the amenities one would expect in any big city and the capital, Canberra, is only a short flight away.

Melbourne

Melbourne, one of the oldest Australian cities, has interesting architecture which blends the new with the old. In the surrounding area there are the following:

- The Dandenong Range of mountains, 36 miles (58 kilometres) east of the city, has mountain ash forests and a wildlife sanctuary preserved in a national park.
- Gippsland is a lush, fertile area in south-east Victoria, dotted with unspoilt lakes, forests and raging river rapids.
- Phillip Island Nature Reserve, 77 miles (123 kilometres) south of the city, is home to koalas and fairy penguins as well as other wildlife only to be found in Australia.

Adelaide

Adelaide in South Australia has a very attractive coastline with excellent white sandy beaches. Adelaide has a very European atmosphere, probably due to the large number of German settlers in the area. German settlers in the 1830s started the wine centre in the Barossa Valley where tourists can take tours through the small villages with their Lutheran churches and German restaurants. Another favourite with tourists in the Adelaide area is a trip along the Murray River on a genuine steamboat, recalling images of the Mississippi in the United States of America.

Summary of Australia

Capital:	Canberra
Currency:	Australian dollar (A$) with one dollar = 100 cents.
Getting there:	*By air* to all the main cities – Sydney, Adelaide, Melbourne, Perth, Brisbane and Darwin. There is a departure tax levied on all international departures. Within Australia there is a wide network of internal flights.
	By sea international cruise liners dock at Sydney, Melbourne, Hobart, Fremantle, Adelaide and Brisbane.
Main interests for British tourists include:	visiting friends and relatives, and adventure holidays.
Climate:	varies from semi-tropical in the south to very dry desert in the centre and hot tropical weather in the north. The summer time in Australia is in December and January.

Banking hours: 09.30–16.00 Monday to Thursday and 09.30–17.00 Friday, although there is variation from these times in some parts of the country.

Shopping hours: large stores open 09.00–17.30 Monday to Friday and 09.00–12.00 Saturday. Late night shopping is until 21.00 on Fridays in Melbourne, Adelaide, Brisbane, Hobart and Darwin. Late shopping is until 21.00 on Thursdays in Sydney, Canberra and Perth. Smaller shops tend to stay open until late every night.

Special note: All visitors to Australia need to obtain a visa.

Far East

As flying becomes both faster and cheaper, long haul destinations are becoming more popular. Figure 8.11 indicates some areas of the Far East, including Singapore, Hong Kong and Thailand which are popular with British tourists.

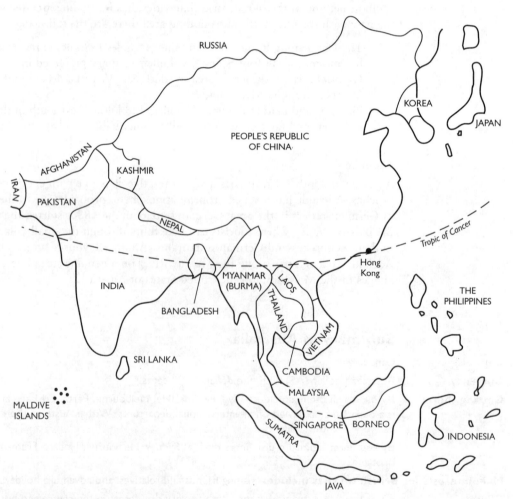

Figure 8.11 The Far East

Singapore

The Republic of Singapore, a former British colony, is an island at the tip of the Malaysian Peninsula, to which it is joined by the Johore Causeway. Singapore is one of the busiest ports in the world and has a vibrant, international atmosphere. The climate in Singapore varies very little throughout the year, being almost always hot and humid, although the Monsoon rains from November to January can bring frequent, heavy downpours. Singapore has many attractions for tourists:

- Van Kleef Aquarium has over 6,000 specimens of fresh and saltwater creatures in attractive landscaped tanks.
- Jurong Science Centre and Bird Park has birds of prey which feature in the daily King of the Skies Bird Show. For children there is also a Parrot Circus and the world's largest walk-in aviary.
- The famous Raffles Hotel, established in 1887 at the heart of the colonial community, was restored to its former glory in the 1980s and caters for visitors with an audio-visual show.
- Haw Par Villa or Tiger Balm Gardens were modernised in 1990 to include high technology attractions alongside traditional Chinese statues.
- Tang Dynasty Village combines a theme park built around pagodas, palaces and terracotta warriors with state of the art film studios.
- Sentosa Island in the harbour has been developed as a modern tourist complex with a beautiful European-style garden plaza with a musical fountain whose water jets dance to music each evening.

It is said by many that it is hard to decide whether Singapore or Paris offers the best restaurants in the world, and certainly Singapore cannot be outdone in its variety of both Eastern and Western food.

Hong Kong

Hong Kong, which is a British territory, will be handed back to the Chinese nation on 30 June 1997. Hong Kong is mainly a business centre and has the highest density of population of any place on earth. With a land area of only 400 square miles, it has a population of over 5 million, giving a density of 12,500 people to every square mile. Compare this with a density of 600 per square mile in the UK, 260 per square mile in France and only 8 per square mile in the USA.

Climate

The climate in Hong Kong is hot and humid in summer, and cool and sunny in winter. Probably the best time of the year for British tourists to visit Hong Kong is in the autumn when the temperature and the humidity drop and days are clear and sunny.

Attractions

There are some attractive islands and countryside to visit around Hong Kong, but most people are attracted by the shopping, entertainment, nightlife and restaurants. Most shopping in Hong Kong is duty free and the area around Cat Street is noted for very cheap oriental antiques, while the Stanley area is excellent for clothes. The Aw Boon Haw or Tiger Balm Gardens appeal to visitors of all ages, and the Sung Dynasty Village on Kowloon recreates a Chinese village of a thousand years ago.

Thailand

For British tourists, Thailand, formerly known as Siam, epitomises all the mysteries of the East. The capital, Bangkok, has over 300 temples, each one a fine example of Thai art and tradition. However, for all its tradition, the city still vibrates to discos, nightlife and what are euphemistically called massage parlours. Bangkok is a shoppers' paradise and bargaining is a must in most places, although the better stores tend to have fixed prices. Good buys include Thai silks, cotton, precious stones, silver, bronze and pottery antiques.

Outside of the city are some beautiful resorts:

- Chiang Mia, known as the Rose of the North, is Thailand's second city and is set in a beautiful fertile valley, 1,000 feet (300 metres) above sea level.
- The seaside resort of Pattaya, two hours' drive from Bangkok, is on the Gulf of Siam and offers an abundance of watersports. The resort is set in cliff-hidden bays with palm-fringed beaches but during the 1980s it became overdeveloped and its beaches were polluted. There is a conscious effort by the Thai government to revive the resort in the 1990s, by strict controls on the use and development of land, protecting and conserving nature and local customs and drawing up plans to reduce crime and accidents.
- Phuket is an hour's flight from Bangkok and lies on the Andaman Sea, a backwater of the Indian Ocean with some of the best beaches in Thailand.

Summary of the Far East

SINGAPORE

Currency:	Singapore dollar (S$), although the currency of Brunei (Br$) is also widely accepted
Getting there:	*By air* to Chiangi airport
	By sea as a port of call with several cruise lines
Main interests for British tourists include:	shopping and an exotic mixture of Eastern and Western attractions and food
Climate:	almost always hot and humid, but the monsoon rains from November to January can bring frequent, heavy downpours
Banking hours:	10.00–15.00 Monday to Friday and 09.30–11.30 Saturday
Shopping hours:	10.00 –19.00 Monday to Saturday but many shops, especially in tourist areas, stay open late and on Sundays
Special note:	Singapore is particularly intolerant of drug taking and selling.

HONG KONG

Currency:	Hong Kong dollar (HK$)
Getting there:	*By air* with a thirteen hour flight from London
	By sea as a port of call with several cruise lines
Main interests for British tourists:	shopping, entertainment, nightlife and restaurants
Climate:	hot and humid in summer, and cool and sunny in winter
Banking hours:	09.00–17.00 Monday to Friday and 09.00–13.00 Saturday but some banks may be open longer
Shopping hours:	long opening hours usually 10.00–22.00 weekdays and many shops are open on Sundays
Special note:	Hong Kong returns to Chinese rule on 30 June 1997.

THAILAND

Capital:	Bangkok
Currency:	Baht (Bt) with one baht = 100 strangs
Getting there:	**By air** to airports at Bangkok (Don Muang), Chiang Mai or Phuket
	By sea on some cruise lines
	By rail through Kuala Lumpur

Main interests for British tourists include: long white sandy beaches of the seaside resorts and lush countryside of the hill country, along with a rich Buddhist culture and the cosmopolitan atmosphere of Bangkok

Climate: tropical monsoon climate in the south around Bangkok; tropical savannah climate from the Thai Gulf to the north. Three distinct seasons with March to May very hot; June to September very wet; and October to February quite cool.

Banking hours: 08.30 –15.30 Monday to Friday

Shopping hours: 10.00–19.00 in department stores and 08.00–21.00 in other shops

Special note:
- Tourists are forbidden to take Buddha figures out of Thailand.
- Many Chinese festivals which are common to Singapore, Hong Kong and Thailand are celebrated in different months according to the lunar year, and up-to-date information should be checked with the national tourist board offices

Revision Questions

Primary level

1 State the capitals of each of the following countries

Australia	India
Thailand	Japan
China	

2 In connection with North America, what do you understand by 'The Fall'?

3 Suggest THREE excursions which a family with a 10-year-old child might take while on holiday in Singapore

4 Name FOUR family attractions within the Orlando area of Florida, USA.

5 Name THREE west coast US cities which are popular destinations for British tourists.

6 Name THREE attractions in the city of New York.

7 Name the capital of Canada.

8 Name TWO seaside resorts in Thailand.

9 Name THREE areas of Australia which are suitable for adventure holidays.

10 Name THREE Australian cities which are popular destinations for the VFR market.

Advanced level

1 Name the country in which you would find each of the following

Yosemite	Pattaya
Phuket	Bondi Beach
Sentosa	Barossa Valley
Ayers Rock	Sea World
Fisherman's Wharf	

2 Suggest THREE excursions which could be made by a business traveller who had a few days for relaxation while visiting Bangkok.

3 Of which countries are the following the capitals?

Kathmandu	Manila
Kuala Lumpur	Jakarta
Rangoon	

4 For each of the following name
- a wine producing area in Australia
- a country famous for its silk garments
- the area in the Far East which has the highest density population
- a tax free shopping paradise in the East
- a small island in the Far East which is an independent republic

- the largest island in the world
- a gambling city built in the middle of a desert
- the smallest US state
- a walled city in North America

5 In which city or town would you find the following

The Freedom Trail
Tiger Balm Gardens
Raffles Hotel
A Canadian Cowboy Festival held in July
The Rockefeller Center

6 Name a gateway airport for EACH of the following

Walt Disney World
Kowloon
Yosemite
Bondi Beach

7 Which major Canadian city is within a few hours' drive of Niagara Falls?

8 Suggest THREE reasons why Thailand is a popular destination for British tourists.

9 How did the Blue Mountains in Australia get their name?

10 What is the currency for EACH of the following countries

Australia
USA
Thailand
Canada
Singapore

Package holidays

9) *Tour operators*

One of the earliest British tour operators was Thomas Cook, who organised his first rail excursion from Leicester to Loughborough for 570 members of the Temperance Association in 1841. Ten years later he organised trips to the Great Exhibition in Hyde Park. One young visitor who travelled to the Great Exhibition with her parents in 1851 told of how Thomas Cook had booked the hotel, the train, on which he provided hot water-bottles, and, best of all, couriers and guides to help his clients at every step of the way.

The Paris International Exhibition in 1855 gave Thomas Cook the opportunity to offer continental trips and from there Cooks Tours became ever more popular and adventurous. In 1872 at a price of 210 guineas Thomas Cook offered a round-the-world trip taking in Hong Kong, Singapore and India and lasting nearly a year. His son John Cook took the first American tour in 1886 and with his three grandsons carried on the successful business into the 1900s.

Others imitated the idea of package tours but some like the Cyclists Touring Club, founded in 1878, and the Toynbee Travellers Club put more emphasis on the educational value of the trips. In the 1880s, Sir Henry Lunn, whose name survives in the Lunn Poly chain of travel agents, was responsible for organising lecture tours to Greece for his nonconformist friends, as well as some of the first skiing holidays.

Tour operators produce package holidays which they advertise in holiday brochures and some tour operators pay commission of about 10% to travel agents to sell the holidays on their behalf. The name tour operator derives from inclusive tours or ITs, the alternative name for package holidays. The first package holidays, offered by such people as Thomas Cook and Sir Henry Lunn, usually involved actual touring around European places of interest. However nowadays a package holiday can have a variety of meanings both as regards the destination and the way in which the holiday is taken.

Main components of a package holiday

Whatever the form of a package holiday, it will usually be offered in a brochure with a fixed price for the main components (Fig. 9.1):

- accommodation
- transport
- ground arrangements, such as transfers from the airport or car hire
- services of a courier or representative.

We considered transportation in Chapter 2, accommodation in Chapter 3, and ancillary travel services in Chapter 4. However, ground arrangements and the services of a courier or overseas representative are peculiar to package tours.

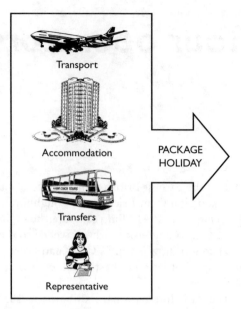

Figure 9.1 Components of a package holiday

Transfers

People travelling independently must find their own way from the airport to the hotel but on a package holiday the tour operator will make these arrangements in advance. Transfers or the transport to the booked accommodation in the resort may be in the form of a waiting taxi, but more usually nowadays it will be by coach. The larger tour operators can have a dozen or more coaches meeting a specific flight so first time holidaymakers should be advised to check their transport carefully. Where transport is by coach an on-board courier usually introduces the clients to the area as they approach their hotel or apartment. Package holidays bring foreign travel within the budget of many people. However, many of these people are travelling for the first time and the support given by the tour operators in their ground arrangements can be very important.

Overseas representatives

To provide ground arrangements and other support for clients, tour operators recruit and train overseas representatives or 'reps' to:

- provide the hotels with rooming lists from information received from the UK office
- meet clients on arrival in the resort
- show clients to their accommodation
- help clients to enjoy their holiday
- assist with general enquiries, usually providing a file of information about the local area, banks, doctors, shops, pubs and excursions
- sort out any potential problems
- look after children, where clubs are provided
- provide entertainment in the evenings, especially on long stay holidays for retired people
- make arrangements for clients who are ill to see a doctor
- make arrangements for clients who need repatriation
- escort clients to the departure point at the end of their holiday

● help clients who have serious problems to fill out a company report giving details of the complaint.

Figure 9.2 shows a typical rooming list which might be used by a rep to show the names of clients, the number of nights they are staying and their required room type, including any special requests.

Reps are sometimes recruited by the UK office, usually with some knowledge of a foreign language. They may be foreign nationals, or Britons married to local nationals, recruited by the overseas office. The reps are usually available for their clients throughout a package holiday. In the larger hotels there will be a team of reps so that at least one is available throughout the day. Smaller hotels and apartments may receive a daily visit but in some more remote areas there may simply be a telephone number for contacting the rep.

ABC TOURS

ROOMING LIST

FOR HOLEL: *Honolulu*　　　　　　　　　　update on ___*22 July*___
ARRIVAL DATE: *24 August*
FLIGHT NUMBER: *BO 123*
FROM: ___*MAN*___
TO: ___*MAD*___

ROOM TYPE	FACILITIES	NO OF NIGHTS	PASSENGER NAMES	REQUESTS
TW	PB, WC, BAL	14	*Mr. J. O'Connor*	*None*
			Mrs. P. O'Connor	
TR	PB, WC, SV	7	*Mr. W. Sharratt*	*lowest possible*
			Mrs. M. Sharratt	*floor*
			Miss. P. Sharratt	
SI	PB, WC,	7	*Mr. B. Sharratt*	
TR + B	PB, WC, SV	14	*Mr. M. Wilson*	
			Mrs. L. Wilson	
			Miss. A. Wilson	
			Miss. C. Wilson	*COT*

SI = single　　PB = private bath
TW = twin　　WC = toilet
TR = triple　　BAL = balcony
+B = extra bed　SV = sea view

Figure 9.2 Tour operator representative's rooming list

Area representatives

For each resort area, a tour operator will have an office and area representative. This local office will:

- supervise the reps in the resort
- check flight details
- make transfer arrangements
- maintain contact with the hoteliers and apartment managers
- maintain contact with the UK office
- organise excursions to local attractions.

Normally these offices are not open to the public because the clients' point of contact should be the rep at their hotel or apartment.

UK representatives

Tour operators' agency sales are promoted by UK representatives who are employed by the tour operators to visit travel agencies. UK representatives have the task of ensuring that travel agents receive sufficient publicity material and brochures and that these are prominently displayed. Some representatives arrive unannounced in an agency to observe the image being portrayed for their company.

The larger tour operators sometimes cooperate with travel agencies in promotions at local travel fairs or with travel trades clubs in sponsorship of entertainment. At these events the UK representatives have an opportunity to promote the latest brochure product.

Brochures

On average it is agreed that it takes eight to ten brochures to produce one firm booking. About 80% of the bookings for the larger tour operators are done by only 20% of ABTA travel agents. In 1971 Cosmos was the first tour operator to restrict distribution of their brochures but now it is common practice. Travel agents can argue that they cannot do bookings if they do not have brochures, but most tour operators will now send brochures only in proportion to the past bookings.

Contracting

In order to be able to offer holidays with certainty the tour operator must contract:

- flights or other means of travel
- accommodation
- services such as transfers or car hire rates.

In negotiating contracts, the tour operator is concerned both to establish the availability of these elements and to obtain a realistic price which allows the holidays to be offered to the public at an attractive price and at the same time be profitable for the company.

Airline contracts

Contracts drawn up with airlines should detail the flights to be used, the costs involved and any penalties to be paid on either side if the contract is not fulfilled.

Scheduled airlines

Scheduled airlines usually agree to an allocation of seats, which means a number of seats made available to the tour operator. A date will be agreed, after which the airline is at liberty to sell those seats to others if the tour operator has not taken the full quota. This date is referred to as the release date.

Charter airlines

Charter airlines usually require the tour operator to pay a deposit of 10% initially and then the balance after each flight. Different types of charters were considered in Chapter 2.

Vladimir Raitz of Horizon is said to have been the first person to negotiate charter seats with an airline. The Horizon offices were opened in 1949 over a tobacconist's shop in Fleet Street. The first charter was a thirty-two seater DC3 to Corsica. For £32 10s. each, the thirty-two clients were flown from London to Corsica and given full board accommodation in tents. Bearing in mind that the average wage per week in the 1950s was about £10, this holiday was not as cheap as it sounds, representing three weeks' wages. Nevertheless it was considerably cheaper and more convenient than travelling independently to Corsica.

Maximising use of aircraft

Aircraft can make money only when they are flying; in fact on the ground they are incurring airport expenses, so the tour operator and airline will aim to make maximum use of each flight. Sometimes the same aircraft can be used to do flights from more than one airport.

If for instance the airline flies from Manchester but does not have an aircraft based at Birmingham, the tour operator may arrange for clients to be taken from Manchester to Malaga, return from Malaga to Birmingham, take clients from Birmingham to Malaga and finally return with passengers for Manchester. This type of flight pattern is known as a W Flight Plan as shown in Fig. 9.3.

In order to keep the aircraft in the air as much as possible it is usual for there to be at least three flights per day in summer and two flights per day in winter for each chartered aircraft.

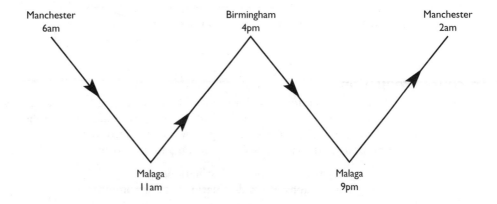

Figure 9.3
W Flight Plan

Accommodation contracts

The contracts for accommodation are drawn up after negotiations by the UK and overseas staff in the larger companies, or with the help of an agent abroad in the smaller companies. The contracts can be of three different forms.

1 The tour operator may be committed to paying for an agreed number of beds regardless of whether or not they can actually be filled.
2 A more popular way of contracting accommodation is by allocation, where a number of beds are available to the tour operator until the release date, which can be four to six weeks before the holiday date.
3 The third way of contracting accommodation is on an ad hoc basis where the tour operator requests accommodation by telex as and when the client requires it.

Figure 9.4 summarises the main advantages and disadvantages of each of these ways of contracting.

Whichever method is used the accommodation contract should include:

- details of the types of bedrooms available, whether they be single, twin, three or four bedded
- the meal arrangements, including special diets
- the reservation and porterage procedures
- any special facilities, such as for disabled people
- fire and safety precautions
- acceptable health conditions in areas such as the kitchen
- personal accommodation for a rep and space for a desk and noticeboard.

	ADVANTAGES	DISADVANTAGES
Tour operator committed to paying for an agreed number of beds	Tour operator can demand a good price	Any unsold beds will add to the tour operator's overall costs
Allocation of a number of beds until an agreed release date	A reasonable price can be negotiated and the tour operator reduces the risk involved	After the release date, the tour opertor will have to telex the hotel about availability
Contract accommodation on an ad hoc basis	No risk involved for the tour operator	More expensive for the client

Figure 9.4 Three types of accommodation contracts

Brochure production

The tour operator's brochure is the client's means of knowing the holiday which is being offered. It is also the basis of the legal contract between the tour operator and the client and it is therefore important for the information in the brochure to be accurate and comprehensive. Tour operators' brochures should have:

- information about the destinations
- photographs of the destinations and accommodation
- details of costs and booking conditions.

Accommodation and price grid

Figure 9.5 shows the kind of information which will be required for printing price tables in the brochure.

The holiday code is used to identify the package holiday in the reservation system. Other details in the grid include:

- the name of the resort
- the name of the hotel or accommodation
- the type of meal arrangements
- the departure airport
- the actual day of the week and time of flying
- the length of the season.

Departure periods

Down the left hand side the price grid outlines the departure periods for pricing. In Fig. 9.5 all departures which fall between 1 and 19 November will have the same price and then the price will increase or decrease in the next band according to the pricing strategy adopted by the company as considered below.

HOLIDAY CODE	ABC 235	
RESORT	ORLANDO	
HOTEL	GRANADA	
MEAL ARRANGEMENT	HALF BOARD	
DEPARTURE AIRPORT	MANCHESTER	
DEPARTURE DAY	FRIDAY	
DEPARTURE TIME	10.30	
FIRST DEPARTURE	4 November	
LAST DEPARTURE	21 APRIL	14 APRIL
NUMBER OF NIGHTS	7	14
Departures between		
1 NOV – 19 NOV		
20 NOV – 3 DEC		
4 DEC – 14 DEC		
15 DEC – 20 DEC		
21 DEC – 29 DEC		
30 DEC – 25 JAN		
26 JAN – 21 FEB		
22 FEB – 31 MAR		
1 APR – 15 APR		
16 APR – 24 APR		

Costs are inserted in these boxes according to the pricing strategy

Figure 9.5 Accommodation and price grid

Basic costings

We have already seen that the tour operator must pay for transport, accommodation and transfers, and in addition brochure costings must take into account the fixed costs of the tour operator, the variable costs of holidays, the commission paid to travel agents and an element of profit.

Fixed costs

Fixed costs include staff salaries, rent, heating, lighting and cleaning for both the UK and overseas offices, advertising and brochure production.

Variable costs

Variable costs include tickets and inflight refreshments. These vary with the number of passengers because they have to be paid only for the people who actually travel.

Seasons

Seasons are the basis of a pricing strategy in many brochures.

High season

The most expensive dates are called the high or peak season, which may be August in a summer holiday, Christmas or February in a skiing holiday or March in the Canary islands.

Low season

The cheapest dates are called the low season, which may be August in Egypt when it is extremely hot or spring and winter in Europe when it is cool. The other dates in the year are referred to as the shoulder season

Load factors

Most package holiday calculations involve the idea of a load factor. This means the percentage of the airline or hotel which is actually used.

A chartered flight has to be paid for whether the aircraft is filled or not and tour operators could make their costings for example on the assumption that the plane would be at least 90% filled. This 90% is the load factor. Some charters hope to achieve an even higher load factor, whereas scheduled airlines often work to a load factor as low as 55% or 60%.

Calculating costs of flights

Assume a tour operator contracts a flight series for a 130-seater Boeing 737 every Thursday at a cost of £12,000 per return flight.

If the season covers 28 weeks and there is an empty leg at the beginning and end of the season, this gives a total of 29 return flights to be paid for:

29 flights at £12,000   = £348,000

There are only 28 return flights with passengers so the real cost of each of these return flights is

£348,000 divided by 28 = £12,429 per flight

The aircraft holds 130 passengers but a load factor of 90% would assume only 90% of 130 = 117 passengers would actually fly.

Therefore 117 passengers are expected to cover the £12,429 cost of the flight.

Therefore the minimum cost to be charged per person will be:

£12,429 divided by 117 = £106.23

If more than 117 persons book then the extra fares are clear profit for the company. If fewer than 117 book then a no profit and even a deficit situation will occur. In this case a decision may be made to consolidate flights and ask clients to fly at another time or from another airport thus saving on the cost of a flight.

Pricing strategies

Now we will consider how the different tour operators might approach a reasonable costing for the brochure.

Small tour operators

The smaller specialist tour operators, who make up most of the ABTA membership, usually cost the basic elements of the holiday and then add a mark-up of 20% to 35% to cover fixed costs, travel agent's commission and profit. There may be very little difference in prices in the brochure throughout the year.

Large tour operators

The larger tour operators are more conscious of the prices of their competitors and their pricing strategy could mean that holidays in the low season are offered at the break even point where no actual profit is made, but holidays in the peak season are inflated to cover fixed costs, travel agent's commission and profit.

Risks of reduced prices

Selling without profit is regarded as better than not selling at all, especially if the tour operator actually owns airlines and hotels. However, the collapse of Court Line and Clarksons in the 1960s and ILG and INTASUN in the 1990s, each among the biggest tour operators of their day, have shown that reducing prices to a bare minimum can be a risky business.

Calculating selling prices

Here is an example of how a pricing strategy might be approached.

If the transport cost per person for the flight was	£106.23
Assume the hotel cost per person per week is	£70.00
Assume transfers come to	£7.00
Minimum cost per person would be	£183.23

Break even point

This £183.23 is required to cover the client's actual costs and now the operator must calculate a price at which fixed costs and travel agent's commission can also be covered. About 3% will also be built in for profit. This final price is referred to as the break even point.

Final calculation

There are two main ways of calculating the final selling price.

First, the smaller operators often add a mark up to cover these costs, so

Cost per person	£183.23
Mark up of 20%	£36.65
Total	£219.88

The small tour operator could then round up £219.88 to a selling price of £220.00 which would be charged throughout the season.

Second, the larger tour operators usually cover the cost of travel agent's commission and then adjust the price according to the season. Refer back to Fig. 9.5 to see that ten different price bands could be used throughout the season.

Travel agents' commission

Most travel agents receive 10% commission from the tour operators, but those who do more bookings than average will receive a bonus or over-rider commission which could be 2% or 3% above this.

If the travel agent is to receive 10% of the final selling price this means that the tour operator must add another one-ninth to the cost arrived at above, so

Cost per person	£183.23
Plus 1/9 for travel agent's commission	£20.35
Selling price	£203.58

Just check this figure back again if you are not convinced about the one-ninth: 10% of £203.58 is £20.35.

Final selling price

The tour operator could now round up this £203.58 to a selling price of £204.00. The pricing strategy might then be to sell the holiday at this price of £204.00 in the low season, knowing that immediate costs would be covered. The price could then be raised to say £250.00 in the peak season and £222.00 in the shoulder season. In this way the clients who travel in the high and shoulder seasons are in effect paying for the fixed costs and profits for the whole year.

This is a very simple example but should serve to show the reasoning which could go into producing a price grid which varies throughout the season. The actual calculations for real brochures would be far more complicated but our purpose at present is simply to understand the reason for a pricing strategy.

Brochure production schedule

The production of a brochure starts up to two years ahead of the actual holidays. Figure 9.6 gives an indication of the timescale for the various activities both in the UK and in the overseas resort.

Booking procedures

Reservations systems, which can be either manual or computerised, are used to keep track of the bookings for various elements of a package holiday.

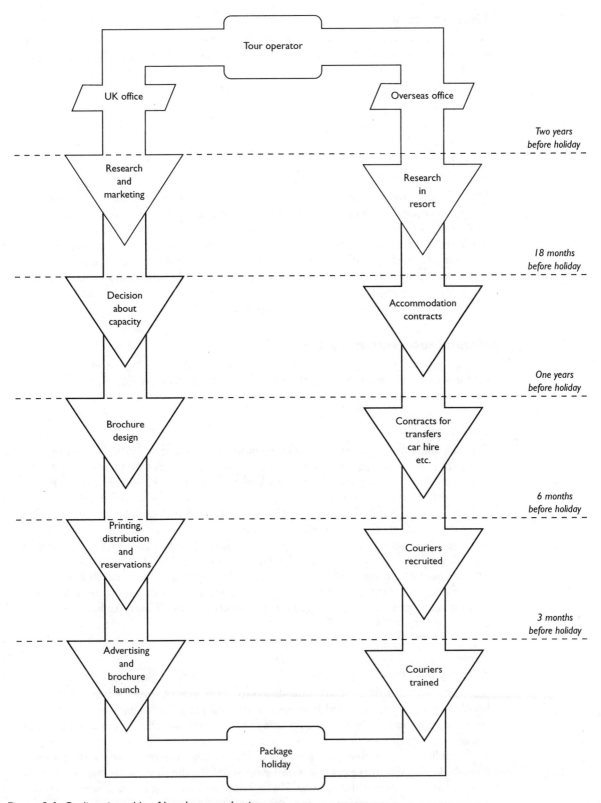

Figure 9.6 Outline timetable of brochure production

Units of stock

All reservations systems work on the idea that there is a stock of holidays and an up-to-date count of what has not been sold is always available. Package holidays can involve reservations for:

- flight seats
- berths on ferries
- car spaces on ferries
- hotel beds
- apartments
- tent sites at camps.

Each of these components is shown as a unit of stock. A twin room will be shown as two units of stock as it can be booked by two people, each of whom will require further units of stock for a flight seat or berth. As bookings are made, so the units of stock are subtracted from the total and the remaining stock is shown as still available.

Pricing on package holidays is crucial and the profitability of the tour operator depends on selling as many units of stock as possible. The current up-to-date situation is therefore very important to the tour operator. The current state of units of stock is also important to ensure that overbooking does not occur.

Manual reservations systems

Manual reservations systems can use wallcharts or cards which are produced at the beginning of the season showing the available units of stock for flights, beds, berths and any other reservable units.

Wallcharts

On each chart there are marks or flags to indicate each unit of stock. When the travel agent telephones the tour operator, a reservations clerk checks the charts and, if the required holiday is available and the booking is confirmed, the reservations clerk crosses off the mark or removes the flag on the wallchart. For a booking of two airline seats and a twin room, four flags would be removed from a wallchart.

The main advantages of a wallchart manual system are that the large wallcharts can easily give an overall picture of the current booking situation and for this reason they are still used by some companies as backup to other systems. Wallcharts are also cheaper than a computerised system for a small independent tour operator.

The main disadvantages of wallchart manual systems are that they are time-consuming to produce and their accuracy depends on several users all keeping the information up to date.

Cards

The card manual reservations system is similar to wallcharts but instead of just showing a mark or flag, a card is produced for each unit of stock. When a holiday is booked the cards are removed from their trays and placed in an envelope. In this system a room in a hotel would have one card showing whether it was a twin, three-bedded or larger room.

If a holiday were booked for a family of three flying to a resort and staying in a three-bedded room, three cards would be removed for the flight seats and one for the room, making a total of four cards. These would be placed in an envelope which is passed to the administration section.

The card system makes more efficient use of the time of the reservations clerk as the trays of cards can be placed near to the telephones. However, it does not give the overall picture of the current booking situation which is achieved by the wallcharts.

Computerised reservations systems

Computerised reservations systems can be accessed through a reservations clerk by telephone or offered by the tour operator for direct access by the travel agent using a viewdata system. Computerised systems have to be interactive so that units of stock can be removed by only one user at a time. This is achieved by the computer programmer, who will also build prompts and safety checks into the system.

Once holidays are confirmed, units of stock are removed and placed on other computerised files of information which are used for invoicing, payments and ticketing.

The basic ideas of a computerised system are similar to the manual systems but the transactions can be made much more quickly.

The main advantage of computerised reservations systems is that the travel agent has more information readily available so that clients can be helped to make alternative choices if their preferred holiday cannot be booked. Computerised systems which are directly available to travel agents mean that the tour operator no longer has to employ as many reservations clerks and such systems are very efficient for the travel agent taking out options, whereby a holiday is temporarily reserved for a client until the end of the following day.

Electronic payment, whereby the tour operator can debit the travel agent's bank account directly at the end of each month, is made possible with computerised systems and the introduction of viewdata systems has made it easier for tour operators to make cheaper last minute holidays available and to keep these constantly updated.

Administration

Key timings

The tour operator's administration section produces invoices, receives payment and despatches tickets to clients and travel agents. Figure 9.7 shows the key timings involved in the booking of a package holiday.

Customer complaints

The customer services department deals with customer enquiries and complaints. In responding to complaints, the customer services department will always refer to the brochure in their initial dealings with a client. The role of this department is one of conciliation as they are expected to placate a disappointed client and come to some agreement whether it be an apology or some compensation, without having to resort to outside intervention.

Sometimes an 'ex gratia' payment is offered to a client. This payment is made on the understanding that the tour operator is not accepting any liability or responsibility for whatever has gone wrong with the holiday. The payment is simply made as a goodwill gesture on their part.

A litigation section within the customers services department will be responsible for dealing with any serious complaints which actually come to court. Chapter 15 gives more details about action which could be taken by ABTA or the courts in the case of unsatisfactory holidays being sold by the tour operator.

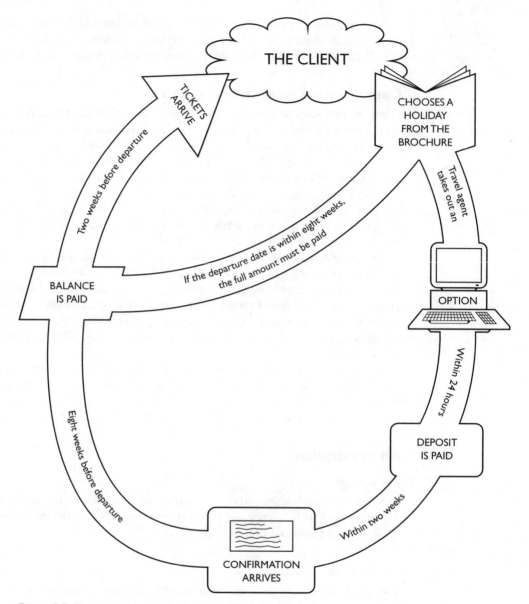

Figure 9.7 Key timings during the booking of a package holiday

Summary of the main functions in tour operating

Figure 9.8 summarises the main functions in tour operating in the UK office and the overseas office.

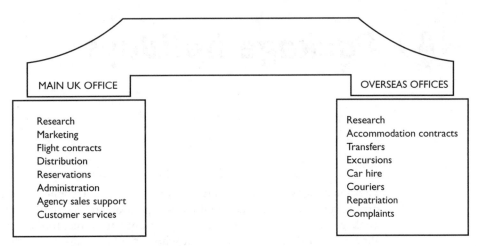

Figure 9.8 Functions in tour operating

Revision Questions

Primary level

1 List THREE major components of a package holiday.

2 Briefly describe FOUR duties of an overseas rep.

3 What name is given to the practice of leasing or hiring aircraft?

4 A tour operator's programme may be divided into three seasons, one of which is the peak season. What are the other two seasons called?

5 List THREE items which should be included in a brochure.

6 What do you understand by the term 'variable cost' in connection with brochure pricing?

7 What is meant by the term 'transfer' in connection with a package holiday?

8 Name THREE items which should be included in a contract between a tour operator and an airline.

9 Name THREE items which should be included in a contract between a tour operator and a hotel.

10 Holiday codes are printed in most brochures. For what are these codes used?

Advanced level

1 Describe THREE ways in which a tour operator could contract accommodation for package holidays.

2 What is the word used to describe the practice of asking clients to change their flight if charter aircraft cannot be filled for a certain time or airport?

3 In connection with an allocation of scheduled airline seats, what do you understand by a 'release date'?

4 With regard to the costing of package holidays what do you understand by the term 'break even point'?

5 On an aircraft what is the term used to describe the number of seats sold as a percentage of the number of seats available?

6 What do you understand by the term 'mark-up'?

7 List FOUR responsibilities of a tour operator's area representative.

8 Other than August in summer brochures, which other month might be high or peak season in a brochure, and why?

9 List FOUR examples of fixed costs which could be incurred by a tour operator in brochure production.

10 What do you understand in relation to package holidays by the term 'empty leg'?

10) *Package holidays*

Package holidays are those which include transport, accommodation, ground arrangements and the services of a tour operator's representative for an all-in-price. Package holidays may be sold by the tour operator direct to the public or more often they are sold through a travel agent who is paid commission for the sale.

Types of package holidays

There are four man types:

- single and multi-centre holidays
- special interest holidays
- touring holidays
- fly/drive holidays.

Single and multi-centre holidays

Many package holidays are to a single destination where the client stays in the same accommodation for the full week, fortnight or however long the holiday lasts. The most common single destination holidays are offered in the summer and winter brochures which are produced by all the large tour operators. Single centre holiday brochures may be produced with a particular group in mind, such as young people under 30, or older people over 55. The destinations, hotels and entertainment offered in the brochures are all planned with that particular age group in mind. Multi-centre holidays are those where the client stays in two or more hotels or other accommodation, usually in contrasting areas. For example a client might book a week on a quiet island followed by another week in a vibrant resort with plenty of nightlife and entertainment.

Special interest holidays

Brochures may cater for special interests as varied as golf or painting. There is a wide range of brochures offering all kinds of activity or sporting holidays. The largest group of these is the skiing holidays. We shall consider specialist holidays in more detail in Chapter 11.

Touring holidays

Some tour operators offer touring holidays for clients to see all the sights of an area. Tours of the Far East can involve a client in spending three or four nights in each of several different countries. For example it is possible within a three week holiday to visit Egypt, India and Thailand. Cruising is a special form of touring with the possibility of three months sailing right around the world or a shorter trip to the

Mediterranean or the Canary islands. Several companies offer fly/cruise holidays to the Caribbean where it is possible to fly out from the UK and then cruise around the islands for a week or two before flying home. We shall look at cruising holidays separately in Chapter 12.

Fly/drive holidays

Some tour operators package holidays which include the flight from UK, hire of a camper or car, and vouchers for hotel accommodation to be used as and when the client wishes. Such touring holidays are particularly popular in the USA and Australia and are referred to as fly/drive holidays.

Booking a holiday

The brochure

A tour operator's brochure should have information about:

- the resort, accommodation and transport
- departure dates and prices
- any extra services such as insurance or car hire
- booking conditions showing clearly the responsibilities of both the tour operator and the client.

The booking form, once completed, must be signed by the lead name, that is the person whose name appears first on the booking. The person who signs the booking form must be over 18 years of age because the lead name is held responsible in law for any charges or subsequent claims if the holiday is unsatisfactory.

The role of the travel agent

Figure 10.1 illustrates the relationship between the tour operator and the travel agent. If a package holiday is booked through a travel agent the client has the right to expect clear and accurate information from the travel agent about the holiday and assistance in making a suitable choice of destination, transport and accommodation. Further assistance might also be given with regard to passports, visas and health regulations, as outlined in Chapter 4.

Options

An option can be taken out by the travel agent if the clients are uncertain about a holiday, need more time to consider it or if they do not have the deposit to hand. This is a provisional booking which is held in the tour operator's reservation system for a short period of time. Sometimes an option is taken for just 24 hours but at times it may be taken for a week and even renewed if this is a possibility on the tour operator's system.

Deposits

A deposit must be paid, once the client has made a final choice, to secure the holiday booking. The deposit is very often 10% of the cost of the holiday but in some brochures a fixed figure such as £25 per person may be stated. The deposit not only secures the holiday for the client but also obliges the client to abide by the booking conditions, which are considered in more detail below.

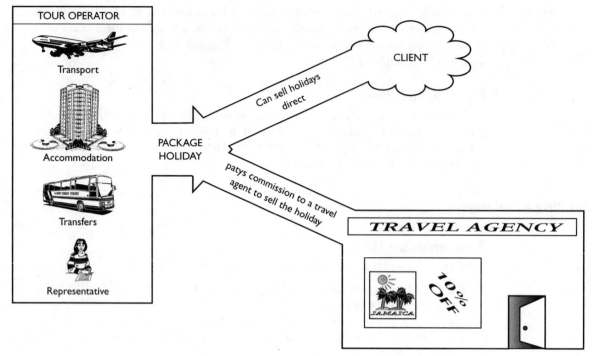

Figure 10.1 The tour operator and the travel agent

Confirmation

Confirmation of the booking will be sent by the tour operator to the travel agent within two weeks of the deposit being paid. This confirmation should be carefully checked by the travel agent who then sends it to the client. Any errors, especially of names for travel documentation, should be corrected at this stage.

Balance of payment

The balance of payment, that is the full price less the deposit, must usually be paid to the tour operator eight weeks before the holiday starts. Tickets are then sent to the travel agent about two weeks before the holiday and again these should be checked very carefully.

Late bookings

Late bookings, which are those made within eight weeks of the start of the holiday, should normally be paid for in full at the time of booking.

Booking conditions

Booking conditions in holiday brochures may be called a fair trading charter or agreement or policy. Whatever the title, the booking conditions should not be printed on the reverse of the booking form which will be retained by the travel agent once it has been signed by the client. The travel agent should point out the conditions to clients, who should retain their own copy.

Booking conditions as a contract

Booking conditions are divided into two sections - one deals with the client's contract with the tour operator, the other deals with the responsibilities of the tour operator to the client.

Client's contract

The client's contract in the booking conditions states that the client will pay a deposit to secure the holiday, pay the balance within a specified time and an amendment fee if any alterations are requested. Amendment fees must be paid for each item of change, for instance if the names of persons travelling are changed or the date of departure is changed. Amendments must be notified to the tour operator in writing and the client is responsible for the amendment fees. Typical amendment fees are £15 per person and per detail changed.

Tour operator's contract

The tour operator's section of the booking conditions usually includes a promise to supply the holiday as in the brochure and a list of circumstances under which the tour operator would be entitled to make changes and whether or not these should be regarded as major changes.

Changes to a package holiday

Cancellation charges

Cancellation charges are detailed in the booking conditions and these usually range from the deposit only if the client cancels early enough, to the full cost of the holiday if it is cancelled on or after the departure date. All cancellations should be sent to the tour operator in writing and it is only at this point that they come into effect. The notification of cancellation must be signed by the person who signed the booking form, that is the lead name.

For example using Fig. 10.2, a family of four had booked a two week holiday to Tenerife departing on Friday 16 June at a basic cost of £650 per person. At the beginning of May they were invited to a family wedding which would take place on

These charges are based on how many days before your booked departure we receive your written instruction – the more notice you give, the less we charge.

These charges are a percentage of the total cost of your holiday, not including your insurance premium.

Period before departure within which we receive your written cancellation	Amount you must pay
More than 42 days	deposit only
29–42 days	50% of holiday cost or deposit if greater
15–28 days	60% of holiday cost or deposit if greater
1–14 days	90% of holiday cost or deposit if greater
Departure date or after	100%

Figure 10.2 Cancellation charges

24 June, the Saturday of their second week. They discussed the possibilities and finally decided on 16 May to cancel the holiday. They wrote to the tour operator and posted the letter with a second class stamp so that it arrived on Friday 19 May. The tour operator cancelled the holiday and charged them £1,560 cancellation fee, that is 60% of the cost of the holiday. If they had made their decision earlier, or indeed used a first class stamp so that the letter arrived by 17 May, they would have been liable for a 50% cancellation fee, that is £1,300, a saving of £260.

Another client and partner had booked a ten day holiday in Majorca at a cost of £370 each, departing on Thursday 13 April from London Gatwick. On 29 March the partner's father died suddenly and they had to cancel. They telephoned the travel agent immediately and sent a written cancellation to the tour operator who received it on Saturday 31 March. Cancellation charges were 90% of the cost of the holiday, that is £666. However, the couple had taken out holiday insurance and, because death of a close relative was included in the cover, they were able to claim the full £666 from the insurers.

Compensation

Compensation must be paid to the client, according to the ABTA Code of Practice for tour operators, if the tour operator changes:

- the resort to a lower category of accommodation than that booked
- the flight time significantly
- the airport of departure or arrival to one which is inconvenient.

For any major alterations the booking conditions specify a scale of compensation fees which could be paid to the client.

For example using Fig.10.3, a group of five young people had booked a two week holiday in Torremolinos departing from Manchester on Saturday 22 July. The tour

If we change your holiday we will compensate you according to these scales. The compensation is based on how many days before your booked departure we tell you of a major change. We will only make one payment for each person in the booking.	
Period before departure within which a major change is notified to your travel agent	**Compensation per person**
0–7 days	£50
8–14 days	£40
15–28 days	£30
29–56 days	£20
more than 56 days	£10
If the change is not acceptable to you, you can cancel your booking. In this case we will refund all the money you have paid to us and will pay you £30 compensation if we have given less than 14 days notice and £15 compensation if we have given more than 15 days but less than 56 days notice. If we have given more than 56 days notice we will not pay compensation, although you are still entitled to cancel your holiday and receive a full refund of money already paid.	
Important Note: We will not pay compensation for changes made because of war or threat of war, riots, civil disturbances, terrorist activity, industrial disputes, natural and nuclear disasters, fire, epidemic or health risks.	

Figure 10.3 Compensation

operator notified them on 13 July that it was necessary to consolidate the Manchester and Birmingham flights and asked the group to fly from Birmingham on 22 July, staying at the same hotel and resort. Coaches would be provided to transport clients at the beginning and end of their holiday between Manchester and Birmingham. The tour operator was obliged according to Fig. 10.3 to offer each person £40 compensation, making a total of £200. Alternatively the group could have cancelled their holiday and each would have received a full refund plus £30 compensation.

Some tour operators use two scales of compensation. A lower scale is used to provide compensation if the accommodation is changed to the same, similar or a higher standard in the same resort or if the time of the flight is changed by more than twelve hours. A higher scale of compensation is used in cases where the changes involve accommodation of a lower standard; a different resort; a change of airport; a change to the length of the holiday; a change of day of departure; or a change from a day to a night flight.

Night flights are defined as those flights which leave the UK between 10 pm and 6 am or which land home between midnight and 6 am. This definition needs to be clear if the client is considering claiming compensation for a change of flight from day to night. It should also be noted that the length of a package holiday is normally counted in the number of nights at the hotel or other accommodation.

Major changes to a package holiday

If the changes made by the tour operator are so drastic that the client is asked to go to a resort in a different country from that booked or to accept a flight which is changed by more than 24 hours, then the ABTA Code of Practice states that the client can regard this as a cancelled holiday and claim a full refund.

Force majeure

Where changes to a package holiday are beyond the control of the tour operator, the tour operator is not required to comply with the compensation scales. Such circumstances are sometimes referred to as 'Acts of God' or 'force majeure'. Examples of such changes would be:

- a hurricane
- an earthquake
- threat of war
- riot
- civil strife
- industrial dispute
- terrorist activity
- nuclear disaster
- fire.

Complaints

The booking conditions also give advice as to how the client can make known any complaint if the holiday goes wrong. Normally complaints should have been notified to the representative in the resort in the form of a written report as well as to the hotel, coach company or other supplier with whom the client has a problem. On return from their holiday clients have a specified length of time, usually about 28 days, to write to the complaints department at the tour operator's UK office. Such correspondence should include the client's holiday reference number; a copy of, or reference number for, the resort report; the client's name and address and contact telephone number.

In the brochure of a registered ABTA member, details will also be given of the special complaints procedure available through ABTA. The ABTA complaints procedure is considered in more detail in Chapter 15.

Costings from brochures

We will approach this topic through a series of examples using Figs 10.4 and 10.5 as a basis. The basic costs of a holiday may have various supplements added and various reductions deducted.

Costing hotel package holidays

Basic costs

Basic costs per person for hotel package holidays are listed in the price table shown in Fig. 10.4 and these depend on two factors, namely the departure date and the length of the holiday.

A couple wish to book a three night holiday at the Grand Hotel departing from London Gatwick on Wednesday 8 November. The cost each will be £205.

Another couple wish to book a ten night holiday at the Grand Hotel departing from London Gatwick on Wednesday 1 November. Their departure date is not listed specifically but it comes within the band 29 Oct to 07 Nov and so, reading across the first line of prices, the cost each for the ten nights will be £325.

Flight supplements

Flight supplements are often charged by tour operators for departures other than London. If either of the two examples above had involved a flight from Manchester then each person would have been charged a further £23. Similar supplements are listed for the other departure airports, together with the day of the flight.

A group of four young people wish to book a two week holiday at the Grand Hotel for Christmas departing from Birmingham on Tuesday 19 December. The departure comes within the band 14 Dec to 20 Dec and the cost per person will be £509 plus £21 supplement for the Birmingham flight.

Room supplements

Room supplements may be charged for extra facilities such as a single room, a balcony or a sea view. These supplements are normally charged for each person according to the number of nights on the holiday.

If the couple who booked the three night holiday on 8 November wanted to book a room with a sea view, the total extra cost for the booking would be

2 adults @ £0.90 for 3 nights
$2 \times 0.90 \times 3 = £5.40$

If the group of four young people having a two week holiday at Christmas decided they wanted a single room each, the total extra cost for the booking would be

4 adults @ £2.95 for 14 nights
$4 \times 2.95 \times 14 = £165.20$

Meal supplements

Meal supplements are charged where half or full board are available but not included in the basic cost. Half board means that the clients would have breakfast and either lunch or dinner in the hotel each day. Full board means that the clients would have breakfast, lunch and dinner in the hotel each day.

Prices are per person in £s at time of going to press						
Accommodation and meal arrangements	**GRAND HOTEL** Bed and Breakfast					
Accommodation code	GRH					
Prices based on	SH WC BL					
Number of nights	3	4	7	10	11	14
Departures between	Adult	Adult	Adult	Adult	Adult	Adult
29 Oct – 07 Nov	229	229	265	325	325	369
08 Nov – 15 Nov	205	205	239	295	295	335
16 Nov – 22 Nov	169	169	205	265	265	309
23 Nov – 29 Nov	149	149	179	235	235	275
30 Nov – 13 Dec	149	149	179	235	235	–
14 Dec – 20 Dec	145	145	–	–	479	509
21 Dec – 27 Dec	359	–	425	519	–	549
28 Dec – 03 Jan	205	205	239	239	279	315
4 Jan – 24 Jan	189	189	215	259	279	279
25 Jan – 7 Feb	195	195	219	275	275	315
8 Feb – 14 Feb	205	205	249	295	295	335
15 Feb – 21 Feb	205	205	245	309	309	365
22 Feb – 13 Mar	209	209	269	369	369	405
14 Mar – 20 Mar	209	255	319	389	399	439
21 Mar – 27 Mar	305	305	335	395	395	425
28 Mar – 03 Apr	249	249	295	349	349	395
04 Apr – 10 Apr	239	239	259	335	335	375
Supplements per person per night	Single Room (SH WC) £2.95 Sea View £0.90 Half board £2.55 Full board £4.25					
Child Reductions (age 2–11 inclusive)	First Child sharing with two full fare paying adults, less 50% Second Child sharing with two full fare paying adults, less 10%					
Reductions per adult per night	3rd adult only sharing £2.50 Twin Room (SH WC) £0.50					
Insurance – Adult	£22.50	£22.50	£25.95	£29.95	£29.95	£29.95
Insurance – Child (2–11)	£11.00	£11.00	£13.00	£15.00	£15.00	£15.00
Flights are available from London Gatwick (Wed); Manchester (Wed, £23); Birmingham (Tues, £21); Luton (Tues, £5); Bristol (Wed, £5); Newcastle (Wed, £19); Glasgow (Tues, £28); Cardiff (Tues, £11)						

Figure 10.4 Price table for a hotel package holiday

If the couple on the ten night holiday departing on 1 November wished to know the relative cost of booking either half or full board, they could be told that the extra cost would be

2 adults half board @ £2.55 for 10 nights
$2 \times 2.55 \times 10 = £51$

or

2 adults full board @ £4.25 for 10 nights
$2 \times 4.25 \times 10 = £85$

Child reductions

Child reductions vary greatly from one brochure to another but normally they apply only to the basic cost and not to supplements. Free child places may be offered but these are usually limited in number and tied to certain departure dates. For these reasons free child places are normally sold out very soon after the launch of a brochure. Some brochures list a child price for the first child in the party and give a small percentage reduction for a second child while other brochures list percentage reductions for each child.

Normally child reductions are only given for up to two children aged 2–11 years of age sharing a hotel room with two full fare paying adults. A few brochures offer a reduction for one child with a single parent.

If a family of two adults and two children aged 8 and 10 were to book a seven night holiday sharing a room at the Grand Hotel, departing on 15 November from London Gatwick, the cost would be

2 adults	@ £239	£478.00
1st child	@ £239 less 50%	119.50
2nd child	@ £239 less 10%	215.10
	total cost	£812.60

Adult reductions

Adult reductions are normally available if a third adult shares a room or if a lower grade of room is booked. Figure 10.4 shows a 50p reduction for each person each night if a twin room without a balcony is booked. On a seven night holiday for a couple this would give an overall reduction on the total cost of the holiday of

$2 \times 0.50 \times 7 = £7.00$

If three adults were to book a four night break at the Grand Hotel departing from London Gatwick on Wednesday 20 March the basic costing would be in the band 14 Mar to 20 Mar

2 adults	@ £255	£510.00
1 adult	@ £255 less (£2.50 × 4)	245.00
	total cost	£755.00

Insurance premiums

Insurance premiums should be added to the total cost and care must be taken with the layout of costings as detailed below.

Costing self-catering package holidays

Basic costs

Basic costs per person for self-catering package holidays are listed in the price table shown in Fig. 10.5 and depend, as for hotel package holidays, on the departure date and the length of the holiday. However, with self-catering holidays a third factor to be considered is the size of the studio or apartment. A studio is usually one room with a small kitchen area, living space, a bed and possibly a bathroom, although this may be shared. An apartment has at least one separate bedroom as well as a bathroom and may have a separate kitchen and even a utility room..

If three adults were to book a week's self-catering holiday in a studio at the Dunes Club, departing from London Gatwick on Wednesday 22 November, the basic cost would be £255 each.

If four adults booked a one bedroom apartment at the Dunes Club for the same week, departing from London Gatwick, the basic cost would be £249 each.

Occupancy supplements

Supplements apply for self-catering holidays if the number of full fare paying adults booking a studio or apartment is less than the capacity of that unit.

If a couple were to book a two week holiday in a studio at the Dunes Club, departing from London Gatwick on Wednesday 13 March, the basic cost would be £325 but each client would have to pay a £2 supplement for each night of the holiday. The costing would therefore be

2 adults	@ £325	£650.00
2 supplements	@ (£2.00 × 14)	56.00
	total cost	£706.00

If the same two adults wished to book a one bedroom apartment rather than a studio, the basic cost would be lower at £319 each but there would be a supplement of £3.65 each for each night of the holiday. The costing would therefore be

2 adults	@ £319	£638.00
2 supplements	@ (£3.65 × 14)	102.20
	total cost	£740.20

If a group of four wished to book a week's holiday in a two bedroom apartment at the Dunes Club, departing from London Gatwick on Wednesday 3 April, the costing would be

4 adults	@ £335	£1,340.00
4 supplements	@ (£1.45 × 7)	40.60
	total cost	£1,380.60

Child reductions

Child reductions vary greatly from one brochure to another. Free child places may be offered as for hotels, although there is usually more availability in self-catering units. A child price may be listed or percentage reductions may be given as for hotels. Very

Prices are per person in £s at time of going to press						
Accommodation and meal arrangements	**DUNES CLUB APARTMENTS** Self Catering					
Accommodation code	DCA		DCB		DCC	
Prices based on	Studio 3 adults		1 Bdrm Apt 4 adults		2 Bdrm Apt 6 adults	
Number of nights	7	14	7	14	7	14
Departures between	Adult	Adult	Adult	Adult	Adult	Adult
29 Oct – 07 Nov	295	325	289	319	279	309
08 Nov – 15 Nov	259	295	255	289	245	279
16 Nov – 22 Nov	255	285	249	279	239	269
23 Nov – 29 Nov	245	269	239	265	229	259
30 Nov – 13 Dec	239	259	229	255	225	249
14 Dec – 20 Dec	235	379	229	375	225	359
21 Dec – 27 Dec	395	445	389	435	375	419
28 Dec – 03 Jan	389	399	379	395	369	379
4 Jan – 24 Jan	279	305	275	299	265	289
25 Jan – 7 Feb	259	295	255	289	245	279
8 Feb – 14 Feb	269	289	265	285	255	279
15 Feb – 21 Feb	295	315	285	309	275	299
22 Feb – 13 Mar	285	325	279	319	269	309
14 Mar – 20 Mar	309	349	305	345	295	329
21 Mar – 27 Mar	355	405	345	399	325	385
28 Mar – 03 Apr	325	375	349	369	335	355
04 Apr – 10 Apr	325	339	315	335	305	325
11 Apr – 17 Apr	329	342	319	339	309	329
18 Apr – 30 Apr	325	–	315	–	305	–
Supplements per adult per night	for 2 £2.00		for 3 £1.25 for 2 £3.65		for 5 £0.60 for 4 £1.45 for 3 £2.90 for 2 £5.85	
Supplements per person per night	Half Board £8.40					
Child Reductions (age 2–16 inclusive)	Up to two children with two full fare paying passengers each receives a 50% reduction					
Insurance – Adult	£22.50	£22.50	£25.95	£29.95	£29.95	£29.95
Insurance – Child (2–11)	£11.00	£11.00	£13.00	£15.00	£15.00	£15.00
Flights are available from London Gatwick (Wed); Manchester (Wed, £23); Birmingham (Tues, £21) Luton (Tues, £5); Bristol (Wed, £5); Newcastle (Wed, £19); Glasgow (Tues, £28); Cardiff (Tues, £11)						

Figure 10.5 Price table for a self-catering package holiday

often, as in Fig. 10.5, up to two children will receive a substantial reduction. A few brochures also offer discounts for a third child and some raise the qualifying age bracket to 2–16 years.

Flight and meal supplements

Flight and meal supplements are applied to self-catering package holidays (where appropriate) in the same way as to hotel holidays.

Layout for costings

Costings should show very clearly:

- the number of people travelling
- the basic cost
- any children or adults receiving discounts or reductions
- any meal or travel supplements
- insurance.

It is useful if this information is listed to the left hand side, then unit costs can be stated in the middle and total costs on the far right. Care should be taken in the column of total costs to keep the decimal points under each other and any amounts without pence should be shown in the format £350.00 rather than just £350.

Using Fig. 10.4

Consider a group of friends who want to book a week's holiday at the Grand Hotel with half board, departing from Glasgow on 20 February and the group consists of two adults and a child aged 7 sharing a room; a couple who want a room without a balcony; and another person who wants a single room. They would all like to have a room with a sea view. The costing would be

basic cost adults	3 @ £245	£735.00
1st child	1 @ (£245 – 50%)	122.50
single room supplement	(1 × £2.95 × 7)	20.65
2 adults (no balcony)	2 @ (£245 – (7 × 0.50))	483.00
half board supplement	6 @ (£2.55 × 7)	107.10
sea view supplement	6 @ (£0.90 × 7)	37.80
Glasgow flight supplement	6 @ £28	168.00
insurance (adult)	5 @ £25.95	129.75
insurance (child)	1 @ £13.00	13.00
	total cost	£1,816.80

Selecting appropriate holidays

Selecting an appropriate destination

Earlier chapters in Part Two of this book gave some indicators as to the most popular destinations with British clients. In making recommendations as to destinations, the travel agent should be aware of the climate at different times of the year, health risks, the range of attractions and distances from the port or airport, all of which could be important for specific clients. Some self-catering apartments and villas can be in isolated locations and it is essential that the travel agent recommends car hire in these cases.

Selecting an appropriate type of holiday

Bearing in mind that certain brochures are designed for specific groups of clients it would of course be totally inappropriate to recommend that a retired client or one with a family of young children should join an 18–30s type holiday. Equally a group of young people aged 17–19 are unlikely to enjoy a winter break in an isolated hotel which caters for long stay retired clients.

Selecting appropriate accommodation

There may be instances where the travel agent can assist clients to choose their grade of accommodation, the location of the accommodation or the type of rooms.

Using Fig. 10.4

> If a family of two adults and three children aged 9, 11 and 15 were to book a seven night holiday at the Grand Hotel, departing on 15 November from London Gatwick, the travel agent would have to recommend two rooms. However, a comparative costing shows whether the family would be better to book the two younger children with discounts and the 16 year old in a single room, or whether, for the sake of 10% reduction, it might be better to pay the full basic cost for a second child.

Alternative 1

2 adults	@ £239	£478.00
1st child	@ £239 less 50%	119.50
2nd child	@ £239 less 10%	215.10
1 adult	@ £239	239.00
single supplement	(2.95 × 7)	20.65
	total cost	£1,072.25

With this booking the family are guaranteed a large room with a balcony but the single room may be small, would not have a balcony and may be in a different part of the hotel.

Alternative 2

2 adults	@ £239	£478.00
1st child	@ £239 less 50%	119.50
2 adults	@ £239	478.00
	total cost	£1,075.50

With this booking, for an extra £3.25, the family is guaranteed two larger rooms, both with balconies.

The travel agent could show the above comparison to the clients and allow them to make an informed choice.

Revision Questions

Primary level

1 Give TWO examples of special interest package holidays.

2 What do you understand by a fly/drive holiday?

3 By whom should a package holiday booking form be signed?

4 What is the reason for clients having to pay a deposit when booking a package holiday?

5 How soon prior to departure can clients expect to receive their tickets for a package holiday?

6 For a booking made five weeks before departure for a holiday costing £350, how much would the client be expected to pay at the time of booking?

7 Booking conditions in brochures are normally divided into two sections: what are these?

8 Using Fig. 10.2, if a client had booked a £450 holiday for 8 June and then cancelled it on 15 May, what percentage of the holiday cost would be charged as a cancellation fee?

9 Using Fig. 10.3, if a tour operator made a major change to a client's holiday which was due to take place on 5 May but informed them of the change only on 2 May, to how much compensation would the client be entitled?

10 Using Fig. 10.4, cost a holiday including insurance for a couple who wish to stay at the Grand Hotel for ten days departing from Bristol on Wednesday 3 April. They would like half board and a room with a balcony and a private bathroom.

Advanced level

1 Briefly describe what is meant by a multi-centre package holiday.

2 Apart from information about the resorts, list FOUR essential items which should be in a package holiday brochure.

3 When is the balance normally due to be paid for a package holiday?

4 Using Fig. 10.2, if a client booked a holiday to depart on 21 February for four people at a cost of £1,350.00, including insurance premiums of £120.00, and then cancelled on 17 January, how much would the fee for cancellation be?

5 Name FOUR items for which a client may be asked to pay a supplement on a package holiday.

6 According to the ABTA Code of Practice for tour operators, compensation must be paid to clients if certain changes are made by the tour operator. Give TWO examples of such changes.

7 Briefly describe what you understand by the term 'force majeur' and give TWO examples.

8 When a client is making a complaint about an unsatisfactory holiday, list THREE procedures which should be followed.

9 Using Fig. 10.4, cost a two week holiday at the Grand Hotel for a family of two adults and two children aged 8 and 10 who want a twin room with a balcony and private bathroom, and a grandparent who wants a single room with a sea view. They will fly from Manchester on Wednesday 24 January and will have only bed and breakfast at the hotel.

10 Using Fig. 10.5, cost a two week holiday at the Dunes Club in a two bedroom apartment including insurance for a family of two adults and three children aged 9, 12 and 14. They will require half board and they will fly from Cardiff on Tuesday 14 November.

11) *Specialist holidays*

There is a great variety of brochures providing specialist holidays from skiing to golf, from wine tasting to honeymoons. Only a selection can be considered in this chapter:

- age-orientated holidays
- city breaks
- skiing holidays
- weddings and honeymoons
- safari holidays.

Age-orientated holidays

The two main age groups which are targeted with special brochures are the 18–30 and the 55-plus groups. Summer holidays for 18–30s are described as 'the pleasure zone' or 'outrageous holidays' while the 55-plus brochures promote winter holidays for the 'young at heart' or those in their 'golden years'.

Holidays for 18–30s

Facilities

Facilities on the seven or fourteen nights 18-30s holidays which differ from regular package holidays include:

- an emphasis on a party atmosphere with descriptions of golden sands and electric nightlife
- hotels which are exclusively for the 18–30 age group
- an opportunity to have shared accommodation arranged for single clients
- excursions to venues such as soul cruises, aquaparks, beach parties, and cabarets, where the meal and drinks are free.

Destinations

Destinations on 18–30s holidays are normally very lively and busy and include:

- Lloret de Mar on the Costa Brava, Benidorm on the Costa Blanca and Salou on the Costa Dorada in mainland Spain
- San Antonio in Ibiza, Magaluf and Palma Nova in Majorca, Playa de las Americas in Tenerife and Playa del Ingles in Grand Canary
- Gumbet and Bodrum in Turkey, Kavos in Corfu, Faliraki in Rhodes, Malia in Crete and Kardamena in Kos.

Holidays for 55-plus

Facilities

Facilities on the seven to eighty-four nights 55-plus holidays which differ from regular package holidays include:

- a choice of very lively or very quiet resorts
- the presence of a chaplain and spouse to lead interdenominational services
- an emphasis on good service, quality and value
- no single room supplements on most departures
- special extras included in the price such as Christmas and New Year Galas, free afternoon tea and biscuits, champagne for anniversaries or honeymoons
- a variety of organised activities such as ballroom dancing, bowling, keep fit, bingo, quizzes, language lessons, card games, rambles, wine tasting and cookery demonstrations, lending library, golf and snooker competitions and painting lessons
- excursions over several days including two day safaris in Tunisia or a visit to Abu Simbel in Egypt.

Destinations

Destinations on 55-plus holidays are, with the exception of San Antonio, similar to those for 18–30s in mainland Spain and the Spanish islands, as well as more exotic destinations including:

- Hammamet, Sousse and Monastir in Tunisia
- St Paul's Bay in Malta
- Portuguese Algarve and Madeira
- Neapolitan Riviera around Sorrento in Italy
- Paphos and Ayia Napa in Cyprus
- Luxor and Nile cruises in Egypt.

City breaks

The most popular city break destination for British tourists is London but other UK cities, European capitals and New York, Boston and Toronto all feature in city break brochures.

London

London breaks are often geared to annual exhibitions, theatre and concert trips, although there is always a market for those who wish to sightsee and shop. Most London packages include accommodation, rail or coach travel, a London Travelcard and discounts in certain shops.

UK cities

UK city breaks may take a theme such as 'Murder and Mystery' or may depend on the surrounding countryside and facilities such as golf or shopping to attract tourists. Gateshead and Newcastle upon Tyne include the MetroCentre on their itineraries and Sheffield has the Meadowhall shopping centre.

Figure 11.1 Charles Bridge, Prague, Czech Republic (*Photograph: Mr Anthony LaRoche*)

European capitals

European city breaks traditionally popular to Paris and Amsterdam have been joined in the 1990s by trips to Eastern European capitals. Prague in particular offers very good value with accommodation arranged in private apartments or houses and an abundance of concerts and operas available at a fraction of the cost in UK (Fig. 11.1).

North America

New York, Boston and Toronto are all favourites for long haul short breaks. The favourable exchange rate on the dollar during the 1990s has made New York a popular shopping destination. Boston is also popular for shopping but has the added attraction of its historical connections and the beauty of the Fall. Toronto is a beautiful city and tourists can take an excursion to the famous Niagara Falls.

Skiing holidays

The most popular winter ski areas for British tourists are in Austria, Switzerland, France and Italy. Scandinavia offers excellent skiing conditions and facilities but as yet is not a major winter destination with British tourists because of the higher cost of living. North American ski resorts however have gained in popularity during the 1990s because the facilities in the USA are excellent and transatlantic travel has become affordable and familiar to many British tourists .

The ski market has increased rapidly since the mid-1970s as shown by the figures from Thomson Holidays opposite.

UK Ski market	1973/4	1981/82	1991/92
booked through travel agents	100,000	200,000	400,000
total market	250,000	500,000	750,000

In European resorts there are two peak seasons, the main month for good skiing is February but December also is a peak time for the British tourists who choose to spend Christmas in a snowy alpine resort.

Types of ski resorts

Ski resorts vary in type from traditional picturesque villages in Switzerland and Austria to purpose built resorts in France and USA.

Traditional resorts

Traditional picturesque resorts have very often grown around a small village, the hotels and guest houses are quaint, at least on the outside, and there are shops and restaurants to visit within the village. However, such traditional resorts can have drawbacks for skiers in that they have not been designed for the large numbers of people who gather there for winter. Figure 11.2 shows the type of lift system which might be found in a traditional resort.

The main lift in a traditional resort takes skiers out of the village and up the mountainside, from where various lift systems fan out. Such a pattern can cause congestion and long queues for the lifts. This can be frustrating for good skiers who are wasting time, and it can be costly for first time skiers who may have been able to ski closer to the village without using the lifts, in a purpose built resort. Mayrhofen in Austria is a typical traditional resort which appeals to all grades of skiers and has a pleasant mountain village atmosphere.

Main lift takes skiers out of the village.
Lift system fans out up the mountain.

Figure 11.2 Traditional ski resort

Purpose built resorts

Purpose built ski resorts have skiing and winter sports as their primary concern and the lift system is designed, as shown in Fig. 11.3, to take skiers away from the village itself

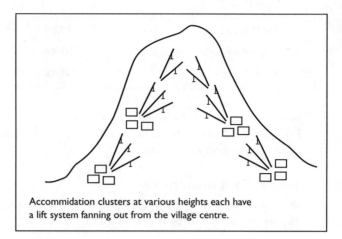

Accommidation clusters at various heights each have a lift system fanning out from the village centre.

Figure 11.3 Purpose built ski resort

as quickly and efficiently as possible. For this reason lifts start right in the village and fan out up the mountain to the various ski runs.

However, the purpose built resorts tend to be functional rather than attractive. Many French purpose built resorts have been constructed high in the mountains so that snow can be guaranteed and sometimes they lack pretty scenery. The architecture of some purpose built villages can also seem rather boring with large blocks of apartments and hotels, lacking the wooden balconies and roofs of more traditional villages. La Plagne in France is a purpose built resort which has excellent facilities for intermediate and advanced skiers as well as for a variety of other sports including tobogganing and hang gliding.

Ski resort facilities

Difficulty of ski runs

Ski runs and the layout of the lift system should be shown on maps of ski resorts in a brochure. The varying difficulty of ski runs is indicated by coloured lines on the maps:

beginners' slopes	green lines
easy ski runs	blue lines
medium ski runs	red lines
most difficult ski runs	black lines

Cross-country skiing

Cross-country ski runs are shown with a dotted line. Cross-country skiing is sometimes referred to as *Langlauf* and it involves covering prepared trails, very often through pleasant scenery, in a sliding, walking action with longer, lighter skis than those used for downhill skiing. The boots are also much lighter and the bindings have only one toe piece, which is hinged to allow the heel to move up and down during skiing. Cross-country skiing is less strenuous and can be a more suitable choice for older or less fit clients.

Lift systems

The lift systems are usually indicated by straight black lines with symbols to show the type of lift.

Figure 11.4
Drag lift symbol

Drag lifts move continuously and consist of T-shaped bars which the skiers tuck into the back of their legs while holding onto the moving line in front of them (Fig. 11.4). The skier is then literally dragged up the mountainside in a standing position with their skis sliding on the ground.

Figure 11.5
Chair-lift symbol

Chairlifts are a continuous cable with chairs into which the skier sits as the chair approaches and is then lifted into the air (Fig. 11.5). The chairs can be single, double or treble but the principle is the same. At the end of the lift the chair descends towards the ground and the skier simply skis off at an angle, as the chair continues around the circuit on the cable.

Figure 11.6
Gondola symbol

Gondolas are enclosed suspended lifts which stop to allow up to six skiers to enter (Fig. 11.6). Often the skis are attached to the outside of the gondola during the short journey.

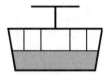

Figure 11.7
Cable-car symbol

Cable-cars can transport up to twenty skiers at one time and are used for longer lifts and greater heights (Fig. 11.7). Skiers stand inside the car with their skis in their hands in an upright position.

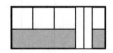

Figure 11.8
Funicular symbol

Mountain railways or funicular lifts are available in some resorts (Fig. 11.8). The carriages in these railways are set on a permanent slant so that the seats inside are always upright, despite the acute angle at which the railway ascends the mountainside.

Après-ski

Après-ski is the French term adopted in most ski resorts to summarise the social activities which take place after a day of skiing. The type of après-ski available may have a bearing on the choice of resort. Some resorts are quiet, offering a few restaurants and maybe a disco. Other resorts offer a selection of bars and discos, nightclubs, cinemas, shopping, fondue parties and Tyrolean evenings.

Other sports

Sporting facilities, other than skiing, are to be found in most ski resorts. These sporting facilities might include tobogganing, ice-skating, curling, sleigh rides, swimming, gymnasium, indoor tennis, squash and prepared paths for walkers. The availability of a variety of sporting facilities can be an important factor when choosing a holiday destination for a group of clients.

Ski holiday destinations

Figure 11.9 shows various ski resorts in Alpine Europe.

Switzerland

Switzerland was the birthplace of modern alpine skiing as a sport. Sir Arnold Lunn opened the first slalom course on 21 January 1922 at Murren in Switzerland. The word slalom derives from the Norwegian words

sla   meaning a smooth hill
laam   meaning a track down

The first slalom races were around bushes but modern races use coloured poles and flags instead (Fig. 11.10).

Nowadays Swiss resorts offer excellent facilities for intermediate and good skiers with charming surroundings and lively après-ski.

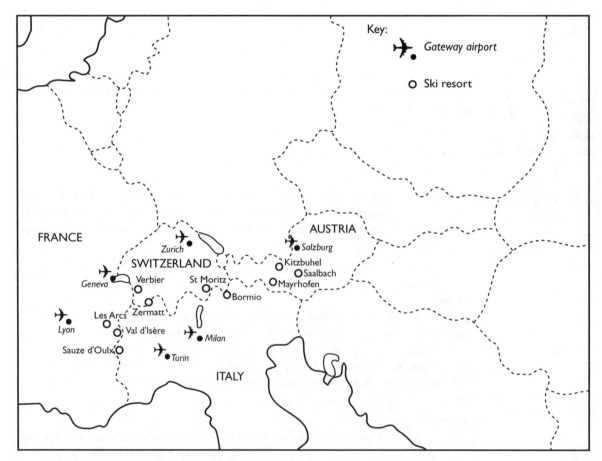

Figure 11.9 Ski resorts in Alpine Europe

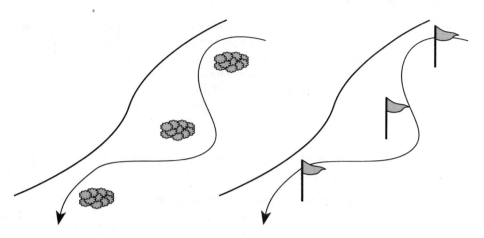

Modern slalom races use flags instead of bushes

Figure 11.10 Slalom course

- Verbier has high, rough and varied ski runs and apart from skiing there is ice skating, tobogganing, swimming, mountain biking, hang gliding and a cinema. The après-ski in Verbier is centred on discos and restaurants and tends to be expensive.
- Zermatt is an excellent resort for intermediate and advanced skiers. Tucked under the Matterhorn and surrounded by three mountains and a glacier, the scenery is spectacular. The pretty traffic-free village also offers swimming, a gymnasium, indoor tennis, ice skating, sleigh rides and a wide range of bars and restaurants. A kindergarten and children's ski school make Zermatt a favourite choice for families.

Austria

Austria is very popular with British tourists because the resorts cater for all abilities and retain the charm of old world villages.

- Westendorf claims to have taught more British skiers than anywhere else and the après-ski is lively.
- Kitzbuhel has good skiing for all abilities, in spite of being the site of the World Cup downhill race, the Hahnenkamm. The nightlife is lively, the hotels are good and there is a variety of non-ski activities. Chic shopping and excursions to Salzburg and Innsbruck increase the appeal of Kitzbuhel to non-skiers.
- Saalbach is a compact village with chalet-style hotels, a modern swimming pool and a lively varied nightlife. A non-ski kindergarten and a children's ski school make Saalbach popular with British families.

France

France has many purpose built resorts which offer an excellent standard of teaching and piste maintenance. However, some villages lack charm and the nightlife can be restricted to a few bars and discos. Nevertheless for those who are interested in a pure skiing holiday, French resorts are probably among the best in the world.

- Les Arcs is the home of Ski Evolutif, a system of teaching skiing using short skis which are gradually lengthened, and over half the instructors are English speaking. Facilities for children are excellent with a kindergarten, mini-club and

children's ski school. However, there is little entertainment for non-skiers, apart from a few bars and discos.
- Val D'Isère has excellent skiing for intermediate and good skiers. Glacier skiing and snow-making canons ensure that there are always good snow conditions. Apart from skiing there is a sports centre, cinema, smart shops, lively nightlife and restaurants, which can however be expensive.

Italy

Italy has resorts which cater mainly for intermediate skiers who enjoy lively but reasonably priced après-ski.

- Bormio is a pretty medieval spa town with winding, cobbled streets and from there skiers have access to other Italian and French resorts. Apart from skiing there is an Olympic-sized swimming pool filled with hot thermal water, tennis, ice skating, mono-skiing, snow boarding, tobogganing, a cinema, horse riding and reasonably priced restaurants. Bormio is particularly popular with British families with older children.
- Sauze d'Oulx is a picturesque traffic-free village which caters for intermediate skiers and again it is a gateway to the Milky Way circus of Italian and French ski resorts. There is a variety of non-ski sports activities, the shops are cheap and the nightlife tends to be both extensive and noisy, appealing to the younger, single British tourists.

North America

USA and Canada have gained in popularity with British tourists during the 1990s. The ski resorts are clustered north of the US–Canadian border in the Rockies and in the state of Colorado (Fig. 11.11). The principal gateway airports are Vancouver, Calgary and Denver.

- Breckenridge in Colorado, USA, is the most popular ski resort with British tourists in North America. The authentic 130 year old Victorian mining town has all the amenities and entertainment of a modern ski resort yet visitors can take a free trolley bus tour of over 300 registered historic buildings. The ski runs cater for all abilities and the Breckenridge ski school has more than 300 qualified instructors.
- Jasper and Banff National Parks, including Lake Louise, are major Canadian ski resorts. Skiing in this vast area is for all abilities with a wide range of runs for each level, in dry powder snow. The non-ski activities include snowmobiling, wildlife tracking, sleigh rides, skating and husky dog sledging. Après-ski tends to be centred around the country and western live music in local bars.
- Whistler, just north of Vancouver, markets itself as the number one ski resort in North America. The season in Whistler lasts from November to March and there are plenty of activities and après-ski.

First time skiers

Clients who are going skiing for the first time may require more specialist attention and knowledge than other package holidaymakers.

Choice of resort

The choice of resort depends on the availability of snow, which depends on the height of the mountain as much as whether or not it is facing the sun from the

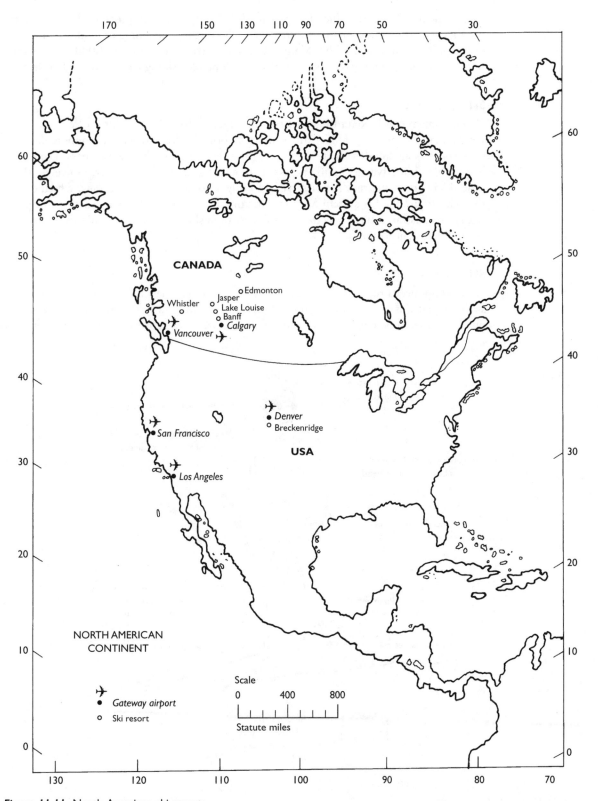

Figure 11.11 North American ski resorts

south. The higher resorts which face north will have snow longer, possibly even into April, but they will also be colder for the first timer who might be standing around listening to instructions or queuing for lifts. Many villages in Austria are as low as 2,000 feet but the resorts in France which have been specially developed for skiing can be over 6,000 feet.

Ski equipment

Ski equipment can be daunting for first time skiers. Most ski brochures offer a ski pack which includes the hire of skis, sticks and ski boots. There is usually an opportunity to purchase lessons in advance at ski school for a few hours each day. Lift passes can also be purchased in advance, giving access to an entire system at the resort. However, first time skiers are sometimes better advised to buy a points card, or coupons, which entitle the skier to use the lift system for a specific number of times. A points card is cheaper than a lift pass and may be better for the first time skier who is not ready to use the entire lift system to the full.

Ski clothing

Ski clothing needs to be both warm and waterproof. The best advice for first time skiers is that it is better to wear several layers of clothing rather than a thick heavy outfit which can be cumbersome and even too warm. Waterproof trousers, ski suits or

Close fitting warm hat

Sunglasses or goggles

Zipped polo necked jersey (avoid nylon clothing)

Waterproof jacket with several thin layers of clothing underneath

Gloves

Bum bag for camera, lip balm, extra clothing and socks

Strap

Waterproof trousers or one piece salopette (never wear jeans)

Poles

Basket

Ski boot

Ski

Bindings which are adjusted so that they will release quickly in a fall

Après-ski boots

Figure 11.12 Ski clothing

salopettes can be hired from some ski shops in the UK and this might be a good idea for first time skiers. Smaller items such as socks, polo or crew-necked tee-shirts, a hat, goggles and sunglasses can all be purchased prior to the holiday. Figure 11.12 indicates the main items of clothing required for a skiing holiday.

Family ski holidays

If the client is booking a family holiday where not everyone is a skier, the travel agent needs to consider the surroundings of the resort and whether or not there will be enough in the way of sightseeing, shopping and other sports, such as skating or swimming, for the non-skiing members of the family. Where there are children in the party the provision of a kindergarten or children's ski school can be crucial to ensure the enjoyment of the entire family. Older children in a family are more likely to be happy with lively Italian resorts or varied Canadian and American resorts where the après-ski may be more to their taste.

Weddings and honeymoons

Brochures promoting weddings and honeymoons in the Caribbean and Indian Ocean are increasing in popularity. Weddings tend to be organised in countries such as Jamaica, the British Virgin Islands or Sri Lanka, which have historical connections with UK. Other countries market themselves as ideal honeymoon destinations, although they may not offer a complete wedding package. In Tonga for instance the bride and groom have to be resident at least twelve months prior to a wedding.

Wedding packages

These packages stress the exotic surroundings of the chosen destination, normally emphasising beaches, palm trees and beautiful gardens. The package includes:

- the services of clergy or a marriage officer
- witnesses if required
- dinner for the couple with champagne and a wedding cake
- the bride's bouquet and the groom's boutonnière
- the ceremony in a beautiful setting.

Safari holidays

Safari holidays come in a variety of packages, from the basic economy holiday which is recommended for the young, or at least 'young at heart', who can live without Western luxuries, to air conditioned, insect proofed holidays in the lap of luxury, living in modern chalets and viewing the wildlife from super deluxe four-wheel drive vehicles.

The main African destinations for safaris are in east and southern Africa. The ideal time of the year to take a safari holiday is from April to November, although the nights in June can sometimes be cold.

Safari details

Game

Safari game in Africa may be the 'Big Five' of elephant, lion, rhino, buffalo and leopard or the plains game such as giraffe, zebra and cheetah. Safaris are an opportunity to observe and photograph the game in their natural habitat and the destinations are often to be found in areas designated as national parks. Game drives are organised at dawn and dusk when the animals are most active.

Accommodation

Accommodation on safari can be in traditional rondavels which are thatched circular chalets having all the appearance of bush huts but in fact containing two rooms, air conditioning, showers and private terraces, all set in a tourist complex. The gates of such complexes are normally locked at sunset. More basic facilities are marked as 'authentic' safaris and tourists are promised that there will not be flush toilets, running water or iced cocktails! Some of the shorter safaris use tented accommodation but usually stress that hot showers will be provided at the end of the day.

Transport

Transport is often in four-wheel drive vehicles which are designed, as shown in Fig. 11.13, so that each member of a small party can have a window seat. The vehicles are also fitted with pop-up roof hatches for wildlife viewing and photography. Due to the confined space in these vehicles clients are normally limited to one suitcase each. An English speaking guide is usually provided for the safari with responsibility for providing information and maintaining the vehicle.

Some safaris to more remote areas may be offered with a flight included in the price, while another more unusual method of transport is on the balloon safaris which depart at dawn and travel over the Masai Mara in Kenya or the Serengeti in Tanzania, finishing with a champagne breakfast.

Clothing

Clothing on a safari should include a hat, sensible shoes and lightweight clothes with a jacket or jumper for cooler evenings. On game drives neutral colours such as browns,

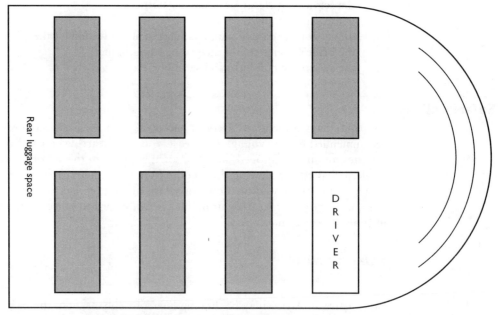

Each of the seven passengers has a full window

Figure 11.13 Safari touring vehicle

beiges and khakis are preferred because bright colours and white may disturb the animals. For the more sophisticated safaris which offer cocktails in the sun, 'smart casual' will be recommended in the brochure and this indicates a collared shirt and slacks for men and a dress or skirt for women in the evening.

Safari destinations

Figure 11.14 shows the most popular safari destinations for British tourists which include Kenya and Tanzania in east Africa and Zimbabwe, South Africa and Botswana in the south.

Kenya

Kenya has long been established with British visitors and can offer different types of safaris in the 40 national parks and reserves which occupy about 10% of the land area of the country.

Figure 11.14 Safari destinations in Africa for British tourists

- Masai Mara Game Reserve, which borders the Serengeti National Park of Tanzania, is famed for its black-maned lions.
- Nairobi National Park, which is just 6 miles (10 kilometres) outside the city centre, is conveniently near and has 25 black rhino for viewing.
- Meru National Park, the home of Elsa the lioness immortalised in the film *Born Free*, is a park of many contrasts at the foot of Mount Kenya, with mountains, swamp, palm trees, forests and thick bush.
- Amboseli National Park is situated right at the foot of Mount Kilimanjaro, Africa's highest mountain, and elephant abound in its forest and swamp areas while cheetah, giraffe and zebra can be seen on the plains. Currently there is a conservation project to renew depleted stocks of indigenous trees in the park and visitors are invited to take an active part.

Tanzania

Tanzania has a concentration of wildlife in a country of huge lakes, mountains, plains, forests and savannah.

- Serengeti National Park, which was declared a reserve in 1929, claims to be the most spectacular game park in east Africa. Each year, after the short rains in November, the wildebeest and zebra gather in their thousands below the Ngorongoro Highlands and in February they move north and west following the rains and fresh grasslands.
- The Ngorongoro conservation area within the Serengeti is a beautiful crater with grasslands, swamp, lakes, forest and shifting dunes and has an abundance of unusually docile animals including black rhino.
- Lake Manyara on the edge of the Serengeti has spectacular views of the Rift Valley and it is easy to find hippo, elephant and buffalo in the area.
- The Tarangire National Park south of Lake Manyara has gentle rolling countryside and is at its best during the dry seasons of June to October and December to March when many migratory species gather at the permanent water of the Tarangire River.

Zimbabwe

Zimbabwe can offer safaris combined with a trip to the famous Victoria Falls. In some Zimbabwean national parks, visitors may take a walking safari led by an armed guide to view the large elephant populations.

South Africa

South Africa was the pioneer of the conservation movement with its first game reserves established in Natal in 1897. South Africa's wildlife can be observed in public or private game reserves. Public game reserves are normally explored by tourists in their own vehicle and generally involve self-catering. The private reserves are open only to residents and provide hospitality and accommodation which is often quite luxurious with game drives off-the-beaten track. The private game reserves are most frequently featured in British brochures.

- Kruger National Park is the location for most of the private game reserves. The park covers an area about the size of Wales and it has a wealth of wildlife including the 'Big Five' game.
- Hluhluwe and Umfolozi public game reserves in the KwaZulu-Natal are both famous for their rhino populations.

- Addo Elephant Park, Mountain Zebra National Park and Bontebok (Antelope) National Park are all public reserves named for the animals to be found within their borders.

Botswana

Botswana is the latest country to offer safaris and claims to be the last unspoilt wilderness in Africa, with some rare opportunities to see wild antelope in their natural surroundings.

Combination safari holidays

Safari holidays in east Africa are often combined with a beach holiday in Mombassa, Dar Es Salaam or Zanzibar, the spice island. Other breaks may centre on Mounts Kenya or Kilimanjaro where five to seven day walking trips are organised. City breaks can be added to the holiday in Nairobi, Cape Town or Johannesburg. Trips to Zimbabwe nearly always include the Victoria Falls, the world's largest sheet of falling water. South African nature reserves are not noted for their wildlife but attract visitors for their scenic beauty and walking and hiking trails. Golf and fishing are available in many of these former colonies at very reduced rates when compared with UK.

Revision Questions

Primary level

1 Name TWO age groups to whom British tour operators target specific brochures.

2 Name THREE destinations featured in both of the age group orientated brochures identified in question 1.

3 Give THREE reasons why, apart from sightseeing, a client may wish to book a short break in London.

4 For both Newcastle upon Tyne and Sheffield name a major shopping centre within ten miles of each city centre.

5 Give TWO reasons why Prague is a popular short break destination for British tourists.

6 Name THREE European countries which are popular ski destinations for British tourists.

7 List TWO advantages of booking a holiday in a purpose built ski resort.

8 Which would be the more difficult ski run, a black one or a red one?

9 Give THREE examples of activities which could be described as après-ski.

10 Give FOUR examples of sporting activities other than skiing which can be found in many ski resorts.

Advanced level

1 Apart from European Alpine areas, which TWO long haul areas have become major ski destinations for British tourists in recent years?

2 List THREE features which would distinguish a traditional ski resort from a modern purpose built resort.

3 What do you understand by the term *langlauf*?

4 When booking a skiing holiday for a family with young children aged 2 and 6, name TWO features that you would look for in the ski resort.

5 Describe briefly how you would explain the advantage of a 'points card' to a first time skier.

6 Name THREE destinations which offer wedding packages for British tourists.

7 Which animals are referred to as the 'Big Five' game on safaris?

8 Name an area in each of the following countries which is used for safari holidays.

Kenya   Tanzania   South Africa.

9 List FOUR items of clothing which you would recommend a client to take on a safari holiday.

10 Which is the highest mountain in Africa?

12) Cruising

In this chapter we consider

- types of cruises
- cruise ships
- life on board ship
- cruise destinations
- booking a cruise.

Cruising can be regarded as the ultimate package holiday in a floating hotel. All arrangements are made for the client. The total relaxation and variety of ports of call are said to be addictive to some people, and cruise companies claim a high percentage of repeat bookings. There is a very lucrative market here for the travel agent because, with the high prices involved, the commission can be very worthwhile. Cruise ships provide:

- all meals, 24 hours a day, from a sumptuous breakfast to a midnight feast
- cabin and table stewards for each passenger with a ratio of one crew member to every two passengers on the more luxurious ships
- public entertaining rooms with a choice of bars, restaurants, and facilities such as a ballroom, fitness centre, cinema and casino.

Types of cruises

Ocean going liners met their demise in the 1960s with the coming of the wide-bodied jet aeroplanes but companies such as Cunard and P&O responded by using the *QE2* and *Canberra* as cruise ships rather than liners. In this way they could take a group of passengers to a number of ports, usually in the Mediterranean or the Canaries, and then back to UK, all within a specific time from ten days to a few weeks. With the success of these cruises, other companies commissioned purpose built ships.

Currently the cruise market worldwide is approximately 3 million passengers with about 80% of these being from North America. To sell cruise holidays, the travel agent must appreciate the sort of person who will take a cruise. Traditionally in the UK, cruising has had an up-market image thought to appeal to the older generation and to be too expensive for the average holidaymaker. Cruise companies now realise that this image is changing and have introduced:

- entertainment for younger clientele
- facilities for children, in order to attract families
- flights out to cruise areas to reduce the time spent actually reaching warmer waters
- themed or special interest cruises.

Cruise companies vary in size from Cunard and P&O liners to Silversea Cruises, which operate luxury cruises in ships that are more comparable to ocean going yachts.

Port to port cruises

At a normal speed, cruise ships can do an average of 400 to 500 miles in a 24 hour period. This speed means that the traditional port to port cruises from UK to the Mediterranean can spend two or three days each way in the Bay of Biscay, an area renowned for poor weather conditions. During the 1980s the popularity of this type of cruise declined, although P&O's *Canberra* and *Oriana* make several trips a year from Southampton.

Fly/cruises

To take clients as quickly as possible to their desired area, fly/cruises were introduced in the 1980s. With fly/cruises the Mediterranean is more accessible and ports such as Miami and Fort Lauderdale in Florida have become major home ports for Caribbean cruising. Over 40% of UK passengers taking cruises start their holiday with a flight from London Heathrow or Manchester airports. Figure 12.1 shows some of the ports used on fly/cruise holidays for British tourists.

Cruise and stay

Fly/cruise holidays are sometimes combined with hotel accommodation for a period of time making the Cruise and Stay holiday. For example, it is possible to fly out to Florida, spend a week in Orlando seeing Disney World and other attractions and then join a cruise from Miami to the Caribbean for a second week.

Round the world cruises

For clients with more available time, there are round the world cruises. P&O offers a choice of ships with 91 day round the world cruises on both *Canberra* and *Oriana* and Cunard has a 120 day cruise on *QE2*. All these cruises sail from Southampton and include visits to:

- the Far East
- Australia
- west coast of USA
- the Caribbean.

Round the world cruise prices on P&O's *Canberra* range from £5,400 to £21,700 and on *Oriana* from £7,500 to £22,000. *Canberra* circumnavigates South Africa via St Helena and the Seychelles, sailing eastwards around the world, while *Oriana* sails west and returns through the Suez Canal and the Mediterranean. Cunard's *QE2*'s full 120 day cruise costs up to £23,500 and includes Brazil in its itinerary. It is always possible to cruise in sectors on world cruises, flying out to join the ship for a period of time and taking in the ports of call of one specific area.

Special interest cruises

Realising that potential clients for cruising are very varied, Cunard and P&O try to offer different images through different brochures. This strategy is called market segmentation. Cunard's *Sagafjord* which operates under the Royal Viking Lines brand has no lavish shows but a fairly sophisticated cabaret in line with its appeal to older clients who are lovers of traditional cruising.

In the United States cruising is being marketed to younger people. Carnival Cruise Lines claims an average age of 35 on their Fun Ships in the Caribbean. Cheaper prices,

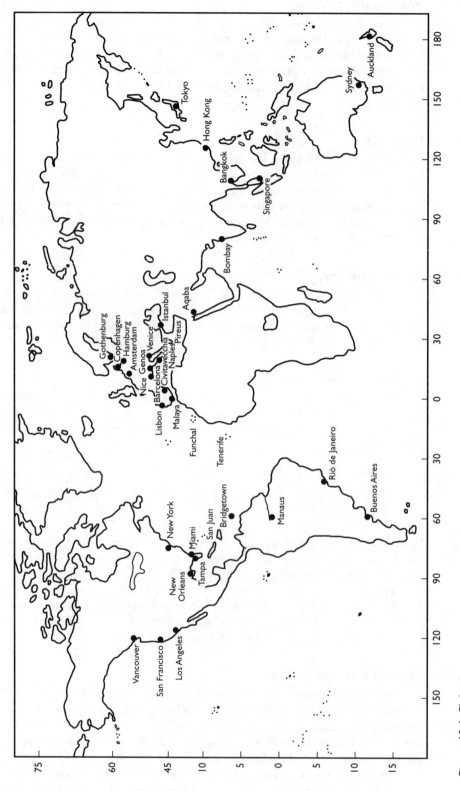

Figure 12.1 Fly/cruise ports

a change in entertainment and the influence of the TV series of the *Love Boat* are all said to have contributed to this change of image.

Other themes used to market cruises have included such unusual topics as gardening, with visits to the Alhambra at Granada from Malaga and gardens in Madeira; historical cruises to the eastern Mediterranean; and musical cruises with well known compères or orchestral groups.

Cruise ships

Density

Cruise ships vary in size and facilities and the density or passenger space ratio (PSR) is one means by which we can measure the space available on a ship in relation to each passenger.

Each ship has its gross registered tonnage (GRT), a figure which indicates the size of the ship. The GRT can be found in manuals such as the *ABC Cruise and Ferry Guide*. The *Guide* also gives the maximum number of passengers on the ship. For the QE2 the GRT is 66,450 tons and it carries 1,877 passengers. If we divide the GRT of the vessel by the number of passengers we arrive at the density of the ship, so

66,450 divided by 1,877 gives a density of 35

For *Canberra*, the GRT is 45,000 and it carries 1,641 passengers, giving a density of 27.

This measurement of density shows that each passenger on QE2 has more individual space than those on *Canberra*. In general a higher figure, and therefore lower density, can be taken as an indication that:

- the cabins are larger
- there is more deck space
- the restaurants are not as crowded.

The *Silver Cloud*, which was purpose built in 1993, carries only 314 passengers with a GRT of 15,000, giving a very low density of 48. The new *Oriana* launched as a superliner by P&O in 1995 has a GTR of 67,000 with 1,760 passengers, giving a density of 38.

Layout

Figure 12.2 is from the P&O Cruises brochure and shows the layout of the *Canberra*. The side view diagram shows the decks in relation to each other and the other diagrams show the positions of facilities and cabins on each deck. Notice that:

- decks on ships are referred to as A Deck, not Deck A
- some decks have names which are indicative of the activities on the deck, such as Games Deck or Prom Deck
- public rooms for entertainment are on separate decks from cabins
- the higher the number or letter of the deck, the lower it is in the ship.

The front of the ship is known as the bow or fore, while the back of the ship is the stern or aft. Looking forward:

- the left hand side of the ship is the port side and has a red navigational light
- the right hand side is starboard and has a green navigational light.

SUN DECK

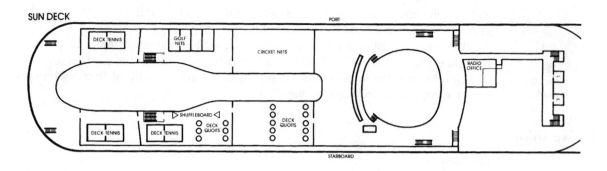

GAMES DECK

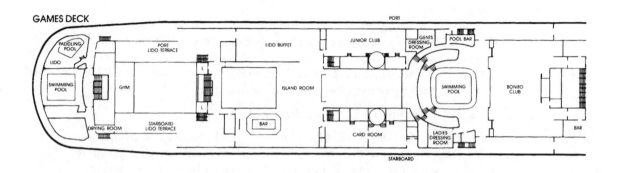

A DECK

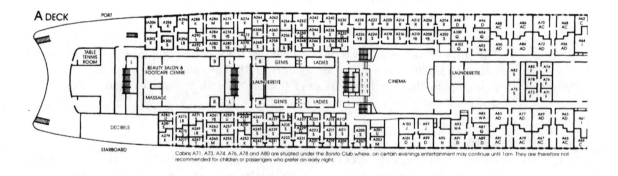

Cabins A71, A73, A74, A76, A78 and A80 are situated under the Bonito Club where, on certain evenings entertainment may continue until 1am. They are therefore not recommended for children or passengers who prefer an early night.

B DECK

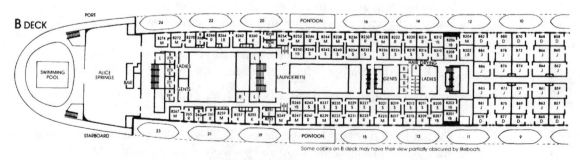

Some cabins on B deck may have their view partially obscured by lifeboats.

Figure 12.2 *Canberra* deck plans *(Courtesy of P&O Cruises)*

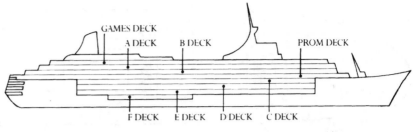

Canberra - 45,000 tons, British built and British registered. Normal operating capacity: 1641 passengers and 800 crew. Nine passenger decks, three swimming pools, children's paddling pool, two restaurants, cinema, theatre, night club, discotheque, dance floors, casino, nine bars and spacious and comfortable lounges. Library, Junior Club, night nursery, hairdressing and beauty salons and four shops.

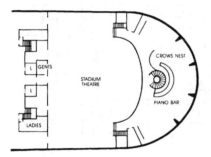

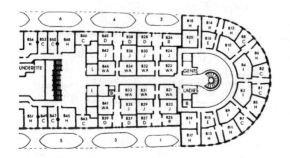

HOW TO CHOOSE YOUR CABIN

First let us say that Canberra is a one class ship and therefore, all public rooms and facilities are there for all passengers to enjoy. But obviously, the price of your holiday depends on the type of cabin you choose. The basic types of cabins, colour coded on both Canberra's deck plans and fares table are as follows:

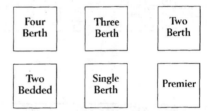

Within these types you have a choice between an inside cabin or an outside cabin with porthole or window or a court cabin (see diagram page 88). There are cabins with bath and WC or shower and WC and certain cabins with shared facilities nearby.

You can tell which cabin is which by the grade letter under the cabin number on the deck plans. For example, if you decide to take an inside two berth cabin with shower and WC - a yellow S grade cabin - just refer to the deck plans and look for a yellow cabin marked with a capital 'S' as below

Simply find the cabin you want, check the grade letter and you can find out your cruise fare from pages 104 and 105.

Please Note: *These deck plans are not to scale and are not shown in relative alignment. There are no passenger decks below the water line.*

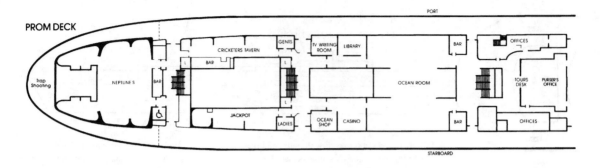

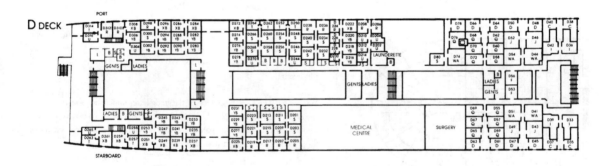

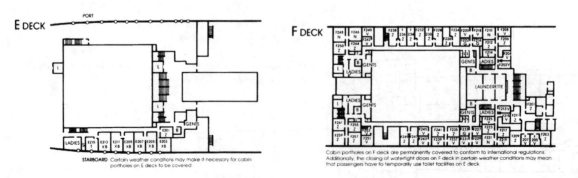

Cabin portholes on F deck are permanently covered to conform to international regulations. Additionally, the closing of watertight doors on F deck in certain weather conditions may mean that passengers have to temporarily use toilet facilities on E deck.

Figure 12.2 Continued

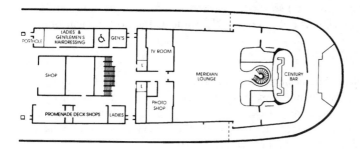

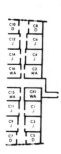

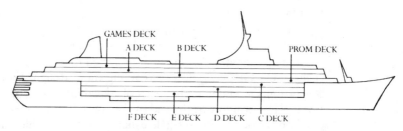

Canberra - 45,000 tons, British built and British registered. Normal operating capacity: 1641 passengers and 800 crew. Nine passenger decks, three swimming pools, children's paddling pool, two restaurants, cinema, theatre, night club, discotheque, dance floors, casino, nine bars and spacious and comfortable lounges. Library, Junior Club, night nursery, hairdressing and beauty salons and four shops.

HOW TO CHOOSE YOUR CABIN

First let us say that Canberra is a one class ship and therefore, all public rooms and facilities are there for all passengers to enjoy. But obviously, the price of your holiday depends on the type of cabin you choose. The basic types of cabins, colour coded on both Canberra's deck plans and fares table are as follows:

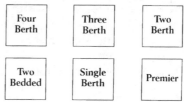

Within these types you have a choice between an inside cabin or an outside cabin with porthole or window or a court cabin (see diagram page 88). There are cabins with bath and WC or shower and WC and certain cabins with shared facilities nearby.

You can tell which cabin is which by the grade letter under the cabin number on the deck plans. For example, if you decide to take an inside two berth cabin with shower and WC - a yellow S grade cabin - just refer to the deck plans and look for a yellow cabin marked with a capital 'S' as below

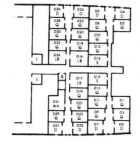

Simply find the cabin you want, check the grade letter and you can find out your cruise fare from pages 104 and 105.

Please Note: *These deck plans are not to scale and are not shown in relative alignment. There are no passenger decks below the water line.*

NOTES

● Connecting Door
B Communal bathroom
S Communal shower

The easy way to remember port and starboard is that the words 'port' and 'left' both have four letters, and port wine is red in colour, the same as the port navigational light.

Cabins

Cabins are sometimes referred to as staterooms and these vary in size and price according to where they are in the ship. The more expensive cabins, referred to as penthouses or deluxe suites, are usually on the higher decks and have their own bathrooms, lounge areas and even verandas. The cheapest cabins are usually on the lower decks and may have only a hand basin with shared facilities for toilets and showers.

Portholes

Another factor which influences price on a cruise is whether or not the cabin has a porthole or window. Those with a porthole or window are known as outside cabins and those without natural light are referred to as inside cabins. Inside cabins are cheaper. On *Canberra*, P&O has an ingenious design shown in Figure 12.3. These court cabins are built so that each of six cabins has a corner window receiving light from a large window at the end of the court. The arrangement gives two three-berth, two two-bedded and two single cabins in a group. This can be useful for families or groups of friends who wish to book adjacent cabins.

Berths

The beds in cabins are called berths but it is important to understand the terminology when booking a cabin.

- A two-bedded cabin will have two beds just as a hotel room might have twin beds.
- A two-berth cabin will have two beds arranged on top of each other like bunk beds.
- Some ships offer large two-bedded cabins which have foldaway berths above and these are good for families with children.
- Not all ships have single cabins, and with some companies it may be necessary to pay quite a large supplement to have the use of a two-berth or two-bedded cabin for single occupancy.
- Deck plans show which rooms have interconnecting doors.

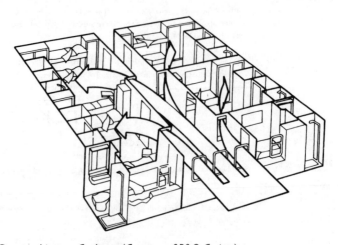

Figure 12.3 Court cabins on *Canberra* (*Courtesy of P&O Cruises*)

Facilities on board a cruise ship

Facilities on board usually include:

- sports and recreation such as deck-tennis, shuffleboard, quoits, a fitness centre or gym, jogging around the deck, swimming pools and sunbathing areas
- a selection of bars, restaurants and shops
- a nightclub, casino, cinema and ballroom
- laundry, hairdressing and beauty salon
- libraries, card room and computer room
- medical centre which will be a mini-hospital with a qualified doctor on most cruises.

The entertainment is organised by the cruise director or entertainments officer and a programme for the day is placed in each cabin every morning. There is of course no compulsion to join in the activities. Not all ships encourage children, but those who do, provide a play room and nurse, as well as reasonable reductions.

Life on board ship

The cruise office

The cruise office or the purser's office is the main source of information for passengers' everyday enquiries. The cruise office normally provides the following services:

- post office and bank
- safety deposit boxes
- exchange of cash or traveller's cheques
- ship-to-shore radio or telephone by satellite
- the handling of all documentation at ports of call including landing cards and liaison with the immigration and port police.

The currency used on board will be specified in the brochure and it is often the currency of the home port, but frequently US dollars are used. Major credit cards are accepted on most cruises, although not for obtaining cash or paying bar bills.

Dress code on a cruise

With regard to dress, advice is sometimes given in the brochure. In general it is safe to say that passengers will need casual clothing for daytime and more formal wear for the evening. The more expensive and luxurious the cruise, the more likelihood of using dinner jacket and cocktail dresses, but all cruises will have at least a few occasions when passengers are invited to dress in style. Fancy dress parties are also usually part of the programme for those passengers who wish to participate.

Tipping on a cruise

Potential cruise passengers sometimes worry about not knowing who is who in the crew. However, they will be assigned a cabin steward as well as a restaurant or table steward who will look after them throughout the cruise. Royal Caribbean Cruise Line has produced an excellent video called *Behind the Scenes* which describes the work done by the crew during a cruise.

Tipping is a worry for some first timers and they can be told that:

- where drinks are signed for at the bar, a 10% or sometimes 15% service charge or tip is automatically added to the bill

- tipping for the cabin and table stewards is at the client's discretion
- a figure of 10% of the cost of the cruise would be an indication of what could be divided between these stewards.

Medical facilities on a cruise

All major cruise lines provide a medical doctor on board and the facilities in the mini-hospital are usually excellent. However, it should be noted that:

- the treatment in these cruise ship health centres does not come under the National Health Service
- passengers should have adequate medical insurance cover
- passengers over the age of 75 are required by some companies to have a certificate of fitness to travel when they book their cruise
- any physical disabilities should be notified before sailing
- although wheelchairs are accepted on cruises, only a limited number will be allowed on any particular cruise.

Shore excursions

P&O give passengers folders with information about each port of call, including a map, a list of principal sights and a brief history of the port and surrounding area. Most ships have a shore excursion office but excursions are optional and usually involve extra cost. For first timers they are probably the best way to make full use of the hours in port because coaches will be waiting to take passengers on trips which have been well organised in advance. The brochure will give details of the number of hours to be spent in port and for any smaller ports it will indicate if the passengers have to go ashore by tender. Tender means using a small boat, very often utilising the lifeboats, to ferry from the ship to the quayside.

Some brochures give information about ports of call with the itinerary and prices, others give the details in a separate section or booklet. Normally precise details about shore excursion are sent to the client after the booking is confirmed.

Cruise destinations

Apart from round the world cruises, the most popular cruise destinations for British tourists are the Mediterranean, the Baltic and the Caribbean.

Mediterranean cruises

Mediterranean cruises generally stay either in the western Mediterranean or in the eastern Mediterranean, but *Oriana* and *Canberra* cruise the length of the Mediterranean from Southampton a few times a year. *Oriana*'s UK to Mediterranean cruises start at £1,400 and *Canberra*'s UK to Mediterranean cruises start at about £1,000. Other cruises from the UK to the Mediterranean go only as far as Corsica or Italy and may include ports of call such as Gibraltar, Malaga, Barcelona, Cannes, Genoa, Civitavecchia for Rome or Livorno for cities and towns in Tuscany.

Cruises to the Greek islands or the Middle East usually start with a flight to Athens or Venice and, in spite of the cost of the flight, these cruises can be done for about the same price as those out of UK ports. However, a few cruise companies do not include the cost of the flight in the total cruise price and this can be misleading. Itineraries can include Cairo for the pyramids of Egypt; Haifa for Jerusalem, Galilee, Bethlehem and Nazareth; Izmir for Ephesus and Istanbul; and Athens for Greek historical sights.

Baltic cruises

Baltic cruises are usually available from May to October and include ports in Norway, Sweden, Denmark and Russia. Many Baltic cruises are offered in the period from the middle of June to the first week in July. At this time of the year it is possible to see the midnight sun in the most northerly regions. The midnight sun occurs during the few short weeks from late June when the sun shines continually both night and day in the far north and this, combined with the spectacular scenery of the fjords, can make an unforgettable sight.

Itineraries to the midnight sun also vary but most will include:

- ancient cities such as Copenhagen with its Tivoli Gardens and St Petersburg with the Hermitage Museum and the Czar's palace at Petrodvorets
- northerly towns such as Narvik and Trondheim, the former Norwegian capital
- beautiful fjords such as Hardangerfjord and Gierangerefjord with their steep cliff faces and waterfalls.

Caribbean cruises

Caribbean cruises are offered all year round and usually involve a flight to join the ship. For British tourists the most popular embarkation or home ports used for Caribbean cruises are:

- Miami in Florida
- Fort Lauderdale
- Port Everglades
- San Juan in Puerto Rico
- the islands of St Thomas and Barbados.

Excluding the flight time, cruises can take from three days to a fortnight and itineraries can be equally varied. All destinations offer the traditional Caribbean palm trees, sand and sun but in addition there is a wealth of different cultures to be sampled:

- St John's, Antigua and Bridgetown, Barbados have English roots and connections.
- Ocho Rios in Jamaica offers a genuine Caribbean atmosphere as well as the beautiful Dunn's River Falls where the roaring cascades make a refreshing change from endless white sands.
- In Martinique the citizens enjoy full French citizenship and the French culture is evident in the shops and sidewalk cafés.
- At St Maarten the jewels and watches for sale remind one of their Dutch heritage.

Booking a cruise

Choosing a cabin

Taking *Canberra* as an example and referring to Fig. 12.2, there are six types of cabins from which to choose: namely four-, three-, two- and single berth, two-bedded and premier. In addition potential passengers need to consider whether they require an inside, a court or an outside cabin and on the *Canberra* the facilities can vary from the Z grade cabins with shared bath and WC to private facilities in the AA grade suites.

The choice of cabin will depend on

- the number of passengers sharing the cabin
- the required facilities with regard to bathrooms and windows

- the price to be paid
- the position of the cabin in the ship.

Each cabin on the plan is shown by a colour indicating its size, the cabin number, which starts with the letter of the deck, and a letter which indicates the grade of cabin facilities.

If a client wished to book an M grade two-bedded cabin as near to the swimming pool as possible on the starboard side of the ship, the travel agent could recommend cabin number B267.

If a client wished to book an M grade two-bedded cabin on as high a deck as possible, on the starboard side but away from lifts, the travel agent could recommend cabin number A203.

Booking forms

When making a cruise booking, great care should be taken to complete all details accurately. Correct information will need to be given for:

- the cruise number
- the cabins required
- decks required
- preferred meal times
- preferred table size
- preferred company at the table
- insurance
- any extras such as subsidised travel.

Figure 12.4 shows the booking form for P&O Cruises. Information about the passport number and nationality of the client are required for immigration purposes.

Costing a cruise

Basic costs

Costing a cruise is usually much more straightforward than costing other types of package holidays. The travel agent's skill is used mainly in recommending appropriate dates and suitable cabins. Most brochures give a table of prices with the most expensive suites at the top and the cheapest inside cabins at the bottom, although P&O lists the cheapest at the top. Below this information will be prices for:

- guaranteed single cabins
- third or fourth adult sharing a cabin
- children aged 2–11 years
- infants under 2 years.

Prices may be the same throughout the season but some cruises are priced as peak, value or economy depending on the popularity of the dates.

Sample costing

For example, for a family consisting of two adults and one child aged 8 who wish to share a twin outside cabin; grandparents who want to have a double outside cabin; and an aunt who wants a single outside cabin; all wishing to book cabins on the same deck for a holiday celebrating a Golden Wedding, the costing would be as opposite using Figure 12.5.

If they all wish to be on the same deck, then the cabins have to be on **D Deck**.

BOOKING FORM - P&O CRUISES 1996 - (Second Edition)

PLEASE COMPLETE THE WHITE SECTIONS OF THIS FORM, USING BLOCK CAPITALS THROUGHOUT

BOOKING REF. No:	SHIP	CRUISE No:	DEPARTURE DATE	EMBARKATION PORT	DISEMBARKATION PORT

Surname (Head of party - enter line 1)	First Christian name and other initial	Title Mr, Mrs Miss etc	Accommodation Offered				Age at sailing	Date of Birth	Passport Number	Nationality as shown on Passport	FARE £
			Grade	Deck	Cabin	Berth					
1.											
2.											
3.											
4.											
5.											

PRIVATE ADDRESS

(It is essential for immigration purposes that your private address is given. If 2,3,4,5 are different please attach seperately)

NB. Please be sure to include your house no. and postcode.

1. Head of party _____

Post Code _____

Tel Number (inc STD code) _____

CABIN BED CONFIGURATION

All Canberra's premier cabins and Oriana's two bedded, staterooms and premier cabins have a choice of a double bed or twin beds. Unless you indicate otherwise these will be made up with twin beds

Double Bed ☐

GROUPS

If you are travelling with a group, newspaper or special promotion, please give the name:

FLIGHTS AND HOTELS

If you're travelling on a **Victoria Fly Cruise** (648 to 738) or **Oriana Fly Cruise** 674A, 674B, 685A or 685B we offer a choice of departure airports. Please tick your preference:

LONDON ☐   MANCHESTER ☐

For Gatwick departures we offer a **Free Hotel stay** the night before. If you would like to take advantage of this, please tick this box: ☐ GATWICK HOTEL

If you are travelling on a **holiday prefixed with the letters H or J** and wish to fly to or from the ship on a different date to that shown for your chosen holiday, fly from a regional airport, travel Club or First Class, arrange a stopover or take one of our one or three night extended stays, please tick this box: ☐

We will then send you an air/hotel request form for you to complete with your requirements and which contains details of the supplements payable.

If you do not tick the box we will assume that you wish to take the holiday as shown in this brochure.

TRAVEL INSURANCE - UK RESIDENTS ONLY

Bishopsgate Insurance premiums (see page 115) to cover everyone listed on this booking form will automatically be added to your fare unless you supply the name of your alternative insurance company (which must offer comparable or better cover) in the space below at the time of booking.

Insurance Co. _____

Emergency Assistance Co. _____

Tel No. _____

RESTAURANT SEATING

Please indicate whether you prefer first or second sitting in the restaurant by ticking the appropriate box.

First ☐   Second ☐

If you wish to be seated with friends please enter names

Details of where you will dine are shown on page 111. When you have read this section please enter your preferences.

Table for: 2 ☐ 4 ☐ 6 ☐ 8 ☐

Smoking ☐   Non Smoking ☐

YOUR HOLIDAY PAYMENT

I wish to pay by: Cash ☐   Cheque ☐   Diners ☐   American Express ☐

Deposit 10% of your fare with a minimum payment of £150 per adult and a maximum of £750 per adult   £ _____

Insurance Cover @ £ _____ per person (Payable in full with your deposit)   £ _____
This will automatically be added to your fare unless you complete the Insurance section above

Card Number ☐☐☐☐☐☐☐☐☐☐☐☐☐☐☐☐   Expiry Date ☐☐☐☐

Cardholder's Name _____

TOTAL ENCLOSED £ _____

Mealtimes on board (Times may vary slightly)	1st Sitting	2nd Sitting
Breakfast	8.15am	9.00am
Lunch	12.30pm	1.30pm
Dinner	6.30pm	8.30pm

We will do all we can to accommodate your request but if there is a heavy demand we may need to allocate in order of booking date.

Please note that tables for 2 are limited on all ships and cannot be guaranteed, that Canberra's Pacific Restaurant has no tables for 8 and her Atlantic Restaurant has no tables for 2 or 6.

DECLARATION

Please read carefully the section 'Health and Safety' on page 115 before completing and signing this declaration

Are the above named in good health (tick as applicable)   YES ☐   NO ☐

In addition, do any of the above suffer from physical or mental infirmities including any which could affect, or partially affect, their mobility during any part of the cruise? If so, **in the interest of their own safety**, please give details below. **Your attention is specifically drawn to condition 22 of P&O Cruises conditions if any of the above use a wheelchair.**

I agree on behalf of the persons named above and I warrant that I have their authority to do so that my/our booking is made upon and subject to the P&O Cruises' conditions as detailed in the P&O Cruises 1996 brochure (Second Edition) and that the holiday which I have booked is detailed in that brochure.

Signature _____   Date _____

Your attention is drawn to the scale of cancellation charges and Holiday Travel Insurance under GENERAL INFORMATION in this brochure.

TRAVEL AGENTS STAMP
(Please include ABTA No. and Tel. No.)

Agent's ref:

A/C Control No:	PUBA

Figure 12.4 P&O Cruises booking form (*Courtesy of P&O Cruises*)

2 adults and one child in a twin outside cabin on D Deck = **Price Band D**	
2 adults @ £2,140	£4,280.00
1 child @ 75% of (£2,140 less 30% reduction)	£1,123.50

Grandparents in a double outside cabin on D Deck = **Price Band B**	
2 adults @ £3,255	£6,510.00

Aunt in single occupancy of a twin outside cabin on D Deck = **Price Band C**	
1 adult @ £2,845	£2,845.00
+ single occupancy @ 50% of £2,845	£1,422.50

Total cost for the party	**£16,181.00**

		CRUISE NUMBER 1503	
Stateroom		Decks	Basic Cost
AA	**Penthouse outside**	**A**	**£5156**
A	Deluxe outside	A, B	£3750
B	**Double outside**	**B, C, D**	**£3255**
C	Twin outside	C, D, E	£2845
D*	**Twin outside**	**C, D, E**	**£2140**
E	Double inside	D, E, F	£1845
F	**Twin inside**	**D, E, F**	**£1745**
G*	Twin inside	E, F	£1645

All fares are per person based on 2 sharing.
Certain cabins in grades C and F are eligible for single occupancy at a supplement of 50% of the basic cost.
* a third and fourth person may occupy the 4-berth cabins on D and F decks at a 30% reduction of basic cost.
Children aged 2–11 sharing with an adult are charged 75% of the appropriate price.
Children over 6 months and under 2 years are charged 30% of the appropriate price.
We regret that we are unable to carry babies under the age of 6 months.

Figure 12.5 Sample cruise price panel

Extra costs and/or reductions

As with ordinary package holidays, the brochure will list what is included in the price of the cruise. The total price usually covers:

- all meals on board
- all entertainment on board
- port charges
- the flight out and back on fly/cruises.

Extra costs can include insurance, local taxes, overnight accommodation at the beginning and end of the cruise and add-on excursions and visits. Fly/cruise holidays usually include the cost of the flight but the price table will indicate the price to be deducted for a cruise-only booking. Deductions may also be made for children and for those clients who book their cruise early.

Tickets for a cruise

About twelve weeks before departure the client will receive an information pack which will include the ticket, details of checking-in times for the cruise or flight and details of the proposed disembarkation or return time. The disembarkation cannot be given with complete accuracy but clients can expect to leave a ship approximately two hours after it reaches the home port.

Cruising is probably one of the greatest potential growth markets in the travel business today. The Passenger Shipping Association is involved in a nationwide training programme for retail travel agents (PSARA) and they produce magazines and seminars to help the travel agent give up-to-date, accurate information to the public.

Revision Questions

Primary level

1 List THREE facilities apart from the meals which could be included in the basic cost of a cruise.

2 List FOUR ports of call which could be included on a Mediterranean cruise.

3 List FOUR ports from which a Caribbean fly/cruise might start.

4 Name two ships which are used for round the world cruises.

5 Name THREE different types of cruises, other than round the world.

6 What do you understand by an inside cabin?

7 Are the medical facilities on board a British cruise ship covered by the National Health Service?

8 What do you understand by the term 'midnight sun'?

9 List FOUR ports of call which might be made on a Caribbean cruise.

10 Name an association which helps travel agents to give accurate information about cruises to their clients.

Advanced level

1 What is the DIFFERENCE between a two-bedded cabin and a two-berth cabin?

2 List FOUR types of sporting activities which could be offered on a cruise.

3 List FOUR quiet pursuits which could be followed on a cruise.

4 What do you understand by 'the port of embarkation'?

5 Calculating the density is one method which helps when appreciating the differences between cruise ships. On the basis of the GRT and the number of passengers carried, which of the following ships would possibly offer your client more space and comfort?

(a) *Sovereign of the Seas,* built in 1988 for Royal Caribbean Cruise Line as a floating resort with a GRT of 73,192 tons carrying 2, 280 passengers.

(b) *Orpheus,* built in 1948 and refurbished for Swan Hellenic in 1989, which carries only 306 passengers and has a GRT of 5,092 tons.

(c) Cunard's ship the *Royal Viking Sun,* which was introduced into service in 1988 with a GRT of 37,845, over a third larger than previous ships in the line, and carrying 740 passengers.

(d) The Sun Line Cruises *Stella Maris* with a GRT of 3,500 tons carrying only 180 passengers on an 'experience of a lifetime' around Italy.

6 What advice would you give to a client with regard to tipping on a cruise?

7 Using Figure 12.5 cost the following cruise booking.

A party of eight wish to book cabins on the same deck on cruise number 1503. The party includes two adults who want an inside double cabin; two adults and two children, aged 10 and 12, who will share an inside four-berth cabin; and two adults who want inside single cabins.

Which deck would you recommend? Cost the holiday for the party.

8 List THREE items, apart from personal items and drinks, which might involve extra cost on a cruise.

9 List THREE types of reductions which might apply on a cruise.

10 List THREE ports of call which might be made on a cruise to the midnight sun.

The travel agent

13) The role of the travel agent

An agent is a person who represents or works on behalf of another person or business. A travel agent works on behalf of the client who is booking a holiday or travel arrangement and also on behalf of the company or principal for whom the agent is making the booking (see Fig. 13.1). In return for making the booking the travel agent receives commission. Commission is payment made to the travel agent on a percentage basis. Travel agents can earn commission at varying rates depending on the company or principal with which they are dealing. More details about commission rates can be found in Chapter 14.

To give advice about	To make bookings for
destinations means of travel accommodation visas, health precautions insurance	independent travellers business travellers package holidaymakers

Figure 13.1 The two main roles of a travel agent

Types of travel agencies

Travel agencies differ according to their size, organisation and their specialism in various markets within the travel scene. Travel agencies may be independent, multiple or implant.

- Independent travel agencies are privately owned, often with a single location, sometimes with a few outlets within a local area.
- Multiple travel agencies generally have more than twenty outlets, often on a nationwide basis. In the UK, most of the major multiple travel agency chains have financial links with the major tour operating companies.
- Implant travel agencies are based within the premises of a corporate customer or within a college, rather than in the public domain.

Travel agencies may also specialise in the customers for whom they cater and these can be distinguished as high street or business house:

- High street agencies cater mainly for the package holiday market, whether that be the cheaper mass tourist market or the more specialised and expensive cruise, long haul and independent markets.
- Business house agencies cater for the regular bookings of companies in commerce or industry.

Very often a travel agency will not specialise totally in either the package or the business market but the latter may be located in a separate office of a high street agency.

Association of British Travel Agents (ABTA)

The Association of British Travel Agents (ABTA) was founded in 1950 in response to a need for travel agents in the UK to support each other in a new and growing industry. Since that time there has been a great improvement in living standards and with it an explosion in the number of people who want to take foreign holidays. Add to this the extra capacity available since the introduction of wide-bodied jets and it is understandable that travel agents and tour operators have flourished in the second half of the twentieth century.

ABTA is a self-regulatory, independent association drawing its members from both travel agents and tour operators. Over the years, ABTA has developed a dual role with responsibilities to the public, as well as to its members. All ABTA members pay a bond which is similar to an insurance policy. The amount of the bond depends on the turnover of the company: the more holidays sold the greater the bond. If a tour operator or travel agent ceases trading, the bond is used to reimburse clients and to bring home those who are abroad.

ABTA's responsibilities to the public have often caused it problems because, by the very nature of the tourist trade, the customer pays in advance for what amounts to a dream – and sometimes the reality, if not actually a nightmare, does not match up to expectations. When things go wrong it usually means unacceptable social problems for the customer as well as damage to the reputation of the travel agent or tour operator. The customer may be affected financially or emotionally by having to endure an excessive flight delay or dirty, unpleasant hotel accommodation. In order to protect both the public and its members, ABTA has devised

- Travel Agents' Code of Practice
- Tour Operators' Code of Practice
- ABTA Conciliation Scheme
- ABTA Arbitration Scheme.

Members of ABTA have to abide by the rules of the association or face fines or even expulsion. More details about the role of ABTA in litigation can be found in Chapter 15.

To assist with training in the travel industry, ABTA has set up the Travel Training Company, a wholly owned subsidiary which is responsible for the ABTA Travel Agents' Certificate (ABTAC) and also works with City and Guilds as the joint lead body for the Travel Services National Vocational Qualifications (NVQs).

Running a travel agency

Travel agency costs

Travel agency costs are either fixed or variable as outlined in Fig. 13.2. The fixed costs are those which are determined by organisations or companies outside the control of the agency and variable costs are those which can be controlled and regulated by the staff of the agency.

Attracting customers

Clients must first be enticed into entering or telephoning the travel agency with an initial enquiry if they are eventually to make a firm booking. The initial attraction can be stimulated by

Fixed costs	Variable costs
Staff salaries	Staff expenses
Rent	Overtime payments
Rates	Petty cash
ABTA bonding	Stationery
IATA subscription	Postage
Electricity fixed charge	Use of electricity
Telephone line rental charge	Telephone call charges
Building insurance premiums	Telex charges
Contents insurance premiums	Printing costs
Computer rental or lease	Advertising costs
Subscriptions to manuals	Sales promotions
	Hospitality

Figure 13.2 Travel agency costs

- word of mouth
- personal recommendation
- the travel agent's window display
- the arrangement of the brochures on the racks within the agency
- the array of late availability cards to be found on the windows or doors of most agencies
- advertisements.

Appearance of staff

General appearance is so important that many travel agencies provide a uniform for their staff. Whether or not there is a uniform, travel agents should aim to be clean in their dress and smart in the way they walk or stand. Travel agents' physique and general health should be such that the long day in the agency does not impair their alertness or cause them to lounge or lean on the counters or desk.

A good appearance can inspire confidence in potential clients who will assume that they will be offered a courteous, efficient service. If the travel agent is untidy and the desk is in a mess, the potential client cannot be blamed for thinking that a person who cannot look after themselves is unlikely to be able to look after a booking with care and attention (Fig. 13.3).

Welcome to clients

The welcome the client receives is very important. It should be friendly and inviting without being too familiar, and it should stimulate further interest or action. Some of the larger multiple travel agents, such as Lunn Poly, put such emphasis on the importance of the welcome given to clients that their staff are trained to give a standard greeting to everyone entering or telephoning the agency.

Window displays

Window displays in travel agencies should attract potential clients by their overall impact and colour. Some agencies prefer to seek professional help from companies which specialise in display techniques and the larger multiples often have a company

Figure 13.3 A disorganised travel agency

directive for changing displays. However, in many agencies it is still a job which is done by the staff themselves.

The display should be arranged to produce definite lines if it is to achieve the greatest impact. Vertical lines give a dramatic appearance while horizontal lines inspire tranquillity. Curving lines are soft and gentle, but diagonal lines can have a startling effect.

Balance is important in a formal display, with an identical right and left side, to imply harmony. An informal display which is not symmetrical has potential to show contrasts. An awareness of colour can help, especially if the display is to have a seasonal effect.

- Red is a strong, emotional and highly visible colour and is especially associated with Christmas.
- Orange is warm and inspires homely thoughts of autumn and harvest time.
- Yellow is cheerful and sunny, implying sunshine, spring and new life.
- Green is a very relaxing colour with associations of calmness and freshness as well as its political use for all that is natural and good for the environment.
- Blue inspires thoughts of quiet and peace as well as water, air and great distance.
- Brown is a drab colour, which is not usually helpful in a display.
- White or black can be very useful as highlights for the other colours.

Brochure displays

Brochure displays can project an image of the travel agent to the potential clients and thus influence their decision whether or not to make that initial enquiry. A cluttered brochure display which lacks order does not promise that the travel agent will deal very efficiently with the booking. A brochure which is out of stock cannot reach its sales potential, no matter how good the advertising campaign associated with it.

Brochures which are displayed to advantage can help the clients to reach their decision about a holiday. The display could be used to supplement a national advertising campaign by one of the tour operators or to reinforce the impact of a television holiday programme, The travel agent should therefore be aware of the importance of positioning brochures to have maximum impact, a technique known in the retail trade as shelf planogram. Some points to bear in mind:

- Position all brochures attractively and make sure that they are well stocked.
- Display preferred brochures at eye level where they are easily accessible.
- Give special attention to the brochures placed to the right of the ones to be promoted. The eyes move naturally from left to right so the products to the right will receive more attention from the client than those to the left.

Some travel agents prefer to rack cards or display copies of brochures so that the client has to ask for a brochure. In this way, it is hoped that the client will be committed more quickly to a selling situation. Most principals agree that it takes on average ten brochures to produce one firm booking.

The larger multiple travel agents have a head office policy on shelf layouts, preferred brochures, shelf strips and lighting, giving a common appearance to their shops throughout the country.

Late availability cards

Late availability cards are used by many travel agents to give clients details of reduced priced holidays which usually have to be taken within the following few days. The cards should be carefully checked each day to make certain that the holiday is still available. Not only can outdated cards be misleading to potential clients, who are disappointed if they enter the shop and find that the holiday has gone, but also the travel agent could in fact be breaking the law. Trading standards officers are very aware of late availability cards and of their potential for offending against the Sale of Goods Act 1979 or the Trades Description Act 1968.

Advertising

Advertising has two main aims

- the obvious one of increasing sales
- the ongoing aim of building up the reputation of the company with the public.

Travel agents can do their own advertising in newspapers and at local events. Sometimes they can share the costs with a principal, if they are doing sufficient business. Principals themselves have nation-wide advertising campaigns, especially at the launch of a new brochure and travel agents should try to build on the impact of principals' advertisements.

A good advertisement should give potential clients information about the product, as well as persuading them that the company has something different and better to offer. In the travel business many companies offer very similar products, so a particular holiday could be to the same hotel, even using the same airport as that of a rival company. To attract the attention of their public, brochures emphasise advantages such as a guarantee of no surcharges, or a selected number of free child places. On transatlantic air crossings, the fare may be the same with different airlines, but the potential client could have to make a choice between a free teddy bear, free in-flight drinks or a free flight bag!

Free gifts not only can attract the client but also help to fulfil the other function of advertising, which is to maintain the image of the brochure or company, so that they stay in the mind of the public.

Making bookings

Reference sources for a travel agent include

- manuals and gazetteers such as the *ABC Guides*
- computerised networks
- other personnel who have been on holiday or an educational visit to a particular destination.

Computerised networks are either viewdata or global distribution systems.

- Viewdata networks enable the travel agent to access a variety of information and computerised reservation systems (CRS). Examples of such networks are PRESTEL, ISTEL and FASTRAK.
- Global distribution systems (GDS) are worldwide communication networks designed for the reservation of airline seats, accommodation, car hire and other travel products. Examples of such networks are GALILEO International and SABRE Travel Information Network.

More information on package holiday bookings can be found in Chapter 9.

Dealing with clients in a travel agency

Attitude of the travel agent

First impressions

First impressions are always important but never more so than in a selling situation where potential clients have to decide in an instant whether or not they can trust the person who is trying to sell them a product. We all make subconscious judgements about each other based largely on our past experiences. If the travel agent is conscious of the impression that is being made, it is possible through sensitivity and experience to increase the influence of certain desirable qualities such as a good appearance, a welcoming form of greeting and a pleasant, attentive attitude.

Greeting clients

The first words of greeting are very important, but equally important is the tone in which they are spoken. When greeting a client it is best to avoid slang, colloquial language and swearing which would almost certainly give offence. The travel agent should not be over familiar because the client is expecting service, not friendship. The question 'Can I help you?' is not a very good way of greeting because it can immediately inspire a response of 'No thank you, just looking'. It is far better to be positive and ask where the person was thinking of going, or even, watching the brochures which take their interest, to start to talk about a particular place.

Voice

The overall impression given by the voice is affected by the volume, speed, pitch and tone of voice. The words 'I'll be with you in a moment' can be said in a number of ways.

- They can be used to imply that the client is a nuisance who is interfering with the travel agent's private thoughts or activity.
- They can be said with sincerity and mean that the client will have the agent's full attention in just a moment, as soon as another important task is completed.

The voice can be affected by the feelings of a person, and if the travel agent is feeling nervous, or even angry, taking a few deep breaths can help to get the voice back under control.

Mental approach

Other qualities are more difficult to define but they are concerned with the travel agent's mental approach. The agent should

- be attentive
- listen to the client
- be confident yet sensitive
- use eye contact to inspire confidence
- have an outgoing friendly attitude.

Body language

A study of body language would help to reveal hidden clues to the attitude of the travel agent. A person who is untidy, who constantly fiddles and clicks a pen, who looks around the room in a distracted manner or sits at the desk eating and drinking will not inspire the confidence of a potential client. Sociability is the art of getting on with other people and the travel agent needs this quality. The agent should be outgoing, helpful and sincere without being either aggressive or too shy. Character or maturity will put the finishing touches to a personality reflecting cheerfulness, honesty, consistency and a sense of responsibility.

Investigating the client's needs

Some potential clients may be very certain of the booking they require, but other clients may have only a vague idea of wanting a holiday but not where they would like to go. It is at this stage that professional selling skills will have scope as the travel agent tries to establish the basic reasons for the person wishing to take a holiday, and then identifies the real needs. The potential clients may want

- a quiet break
- a week in the outdoors
- to learn how to hang glide
- a pilgrimage to Lourdes or Mecca
- a lively week with as much cheap alcohol as possible.

Without establishing these very different needs, the travel agent cannot hope to recommend a suitable arrangement and sell a holiday.

Open and closed questions

In the course of a conversation, the aim is to establish the client's needs and to create rapport, which is an atmosphere of harmony and mutual understanding. The client's needs can be established by the use of both open and closed questions. Open questions are used to give the client an opportunity to express a preference and will help the conversation to continue, so that more needs can be identified. For instance 'Do you want to fly from Manchester?' is a closed question which can elicit a response only of 'yes' or 'no'. On the other hand an open question such as 'From which airport would you like to fly?' gives clients an opportunity to consider other options and to discuss their needs. The secret of formulating open questions is to use the questioning words of

- where
- when
- who
- why

- what
- which
- how.

Closed questions can be useful when the travel agent needs to investigate the client's needs in more detail by establishing facts about the client or alternatively if the client is over-talkative.

Offering a holiday

The next step is to offer the client a suitable holiday. This will most probably involve the skilful use of brochures and viewdata systems to display the holiday's benefits for that particular client. The holiday should be appropriate to the needs that have already been identified, but if there is still some doubt it can be useful to recommend an expensive rather than a cheaper holiday. This will flatter the client and is almost bound to stimulate a reaction of either pleasure, or regret that it is out of the question. Further investigation could then establish the actual needs more clearly. Any objections raised by the client can be used to clarify the real needs if the travel agent is sufficiently alert and sensitive.

Telephone technique

When a client is making enquiries by telephone, the conversation should be controlled by the travel agent so that the required information can be elicited. A checklist is helpful to remind the travel agent to ask all the necessary questions and the effective use of the voice is very important, especially when we realise that most of us only listen to about a third of what is said to us. When using the telephone the travel agent should make a conscious effort to

- listen to the client
- limit the information given over the telephone
- summarise and check details at the end of the call.

Phonetic alphabet

In summarising the details of a booking and when giving the client a reference number for the booking, the use of the phonetic alphabet can help to avoid misunderstandings.

Phonetic alphabet

A	Alpha	B	Bravo
C	Charlie	D	Delta
E	Echo	F	Foxtrot
G	Golf	H	Hotel
I	India	J	Juliet
K	Kilo	L	Lima
M	Mike	N	November
O	Oscar	P	Papa
Q	Quebec	R	Romeo
S	Sierra	T	Tango
U	Uniform	V	Victor
W	Whisky	X	X-ray
Y	Yankee	Z	Zulu

Presenting the product to the client

Once the client's needs have been established, the travel agent must use knowledge, skill and experience to select and present a holiday or travel arrangement best suited to that client's needs. The presentation can be made more personal by generating enthusiasm and personalising statements so that a description of the features of a holiday are turned into a list of benefits for the client. For example

The hotel has a disco in the basement can be personalised

- for a young person by saying that there is a disco on site which means that there is no need to be out late at night and go to the expense of taxis
- for an older person by saying that the disco is in the basement which means that potential noise is well away from the bedrooms.

The key phrase to creating a benefit statement is 'which means that' followed by the personal benefit to the client. So, 'The hotel has three restaurants' could be expressed as, 'The hotel has three restaurants, which means that you can have a variety of meals and décor, all without even having to leave the hotel complex.'

Benefit statements should not however be used to pressurise clients into making a booking because this could mean that the clients would cancel when they reconsider the holiday later. Worse, they may take the holiday and return with a list of complaints and grievances which the travel agent would have to sort out. Either way the pressurised sale has no place in a travel agency.

Closing the sale

Finally, the sale must be closed and this should be done in such a way that the client, impressed with the travel agent's efficiency and care, will want to return to that particular agency for future bookings. The object of the earlier points is to elicit a commitment from the client. Ideally the client will pay a deposit and make a firm booking, but failing this, the travel agent should try to get the client to take out an option. This means that the booking is accepted by the principal's computerised system and is held in the client's name for a specific period of time, such as 24 hours, giving the client time to pay the required deposit. If the booking is not confirmed within that period of time, the holiday arrangements are placed on sale again. More details about options, deposits and firm bookings can be found in Chapter 9.

The travel agent should avoid finishing a potential sale with the client promising to get in touch, unless the travel agent has the means of making that contact possible. The client who is ready to make a commitment will often give the travel agent a sign or clue by using a phrase such as, 'That sounds fine', or 'Right, that's OK'. The travel agent should now close the sale with an assumption that the client is committed.

Provisional bookings

In attempting to close a sale it is not helpful to use a closed question such as 'Would you like me to see if it is available?', because this could prompt a negative response. It is far better to assume the client is going to book and say 'I'll make a provisional booking for you'. At this stage fear could even be used as a stimulus by saying, 'I suggest you book now to avoid disappointment'. This is a form of pressurised selling and should really be used only when an indecisive client has to be encouraged to make a final decision.

If viewdata is being used, the travel agent could indicate the details on screen, which will probably be personalised with the client's own name. Seeing the details on screen and being invited to book now while the holiday is available will stimulate most people into a decision.

Other ways of closing the sale would be

- by directly asking the clients if they are ready to pay the deposit today
- to physically pick up the phone or dial into a viewdata system to check the availability
- if several alternative holidays have been discussed, the client can be invited to make a choice so that the booking can be made.

Giving more details

If the clients still hesitate at making a decision, the travel agent could summarise the details again and ask if there is anything else they might need. Clients may simply need encouragement, time to discuss the arrangements with another person, or they may indeed have a genuine objection. If clients continue to ask questions then the situation can be clarified. If they do not, then the agent may have to ask more questions to investigate needs which have been left unstated.

Dealing with objections

For the client who raises actual objections, the travel agent's best approach is to agree to those objections as far as possible, but to use them to state benefits. For example, if the client says the apartments seem to be away from the shops, the travel agent might say, 'Yes, there is a short walk to the shops, but that makes it quieter at night because you are away from the discos and bars'. If the client says the holiday is too expensive, the agent should offer a cheaper one but should also point out the benefits which will be lost.

Whatever the objections, the travel agent should listen, try to clarify the situation and use open questions which will elicit more information. If the clients say, 'I was wondering about the luggage allowance', then the travel agent should try to clarify the problem by asking what they intended to take with them.

Follow-up

Once objections have been overcome the travel agent should recap on the details of the arrangements and make sure that all the necessary information for the client is available. The follow-up to the sale continues right through to the point where the client receives the correct tickets for the journey. Picture postcards displayed in some agencies testify to the many satisfied clients who remember their travel agent while on holiday.

Dealing with difficult clients

There are two things to remember about difficult clients:

- They probably do not see themselves as being difficult.
- Their awkwardness is probably part of their make-up, whether it be a result of their personality or just nervousness, and they act the same way with everyone.

So the travel agent should not take it personally if clients are difficult and should take consolation in remembering that they will probably be just as awkward with someone else within the same week or even the same day. Junior travel consultants can always refer really difficult clients to a senior assistant or manager.

Among the most difficult clients are those who could be called the

- indecisive
- 'just looking'
- disagreeable
- talkative.

Indecisive clients

The indecisive client can be very difficult to deal with. However, they may simply want their self-confidence boosted a little and to do this the travel agent should emphasise the benefits of the arrangements. With indecisive clients it is usually more useful to use closed rather than open questions. If this is done with skilful questions which inspire a 'Yes', the client can be helped to make a decision.

'Just looking'

When clients say they are 'just looking' this really means that they do not want to be pounced on and so they should be approached with caution. With browsing clients, the travel agent should be observant and try to identify the clients' interests, by the brochures which take their eye, then build on this with further information or a few specific facts.

Disagreeable clients

Disagreeable people will enter the travel agency at some time, whether they are angry about a problem or are just abrupt, argumentative or unreasonable by nature. The golden rule is to avoid antagonism with these people and to make an effort to listen. With disagreeable clients, sales talk should be kept to a minimum and questions should be asked only to clarify a situation. If the client is angry about a particular incident or problem, the conversation should be guided to the future and what can be done, rather than repeating details of a bad experience. Junior staff should always remember to refer a serious problem to more senior staff.

Talkative clients

Talkative clients can be irritating, and the secret with them is to listen at first, until an interest has been identified. The travel agent should then attempt to take control by using conversational gaps to get straight to the point. With talkative clients, sales talk should be kept to a minimum, as should questions. If a sale is to be made, however, the conversation should be maintained in a pleasant and courteous manner. Direction can be given to the conversation with clear choices being offered to the client such as 'Which hotel would you like in Fuengirola?' rather than a vague 'So you have decided on Fuengirola?' The tone of voice is as important as the words, because a business-like attitude, rather than a chatty, intimate atmosphere, will achieve the close of sale more easily.

Revision Questions

Primary level

1 What do the letters ABTA stand for?

2 Name the TWO types of membership of ABTA.

3 What do you understand in connection with the travel industry by the terms agent and principal?

4 Most tour operators' reservations systems are accessible to travel agencies through one or both of two computerised network systems. State the name of ONE of these systems.

5 How many displayed brochures are usually needed to produce one firm booking in a travel agency?

6 Give TWO reasons for keeping a tidy desk or counter in a travel agency.

7 What connecting phrase could be used to turn a statement of fact into a benefit statement for a client?

8 Name FOUR ways in which a travel agent can attract clients into an agency.

9 A client comes into your agency to choose a holiday. She does not know where she would like to go. Give THREE questions you would ask to help her choose.

10 A client comes into your agency to book a specific cruise to the Mediterranean. The particular cruise is already booked up for the price he wished to pay. State briefly the strategy you could adopt to retain this client.

Advanced level

1 A customer is overseas on a holiday booked through an ABTA tour operator. Halfway through that holiday the tour operator ceases trading. State TWO ways in which ABTA might protect this customer.

2 Which THREE of the following cost areas in a travel agency could be termed 'fixed'?

petty cash ☐
stationery expenses ☐
ABTA bond ☐
telephone bill ☐
rental of the premises ☐
travel expenses ☐
standing charge for electricity ☐
postage ☐

3 In a travel agency display, which colours could be associated with the following themes? Match up the corresponding letters and numbers.

A	Christmas	1	yellow
B	cruising	2	red
C	autumn	3	blue
D	calmness and freshness	4	orange
E	sunshine	5	green

4 Open and closed questions are important within sales conversations. Of the questions below, identify which are closed and which are open.

	OPEN	CLOSED
(a) Where will you want to go?	☐	☐
(b) Will you fly from Manchester?	☐	☐
(c) Do you have a British passport?	☐	☐
(d) Will you be travelling alone?	☐	☐
(e) What time do you want to depart?	☐	☐
(f) Have you booked a cruise before?	☐	☐

5 Give ONE reason why open questions are important in a sales conversation.

6 Give ONE reason why closed questions are important in a sales conversation.

7 Describe ONE strategy you would use in dealing with EACH of the following difficult clients:

(a) an over-talkative client
(b) an angry client
(c) a hesitant client.

8 A travel agent sells by stressing benefits which satisfy a particular client's specific needs. Rewrite EACH of the following statements to emphasise their benefit to a group of five single people aged 19.

(a) The hotel is on a main road.
(b) The flight takes one hour.
(c) You will have half board at the hotel.

9 A travel agent sells by stressing benefits which satisfy a particular client's specific needs. Rewrite EACH of the following statements to emphasise their benefit to a couple in their early 30s with two children aged 2 and 4.

(a) A coach will meet you at the airport.
(b) The hotel has two restaurants and a coffee shop.
(c) The return flight leaves at 8 pm.

10 What are the TWO main roles of a travel agent?

14 > *Administration, finance and security*

Without income and profit a travel agent will not stay in business. The main sources of income for a travel agent are:

- commission from principals
- service charges
- interest on money held
- referral vouchers
- utilising office space.

These sources of income will be considered in detail later in this chapter but the travel agent needs to establish administrative, financial and security procedures which will help to maximise income and minimise waste.

Administration

Good practice in a travel agency

Within a travel agency, agreed procedures need to be followed with regard to payment and refunds, and routines need to be established for various tasks to be completed at the appropriate times.

Daily procedures

On a daily basis it is good practice to:

- open the agency in accordance with standard security procedures
- re-set dates on validation equipment and stamps
- sort incoming mail
- check the telephone answering machine for messages
- check computerised systems for incoming messages
- check and replenish brochure racks
- check diary entries in relation to current bookings for tickets to be issued, balances to be paid, etc.
- update diary entries to record future actions required
- deal with customers' enquiries and bookings as they arise
- sort, stamp or frank post
- check, balance and reconcile till, foreign currency and traveller's cheques stock against the day's takings
- prepare cash and cheques for banking
- place all tickets, traveller's cheques, cash and valuables in the safe
- set telephone answering machine to receive out-of-hours messages.

Weekly procedures

On a weekly basis it is good practice to:

- check brochure supplies
- check petty cash and replenish if necessary
- check stocks of tickets, traveller's cheques and foreign currency
- check principals' weekly statements.

Monthly procedures

On a monthly basis it is good practice to:

- pay principals' sales returns where appropriate
- check Bank Settlement Plan (BSP) statement prior to direct debit payment
- review unpaid corporate accounts where appropriate
- process staff salaries
- check performance against sales and expenses budgets
- check all office equipment and apparatus on a monthly rotation.

Annual procedures

On an annual basis it is good practice to:

- review sales of previous year and effectiveness of promotions and policies
- review any rental or lease agreements
- prepare annual accounts
- prepare marketing plan
- prepare sales budget
- prepare expenses budget
- review preferred principals and racking policies
- plan training programme.

Keeping track of bookings

A travel booking, for transport, accommodation or a package holiday, will often be paid for in stages. When clients have chosen a travel arrangement they may be given the opportunity to take out an option which means that they have a specific period of time such as 24 hours to confirm their choice with payment. If the travel arrangement is to take place within about eight weeks the travel agent should ask for full payment. If the travel arrangement will take place later than eight weeks from the time of the booking the travel agent may ask for a deposit, such as 10% or a stated amount indicated by the tour operator, to confirm the booking. The balance, which is the amount still outstanding after the deposit has been paid, must then be paid to the travel agent at least eight weeks before the travel arrangement comes into effect. Management systems are used to keep track of accounts, provide management information and monitor the effectiveness of marketing.

Manual management systems

Manual management systems are kept in ledgers recording enquiries, bookings, money paid, and critical dates such as those when the balance is due or tickets should be sent. A well designed enquiry or option form will help the travel agent to record necessary information in the first instance. A good enquiry form will include spaces for

- client's name, address, and telephone number
- date of travel
- departure point
- destination required
- number of nights for a holiday
- chosen hotel or apartment
- means of transport
- preferred brochure or travel company
- names of other members of the party
- ages of any children who will be travelling.

Files are opened for each client who confirms a booking and these are kept under the departure date to enable the travel agent to keep track of the booking. The client's file can in fact be moved into different sections or drawers of the filing cabinet according to the current status of the booking. As shown in Fig. 14.1 the sections of the filing system could be

- initial enquiries
- confirmed bookings
- bookings on which the balance has been paid
- bookings for which tickets have been received
- dead files.

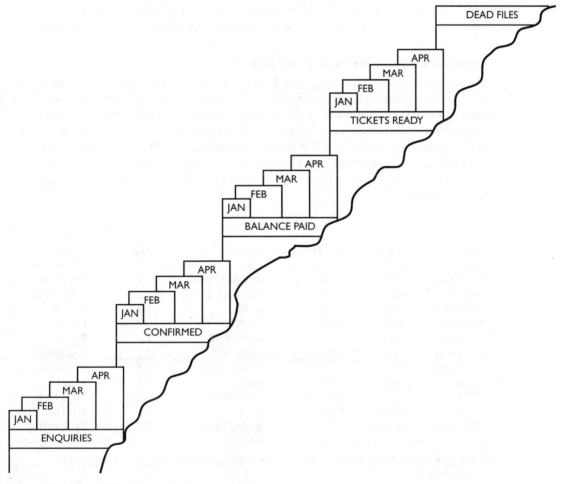

Figure 14.1 Manual filing system by departure date

Filing by departure date in each section means that the travel agent can easily check those bookings for which full payment needs to be sent to principals, eight weeks before departure, or those bookings for which tickets need to be sent to the client, two weeks before departure.

Once the client has taken a holiday, the file is kept in a separate area, sometimes called the dead file, for at least two years just in case there should be any problem or claim made at a later date.

Ledgers can also be kept to record briefly the enquiries and bookings made on particular dates. A reference number can be used to refer to the client's file which holds the complete details but the ledger would normally include the following information

- the date the enquiry was made
- the date the booking was made
- the lead passenger name
- the number of passengers
- the booking reference
- the principal used.

Such information can then be used for marketing purposes to establish the number and types of bookings made with each principal at different times of the year. Once the information is analysed the travel agent can build on it to launch a promotion, possibly with a particular principal in the following year. The ledger can then be used in the following year to assist in judging the effectiveness of a promotion or marketing campaign.

Personal computers in a travel agency

A personal computer in an agency can be used with an integrated software package of word processor, database and spreadsheet to keep track of bookings and administrative tasks. Information can be entered into a database as it might into a manual filing system but the data entered can be re-ordered in a matter of seconds. The same file of information could be used to select bookings which have been made in a particular month arranged alphabetically; or showing those clients who are departing from Manchester Airport; or even those who are staying at a particular hotel (Figs 14.2, 14.3, 14.4 and 14.5).

date	airport	destination	hotel	nights	client
02 June	LHR	PMI	ALHAMBRA	7	O'Connor
05 June	MAN	PMI	GRANADA	7	Armstrong
06 June	LGW	PMI	AZUL	14	Davies
08 June	MAN	PMI	AZUL	7	Eden
10 June	LHR	PMI	GRANADA	14	Ryan
15 June	MAN	PMI	GRANADA	14	Williams
17 June	NCL	PMI	ALHAMBRA	7	Gardner
20 June	LGW	PMI	AZUL	14	Marks
22 June	MAN	PMI	GRANADA	7	Mitchell
28 June	MAN	PMI	AZUL	7	Thorpe
30 June	LHR	PMI	ALHAMBRA	14	Pickering

Figure 14.2 Computer printout showing clients' holidays with June departures arranged by departure date

date	airport	destination	hotel	nights	client
05 June	MAN	PMI	GRANADA	7	Armstrong
06 June	LGW	PMI	AZUL	14	Davies
08 June	MAN	PMI	AZUL	7	Eden
17 June	NCL	PMI	ALHAMBRA	7	Gardner
20 June	LGW	PMI	AZUL	14	Marks
22 June	MAN	PMI	GRANADA	7	Mitchell
02 June	LHR	PMI	ALHAMBRA	7	O'Connor
30 June	LHR	PMI	ALHAMBRA	14	Pickering
10 June	LHR	PMI	GRANADA	14	Ryan
28 June	MAN	PMI	AZUL	7	Thorpe
15 June	MAN	PMI	GRANADA	14	Williams

Figure 14.3 Computer printout showing clients' holidays with June departures arranged alphabetically by name of the client

date	airport	destination	hotel	nights	client
05 June	MAN	PMI	GRANADA	7	Armstrong
08 June	MAN	PMI	AZUL	7	Eden
15 June	MAN	PMI	GRANADA	14	Williams
22 June	MAN	PMI	GRANADA	7	Mitchell
28 June	MAN	PMI	AZUL	7	Thorpe

Figure 14.4 Computer printout showing clients departing from Manchester Airport in June, arranged by departure date

date	airport	destination	hotel	nights	client
05 June	MAN	PMI	GRANADA	7	Armstrong
22 June	MAN	PMI	GRANADA	7	Mitchell
10 June	LHR	PMI	GRANADA	14	Ryan
15 June	MAN	PMI	GRANADA	14	Williams

Figure 14.5 Computer printout showing clients who are staying at the Hotel Granada in June, arranged alphabetically by client's name

An integrated software package enables the travel agent to transfer information from the database to the word processor for documents and customised letters or to the spreadsheet for calculations and graphs.

Data Protection Act 1984

The Data Protection Act 1984 sets standards which must be observed where a computerised filing system is in use. Briefly, if information about living people is input and/or processed on a computer the person using the computer is subject to the Data Protection Act 1984 and should register the fact on the Data Protection Register and then take care to observe the eight data protection principles below:

1 the information must be obtained and processed fairly
2 data should be held only for specified and lawful purposes
3 data should be used and disclosed only in the manner described on the Data Protection Register
4 data should be adequate and relevant
5 data should be accurate and up to date
6 data should not be kept longer than is necessary
7 individuals may be entitled to be told what information is held about themselves and to have it corrected or erased, if appropriate
8 data must be held securely.

The Data Protection Act 1984 protects the individual against the misuse of personal details held on a computer or word processor and gives the individual a remedy if the details are inaccurate. If a person wishes to know what information is held about them, the data user has 40 days in which to disclose the information. A court may order data users to pay compensation for damage caused by lost, destroyed or inaccurate data or by unauthorised disclosure, that is to a person or organisation not named in the registration. If there were a transgression of the law it is the individual member of staff, not the travel agency which could be held liable.

Computerised management systems

Computerised management systems have been developed mainly by the world's major airlines. TravelBase, which is used by many multiple high street travel agencies, is a computerised system provided within SABRE, the booking system developed by American Airlines. Travel Manager, which is used by many business houses, is provided within GALILEO, the booking system jointly owned by several airlines, including British Airways.

Below is a simple guide through computer jargon, from definitions of commonly used words to descriptions of computerised travel agency systems.

AMADEUS GDS owned by Lufthansa and Air France used by 60% of European travel agents

cache memory acts as a buffer which helps to speed up the work of the CPU

CATS computer aided telephone systems where the caller can select from a range of services by pressing a key on a touch-tone phone; the system also provides a sophisticated form of telemarketing where the numbers of potential clients are automatically dialled

CD ROM a compact disc with read only memory where data is stored by means of laser light pulses

Chameleon a PC-based network which currently supports viewdata systems but also has the capability of supporting PC-based technology which can be down-loaded on the dedicated data line connected to the Midland Network Services (MNS)

chip microelectronics in a piece of silicon

CPU the central processing unit which is the core of the computer

CRS computerised reservations systems usually accessed through viewdata

CUG closed user group is a set of pages on viewdata which can be accessed only by using a password

data raw facts

database software for highspeed filing, sorting and reporting

DTP desk top publishing software used to produce newsletters, graphics and posters

EasyRes GDS owned by Reed Travel Group which is provided free to all ABTA and IATA travel agents through PRESTEL, ISTEL and FASTRAK to book the cheapest available seats, hotels and car hire reservations

E-Mail electronic mail, a means of sending a message directly from one computer user to another

FASTRAK a viewdata system which is a subsidiary of Midland Network Services (MNS) which grew out of Midland Bank, the owners in 1984 of Thomas Cook travel and financial services; FASTRAK provides travel agents with access to all major tour operators including Thomson Holidays, ferries and scheduled airlines

floppy disk magnetic storage on a portable disk

GALILEO GDS jointly owned by more than ten airlines, including British Airways, Alitalia, Aer Lingus and United Airlines, used by 40% of European travel agents

GDS global distribution system, a purpose built computerised reservations system for travel agents used for the sale of airline seats, hotels and car hire worldwide

hard disk magnetic storage area which is integral to the computer

hard wiring dedicated lines or cables used to send data

hardware electronic components that make up a computer

impact printer cheapest kind of printer, which is quite noisy as the tiny pins hit the paper forming the letters

information a collection of data organised in a meaningful way

inkjet printer middle-of-the-range printer in price, with a high quality print and low noise level since the characters are formed by magnetising an ink spray onto the paper; a new cartridge also contains a new head each time

ISTEL a viewdata system which is a subsidiary of the US based AT&T (American Telephone and Telegraph Company) and is widely used in travel agencies to access principals' CRSs

LAN local area network, which allows computers within a building to share data and processing power

laser printer most expensive printer producing high quality print, very quickly and silently

33megahertz indicates that the 'clock' in the computer chip 'beats' at the rate of 33 million turns each second and a part of a calculation is done in each 'beat'

modem a means of converting telephone signals to computer data and vice versa, used to enable a PC user to access another computer

monitor computer screen

mouse a pointer and clicker device used with WINDOWS software

operating system controls which program is run; MSDOS (Microsoft Disk Operating System) is the most popular

PC personal computer

PRESTEL the earliest viewdata system developed in the UK by British Telecom to provide information and access to some CRSs

RAM random access memory, the main memory in a computer, which is lost when the power is switched off

ROM read only memory, which remains within the computer even after the power is switched off

SABRE GDS owned by American Airlines and used by 10% of European travel agents, including Thomas Cook, and 44% of US travel agents

scanner copies printed text or pictures in a format which can be used by the computer

software a set of instructions or program which runs inside a computer

spreadsheet software for highspeed budgets and financial analysis

TAB Thomson Automated Banking for the electronic transfer of funds to ensure payments are made on time, used by independent travel agencies

TARSC Travel Agency Retail System Concepts, the leading UK agency management system for independent high street travel agencies which provides a point-of-sale workstation, accounts, management, back office and marketing information

TOP computerised reservation system of Thomson Holidays

TravelBase computerised financial management system developed by SABRE and used in many UK multiple travel agencies

TravelManager computerised financial management system developed by GALILEO and used in many UK business house travel agencies

Videotex called viewdata in the UK, allows computers over a wide area to communicate with a central computer by a local telephone link

WINDOWS a Microsoft operating system which uses pictures and colour to make the computer easier to use

word processor software for high speed typing with easy layouts and styles, usually providing spell-checker and thesaurus facilities

Finance

Sources of income in a travel agency

Commission from principals

Commission is the main source of income in a travel agency. Commission is payment made to a travel agent by a principal such as a tour operator, airline or ferry company. The payment received is a percentage of the value of the booking made and that percentage varies between 1% on traveller's cheques to 37% or more on insurance. The average package holiday tour operator gives the travel agent 10% commission, but for selling scheduled international airline tickets the travel agent can earn 9% with only 7.5% on domestic tickets and about 9% for car ferry bookings. Figure 14.6 analyses possible turnover in a travel agency.

With a massive 37% commission on insurance it is understandable that most travel agents try to sell their own rather than the tour operator's insurance. Travel agents sometimes use part of their potential insurance commission to fund reductions for clients who take out their insurance.

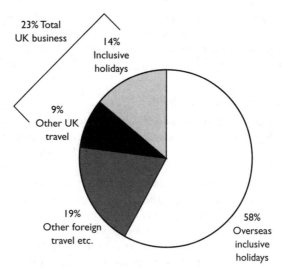

Figure 14.6 Analysis of turnover in a travel agency
Source: Survey of the UK domestic holiday market (1990) (Travel and Tourism Research Ltd)

If a package holiday costs £550 per person and there are four persons travelling, then the total value of the booking is £2,200. A commission of 10% would yield £220 in earnings.

If the booking were for two people taking a cruise at a cost of £3,800 each, the total value of the booking is £7,600 and the commission earned at 10% would be £760.

The effort of making the bookings would probably be the same in each case but the financial return is very different. The travel agent usually tries to predict the expected business for a particular principal and then calculates the expected commission or income before deciding which brochures to stock, and these are known as preferred brochures.

Coach operators usually give 10% commission and, with an average price of a ticket taken at £15, a booking for four people would yield a £6 commission. British Rail give only 7% commission but the prices of average train journeys are greater than for coach trips, thus increasing the total commission paid. However, balance this with the greater time which could be spent in recommending a rail route and not all travel agents choose to become British Rail agents.

Incentive commission, which is a higher rate, is offered by some principals to those travel agents with a higher turnover of business. In some cases a travel agent might be appointed as the 'sole agency' for a principal in a particular locality. If these travel agents accept bookings from other travel agents in the area then they receive over-rider commission which allows them to pay the standard commission to the other travel agents.

Service charges

Service charges may be made by a travel agent just as they can be made in any retail outlet. Normally they are not a great source of income but are simply a means of recouping money on a transaction which might otherwise cost the travel agent some of the commission. A service charge may be made on a theatre booking to cover the cost of the telephone call to the booking office of the theatre. A service charge may also be made if the travel agent applies for a visa on behalf of the client. For business travellers there may be service charges in connection with the delivery of tickets and the revalidation or reissue of tickets. In nearly all cases service charges are made simply to cover the cost of the telephone calls, telexes or postage and in no way can they be regarded as a main source of income. However, it should be remembered that all service charges are subject to VAT and this is considered below.

Interest on money held

Interest on money can be a major source of income and such money held by a travel agent is sometimes referred to as pipeline money because it has been received from the client but has not as yet been passed on to the principal. Monies to principals are normally paid monthly, very often by direct debit on a specific date. Monies paid for bookings processed just after that date can be held for up to a month in the travel agent's bank earning interest. Arrangements can be made with the bank to automatically transfer any credits over an agreed amount to a higher interest account and such adjustments can be made by the bank on a daily basis.

Money which has been paid by a client, before a booking is confirmed, is held in trust for that client. This means that, should the principal be declared insolvent, the money will be returned to the client. If, however, a booking has been confirmed, then the travel agent holds the money in trust for the principal, and should the latter's business fold, the client would have to make a claim as a creditor just as if the money had already been paid over to the principal. While it is possible to run a travel agency using only one bank account it is more usual to have at least two – one for the clients' money and the other for the office account.

Referral vouchers

Referral vouchers which are issued by principals in exchange for the travel agent's recommendations to clients can be a useful source of income. For example a client may be booking an independent holiday and the travel agent may recommend a particular hotel or car hire firm, giving the client referral vouchers to present when making the booking. The travel agent then receives commission or a standard payment once the client has booked and paid directly for the hotel or car. Referral vouchers involve the travel agent in very little extra work but they are a useful source of extra income.

Utilising office space

Finally the travel agent could use any extra space in the office as a source of income. Part of the office could be sublet to a building society, a photo machine could be installed or the travel agent could sell travel related products such as adapters, baggage, and accessories.

Value Added Tax (VAT)

VAT is a tax imposed by Customs and Excise who provide a series of leaflets explaining the many intricacies of the tax. All traders whose turnover reaches a certain threshold are bound to register, receive a VAT registration number and be responsible for collecting VAT at the current rate from their customers. Accounts have to be kept in order and a regular return must be sent to the Customs and Excise. All financial records for the company should be kept for at least six years and must be made available to the Customs and Excise as and when required. Most items of travel, including the commission paid to travel agents, are subject to VAT. However, once a company is registered with Customs and Excise it can in its turn reclaim the VAT element of any costs incurred in the running of the business.

VAT is a highly complex subject but with the advice of an accountant a travel agent should be able to cope, as does any other high street retailer. Some travel agents may have a further complication to their books if they themselves are acting as principals on occasion. This could happen if they sell hotel accommodation directly to clients or they charge for services such as providing a guide, booking a theatre ticket or providing passports and visas. In these cases where travel agents act as a principal they must in their turn charge VAT. However, in their main capacity as agents for tour operators, the travel agent can expect the VAT element to be identified in their accounts from the principals.

Methods of payment

Clients can make payments by

- cash
- debit cards (such as Connect or Delta)
- cheques
- credit cards (such as Visa or Access)
- charge cards (such as American Express or Diners Club International)
- traveller's cheques (usually by foreign visitors booking tours).

Cash

Cash is normally used for smaller transactions such as rail or coach tickets or insurance. However, large amounts should be counted and checked in the presence of the client with a colleague and immediately transferred to the safe.

Bank notes over £10 should be checked for the following security measures

- texture of the paper
- quality of the print, which should not be raised above the paper
- the metal strip, which should appear as a dotted line until held up to the light, when it appears as a solid line
- the watermark, which is visible only when held up to the light and should not be fudged in appearance.

If the travel agent is in any doubt about a note it can be compared with another good note already in the till.

Debit cards and cheques

Debit cards and cheques both authorise the amount to come out of the current account of the client. Debit cards are processed in the same way as credit cards but cheques should be guaranteed with a banker's card and the card number should be noted on the reverse of the cheque by the travel agent.

Items to be validated on a cheque include:

- the date, remembering that cheques are valid for presentation within six months of the date of issue
- the cheque should be made out to the travel agency, not the principal
- the amount in figures and words should be the same
- the signature should be that of the person named on the cheque
- any mistakes should be altered and accompanied with a signature.

Cheques normally take a week to clear the banking system and tickets should not be released unless the amount is backed by the banker's card. Building society cheques do not need special clearance and tickets may be released immediately.

Credit cards

Credit cards can be imprinted manually or they can be swiped on an automatic machine giving direct approval of the client's credit rating. Acceptance of the credit card involves a charge to the travel agent by the credit card company.

Items to be checked on credit cards include:

- validity dates
- cardholder's account number is not on a warning list
- cardholder's name matches that of the signature
- the signature matches that on the reverse of the card
- the credit card company hologram appears on the card.

Charge cards

Charge cards are processed in a similar manner to credit cards but attract even higher charge rates from the card company. However, clients are obliged to clear their charge card account at the end of each month and therefore these cards often carry a higher credit limit than credit cards. In the main charge cards are used for business travel.

Traveller's cheques

Traveller's cheques should be counter signed in the presence of the travel agent and the signature should tally with the original signature which was made in the presence of the person who issued the cheques. Sterling cheques can be accepted at face value but commission is normally charged when a foreign currency transaction is involved.

Receipts

Receipts should be issued for all money received, including cash, cheques, and card transactions. For security, receipts should have serial numbers and each one must be accounted for. If a mistake is made on a receipt it should not be thrown away, but the receipt can be made void with a line right through it. The information on a handwritten receipt should include the amount, the client's name and address, and the date of the transaction. It should also include the name of the principal, the travel agent's name and ABTA and VAT numbers (Fig. 14.7). It is usual to have at least three copies of a receipt, one for the client, one for the file and a third for the travel agent's accounting system.

Refunds

Refunds of unused rail, coach or airline tickets should be made in accordance with company procedures and those of the principals involved.

Controlling costs

In Chapter 13 fixed and variable costs were described. While the fixed costs cannot be controlled, the travel agent should make every effort to control the variable costs.

Petty cash

Petty cash is used to buy small items such as paper clips, sellotape, drawing pins, staff refreshments, or donations to local causes. Each item is small in itself but added together they can amount to significant costs. Petty cash spending should be analysed

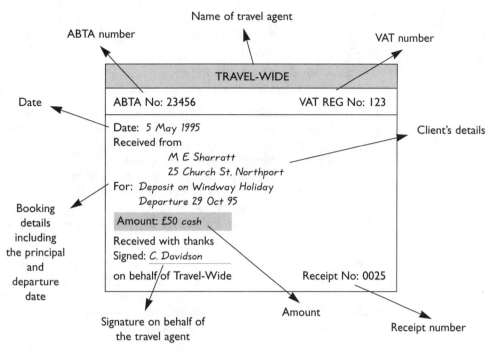

Figure 14.7 Sample travel agent receipt

on a regular basis because if items such as paper clips and sellotape are bought at local shops then VAT is included in the price and as a registered VAT company the travel agent could reclaim the VAT content of the price. However in order to reclaim VAT all receipts must be acceptable to the VAT authorities and it may be easier and cheaper in the long run to buy such items in bulk from 'cash and carry' warehouses.

Overtime

Overtime payments need to be considered at certain times of the year when the agency is particularly busy but care should be taken that such payments are not excessive and the possibility of a part-time member of staff could be considered.

Stationery

Stationery is cheaper if ordered in bulk and this also gives more opportunity for reclaiming the VAT element of the cost. Stationery should not be wasted and notepads should be used for messages or notes, not for doodling!

Heating and light

Heating and electricity running costs should be monitored so that while a warm, bright, inviting atmosphere is maintained in the travel agency for customers, excessive or wasteful use is not encouraged.

Telephone

Telephone calls can be monitored to ensure that personal calls are neither made nor received by staff during working hours. Incoming personal calls can block the line so that clients are unable to contact the agency and unnecessary outgoing personal calls are obviously a waste of the agency's resources. Wherever possible cheap rate calls should be made, using

- 0800 numbers for free calls
- 0345 numbers for local charges.

In larger travel agencies, particularly business houses, management may choose to use call monitoring to know how may calls are received a day, what the busiest hours of the day are, how many calls are lost during the busy period, what the average speed of answer is and whether there are enough exchange lines to cope with potential business.

Call monitoring devices can be connected into the agency's telephone system to automatically monitor all incoming and outgoing calls. Results can be analysed at the end of each day and printed reports can be compared from day to day. Call monitoring devices can be purchased outright or alternatively rented to observe calls for a period of time.

Postage

Postage costs can be controlled by using second class for mail which is not urgent, although it would be false economy to suggest that no mail goes first class. Electronic mail (E-mail) can be used to order brochures and communicate with principals wherever possible and this method is both quick and economical.

Other costs

Hospitality, sales and advertising costs should all be calculated in relation to the return the agency hopes to receive in the way of business. Travelling expenses of staff should also be monitored in relation to the business they support in terms of contacts or improved effectiveness of staff following training.

Reconciliation

At the end of each day, whether records are manual or computerised, the cash, cheques and refunds need to be reconciled prior to banking surplus cash and cheques. Figure 14.8 shows an example of a manual daily cash reconciliation sheet. The serial numbers of receipts issued during the day are recorded along with the total amount of money taken. Any refund issued is taken from this amount and a net figure is shown on the left hand side of the form. A record is also kept of any petty cash spent during the day. Finally the amount to be banked for the day is summarised in the bottom right hand corner. The banks provide paying-in slips to record this amount at the bank.

Security

The main concerns with regard to security in a travel agency are

- protecting premises against intruders
- preventing internal fraud
- fire emergency procedures.

Protecting premises against intruders

A travel agency needs to protect cash, blank cheques, foreign currency, blank tickets, ticket validators and office equipment against intruders. Police crime prevention officers can be asked for advice but the main basic precautions are

TRAVEL-WIDE						
Daily Cash Settlement Date: 5 May 1995						
Counter Receipts	Receipt No:	cash	cheque	c.card	Petty Cash brought forward	17.30
deposit	0025	50.00			items purchased today	cost
balance	0026			537.00	milk	75p
deposit	0027		50.00		stamps	2.00
2 × coach	0028	26.00				
					total spent today	2.75
Totals Receipts		76.00	50.00	537.00	Petty Cash Balance	14.55
Refunds	Client	cash	cheque	c/card		
1 × coach	Jones ref 35	12.00				
Total refunds		12.00				
Total Net Receipts		64.00	50.00	537.00		

Figure 14.8 Manual daily cash reconciliation sheet

- a fireproof safe
- secure all doors, using strong bolts
- secure the main door, using a five lever mortice lock
- secure all windows, using bars if necessary
- fireproof storage for client records
- intruder alarm
- lighting at night
- a closed circuit television system within the agency
- secure areas for staff property.

Preventing internal fraud

Procedures within the agency should be designed to prevent fraud and these should include such basic precautions as

- take care in opening the post
- keep checks on the use of postage stamps
- make full use of the agency safe
- keep the bulk of tickets in the bank
- use a stock book to keep track of tickets

- vary the pattern of banking
- ensure adequate insurance cover
- give refunds only with the principal's authorisation
- train staff to handle cash, credit cards and cheques properly.

Fire emergency procedures

Evacuation routes in the event of an emergency should be clearly posted in the agency and all staff should be aware of the routes. In an emergency fire extinguishers should be used only by those staff who are fully conversant with the different types of extinguishers.

Revision Questions

Primary level

1 List FOUR procedures which you would regard as good practice in a travel agency on a daily basis.

2 List FOUR procedures which you would regard as good practice in a travel agency on a monthly basis.

3 List FOUR items of information which should be included in a travel agent's option or booking form.

4 Which is likely to yield a greater percentage commission for a travel agent – selling traveller's cheques or selling insurance?

5 What do you understand by 'incentive commission'?

6 Give TWO examples for each of the following

debit cards
charge cards
credit cards.

7 State THREE security checks which could be made with regard to a £20 note.

8 In relation to a credit card state FIVE items of information which should be obtained from a client when taking a credit card payment over the phone.

9 Give THREE examples of items which might be bought from petty cash.

10 What do you understand by 'reconciliation' at the end of the day in a travel agency?

Advanced level

1 List FOUR sources of income for a travel agent.

2 List FOUR procedures which you would regard as good practice in a travel agency on an annual basis.

3 Explain briefly why a travel agency manual filing system is often based on departure dates.

4 The Data Protection Act 1984 is designed to protect clients' interests. Briefly describe THREE ways in which the law gives this protection.

5 In relation to computerised travel agency management, what do you understand by

GDS   mouse
modem   SABRE
monitor

6 Some tour operators 'direct debit' travel agencies for amounts outstanding. Explain briefly what is meant by the term direct debit.

7 State TWO actions that travel agency staff can adopt to reduce the cost of telephone calls.

8 State TWO additional functions which may be available on a personal computer with viewdata access, but would not be available on a dedicated viewdata terminal.

9 For how many years should VAT financial records be available for Customs and Excise inspection?

10 State FOUR precautions which a travel agency manager could take to prevent fraud.

15) *Legislation*

Contracts

A client who books a package holiday enters into a legal contract with the tour operator to provide the holiday as presented in the brochure and in booking the package holiday, the travel agent acts on behalf of the tour operator, or other principal. Once the booking has been confirmed and the deposit paid, there then exists a contract in law between the client and the principal. The basis of the contract is the booking conditions, which were considered in Chapter 10.

The travel agent also acts as the agent of the client, who can expect professional advice and information from the travel agent. Services offered by the travel agent, such as giving advice about passports, visas and health regulations, were considered in Chapter 4.

If problems occur with a package holiday it is very important for the travel agent, who may be the first person contacted by the client on returning from holiday, to be aware of possible consequences. Problems may be the fault of:

- the tour operator
- the hotelier
- the airline
- the travel agent
- the client.

Kinds of contracts

A contract is an agreement which can be either written, oral or implied.

Written contract

A written contract is one where the details are written down and the contract is signed. The written contract may come as the booking form and its details would be outlined in the booking conditions.

Oral contact

An oral contract is one which is spoken and agreed between the parties. This can happen where a client phones for a late booking, pays by credit card and arranges to pick up the ticket at the airport. The client has not signed any contract but nevertheless the ticket ought to be waiting at the airport.

Implied contract

An implied contract is where the client has every right to assume that certain items or conditions are included in an agreement. For example, if a client books a hotel room, the presence of a proper bed and bed linen in the room is implied.

The role of ABTA

ABTA's advice to the public in the event of things going wrong with a holiday is first that they should approach the tour representative or the hotel manager on the spot. If the matter cannot be resolved in this way, then the complaint should be recorded on the tour operator's official forms which will be available from the representative. On return to UK the client should then make the complaint known to the travel agent and tour operator. If the dispute cannot be resolved amicably, ABTA provides a free conciliation service or the use of their independent arbitration scheme.

ABTA conciliation service

The ABTA conciliation service requires the client to write to ABTA enclosing

- photocopies of any correspondence with the company involved
- the confirmation invoice
- any photographs or other evidence
- an indication of what action is expected from the tour operator, whether it be an apology or some financial compensation.

ABTA arbitration scheme

The ABTA arbitration scheme is run independently by the Chartered Institute of Arbitrators. It is cheap, concerned with written evidence only and available for up to nine months after the holiday. However, it is not available for claims involving physical injury or illness. If clients choose to use the arbitration scheme, then this must be regarded as an alternative to going to court, as they must agree to abide by the decision of the arbitrators.

The role of the courts

England and Wales have the same legal system. Scotland and Northern Ireland each has its own legal system. Here we shall consider only the system for England and Wales, but similar information is readily available for the other systems. In England and Wales there are criminal courts and civil courts.

Criminal offences and the law of tort

The Norman-French word 'tort' simply means a wrong. In law in England and Wales the word is used to identify wrongs which are serious enough to merit damages being awarded but which are not actually criminal offences.

Serious wrongs such as murder are called crimes which are punished by the state; the offender is prosecuted in a criminal court by the Crown. The law of torts is to do with lesser wrongs, which are not punished by the state, but compensation may be awarded in the form of damages to the injured party who will have sued in a civil court.

Criminal courts

Criminal prosecutions are normally brought first to a Magistrates Court. There is no jury in a Magistrates Court and there is a ceiling on the penalties which can be imposed. A person convicted in the Magistrates Court may be entitled to appeal against the decision to a higher court. The higher criminal courts are

- the Crown Court
- the High Court
- the Court of Appeal
- the House of Lords.

Civil actions

Civil actions are normally heard in the County Court, which is presided over by a circuit court judge with a jury. There are limits to the size of the claim which may be considered in this court. A person dissatisfied with the verdict in the County Court can appeal to the High Court where jurisdiction is unlimited. Appeals can still be taken to the Court of Appeal, then to the House of Lords, and ultimately to the European Court of Justice.

Small claims procedure

The 'small claims procedure' which comes within the County Court is provided for those people who may not wish to embark on what could be a costly court case. This is a form of arbitration where the claim must come below a certain limit. The cost is reasonable, but neither side may claim their legal costs. This procedure is popular for smaller claims such as complaints about holidays where the amount of compensation being sought is relatively small.

Figure 15.1 summarises the points above with regard to offences, courts and possible outcomes. Current levels of costs, fines, punishments and compensations can be established by enquiring at the local courts.

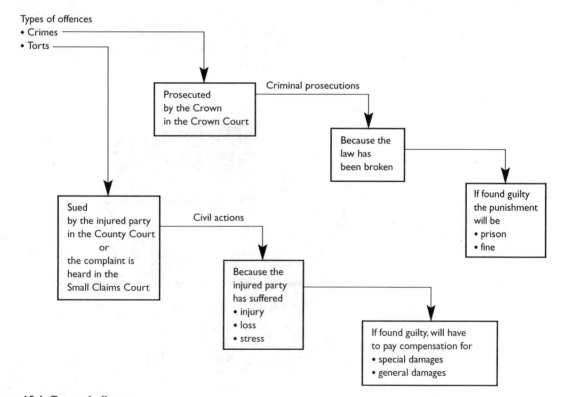

Figure 15.1 Types of offences

Travel law

Travel law, as indeed any other branch of law in the UK, is based on case histories and Acts of Parliament.

Case histories

Case histories are judgments which have been made in the past by a judge in a court. Some of the stories below may seem to be about problems which occurred with holidays a long time ago. However, the decisions made in the courts have implications for other cases which can be shown to be similar and such problems should not happen again for clients in the 1990s.

Jarvis v *Swan Tours Limited* (1973)

The first case history we shall consider is that of Mr Jarvis who booked a fifteen day skiing holiday in Morlialp, Switzerland from the 1969/70 brochure. The brochure promised a 'House Party' atmosphere, with a special resident, English speaking, host and excellent skiing conditions. In fact there were only thirteen people in the hotel during the first week and he was entirely alone for the second week! The hotel owner could not speak English and the entertainment was provided by a local man in his working clothes singing a few quick songs one night. The food was very poor and the bar opened only one night – hardly a 'House Party' atmosphere! Add to all this the fact that there was no representative available in the second week and the ski runs were far away from the hotel and Mr Jarvis' disappointment and frustration were understandable (Fig. 15.2).

The trial judge decided that the tone and wording of the brochure were misleading and he awarded Mr Jarvis damages of half the cost of his holiday for breach of contract.

However, the story did not finish there, because Mr Jarvis appealed and the appeal judge then decided that not only had he been a victim of breach of contract but also he

Figure 15.2

had suffered mental stress as a result of the holiday. The appeal judge awarded
Mr Jarvis twice the original cost of the holiday, considering the mental stress caused by
his disappointment and vexation.

R v *Sunair Holidays Limited* (1973)

Sometimes a case is brought to court by the Crown prosecutor rather than by an
individual person. These cases can be recognised by the use of 'R' for Regina or Queen
in their title and they are criminal rather than civil cases. The difference between these
types of offences was explained above.

In this case the Sunair brochure had stated that a swimming pool was being
constructed for the following season. When the client arrived in the resort the pool was
almost ready but could not be filled (Fig. 15.3).

The trial judge found that the tour operator was guilty but on appeal the second
judge decided that the brochure did not actually say that the pool would be ready, only
that it was being constructed for that season. The appeal judge decided that the tour
operator could not be held liable for statements made about an event in the future.

Figure 15.3

R v *Thomson Holidays* (1974)

In 1974 Thomson Holidays were brought to court because the amenities in a Greek
hotel did not match up to the standard described in the brochure. The interesting point
about this case is that in fact there were two cases heard. Thomson Holidays pleaded
guilty to the first case and then on the second case they tried to claim that they could
not be convicted a second time for the same offence.

However, the judge ruled that in fact an offence was committed every single time a
client read the incorrect information in the brochure, so long as no steps were taken to
correct it.

Jackson v **Horizon Holidays** (1975)

Another story, which took place in Sri Lanka, was that of Mr Jackson who booked an Horizon holiday for himself, his wife and two children. The hotel was supposed to be of the highest standard and he requested a communicating door between the two bedrooms booked. Not only was there no communicating door, but also the children's room was unusable due to mildew and fungus; there was a dirty shower rather than a bath as promised; and several hotel amenities, including the swimming pool, were non-existent.

Mr Jackson was successful in claiming substantial damages not only for himself, but also on behalf of his family, because his was the lead name on the booking form. The lead name is the first name on the booking form and it is this person who should sign the booking form.

Adcock v **Blue Sky** (1980)

In 1980 Mr Adcock was able to obtain damages for himself and a party of friends. In this case the party had booked a skiing holiday in Italy, but the standard of hygiene was very poor, the central heating intermittent and the general atmosphere and comfort of the hotel left a lot to be desired.

The trial judge awarded damages and when Blue Sky appealed, the appeal judge more than doubled the damages awarded because of the irritation, inconvenience and distress caused to all members of the party.

Wall v **Silver Wing** (1981)

In 1981 Mr Wall booked a holiday from the Enterprise brochure at the Marina Apartotel in Puerto de La Cruz, Tenerife. During his holiday he suffered serious injury because a fire exit could not be used, as the door had been locked. It had in fact been locked by the hotel management to prevent burglars getting in, but Mr Wall claimed that he was entitled to presume that he would be safe in the hotel selected by the tour operator. Enterprise however responded by saying that the door was not locked when the hotel was inspected by their representative.

The judge decided in favour of the tour operator, saying in effect that Enterprise could not be held responsible for the day-to-day running of the hotel. A tour operator is however obliged to take care and attention in selecting hotels and should carry out regular checks to satisfy themselves that they continue to be suitable for their clients.

Wings Limited v **Ellis** (1984)

In 1984, Mr Wade booked a holiday in the Wings Faraway Holidays Winter brochure. His holiday was to be in an air conditioned hotel in Nogombo, Sri Lanka, and a photograph of the hotel was shown in the brochure. As it transpired the photograph was of the wrong hotel and in fact there was no air conditioning.

The magistrate found Wings guilty, but the tour operator took the case to the appeal court. The appeal judge then decided that in fact they were not guilty of recklessness because they had informed travel agents and clients of the mistake as soon as they found it. Unfortunately, in this particular instance, the system had broken down and Mr Wade had not received the corrected information in time. This was regrettable, but not a criminal offence. So long as the tour operator sets up a system to inform travel agents and clients of a mistake they have done all that can be expected in the circumstances.

Acts of Parliament

Trades Description Act 1968

The Trades Description Act protects customers against false descriptions by those who are selling or providing services. The providing of services is interesting because it means that the Act applies in a wider context such as car hire. The Act does not require that there be an intention to deceive the customer nor does it imply that anyone has actually been deceived.

As we have seen from *R* v *Sunair Holidays Limited* (1973) the descriptions have to be false at the time when they are made and cannot relate to the future. The case of *Wings Limited* v *Ellis* (1984) shows us that if a statement is correct at the time when it is made but circumstances then change, a system must be set up to inform customers of the change. If such a system is not set up then offences continue to be committed as in *R* v *Thomson Holidays* (1974).

Fair Trading Act 1973

The Fair Trading Act forbids any unfair or unreasonable terms or conditions being imposed on the clients. For example, tour operators cannot say in their booking conditions that all complaints have to be reported within 24 hours of returning from the holiday. This would be unreasonable because clients may have suffered injuries or distress which meant they were not in a position to complain immediately.

When signing the booking form a client is in effect agreeing to the booking conditions and entering into a contract with the tour operator. As the agent of both the tour operator and the client, the travel agent should be sure that the client understands these conditions and is over 18, and therefore an adult in law able to enter into the agreement.

Unfair Contract Terms Act 1977

The Unfair Contract Terms Act forbids the tour operator to try to say that they are not responsible for any problems which might arise on a holiday. For example, tour operators cannot write into the booking conditions that they are not responsible for what happens on a holiday because they do not own the hotels. Whether or not they own the hotels, tour operators are still responsible for seeing that the hotels meet acceptable standards, as described in the brochure.

Sale of Goods Act 1979

This 1979 Act updated the original Sale of Goods Act 1893. The Act applies to tour operators because they repackage accommodation and transport and sell ready made holidays to the public.

Tour operators are not simply acting as agents and, as the case histories above have shown, they must exercise due care and attention when selecting the elements of the holidays. Once tour operators have done this, they cannot be held responsible for the day-to-day running of the services that they have contracted. However, remembering *Jarvis* v *Swan Tours Limited* (1973), tour operators should not be too glowing in their description of the services and should avoid giving what amounts to a guarantee of a good time.

Clients should understand the nature of what they are buying. If the holiday is a late availability one where clients leave the choice of hotel to the tour operator, the price of the holiday may be vastly reduced. However, clients should beware of imagining that the holiday will actually be of a higher standard than is described in the brochure. Similarly, the photograph of a swimming pool in the brochure will normally show the whole pool, and the client should be discouraged from imagining that it is only the corner of a larger pool!

On no account should travel agents be responsible for making misleading statements to clients by claiming to know resorts or hotels with which they are not in fact familiar.

Supply of Goods and Services Act 1982

This 1982 Act extended the protection of the Sale of Goods Act 1979 to give some protection not only to the buyer but also to those who hire or contract services. The goods and services should be up to an acceptable standard and fit for the purpose for which they were intended. The seller or provider should exercise 'reasonable care and skill' in providing the service. As we saw above in *Jackson* v *Horizon Holidays* (1975) and *Adcock* v *Blue Sky* (1980), damages can be claimed for the family and friends who holiday with a person who is not satisfied with the standard of service which is offered.

The implications of this Act for the tour operator are that great care should be taken when selecting the accommodation or transport for the holidays and any services provided, such as that of a courier, should be of an acceptable standard.

The travel agent too should be careful when providing advice that such advice is of a professional standard. For instance, late availability cards displayed in the window should relate to holidays which can actually be booked.

Data Protection Act 1984

This Act sets standards to which both tour operators and travel agents must adhere. The Act was considered in detail in Chapter 14.

Package Travel, Package Holidays and Package Tour Regulations 1992

The EC Directive on Package Travel, Package Holidays and Package Tours was adopted on 13 June 1990 and has implications for both tour operators and travel agents. Member states of the European Union were required to introduce measures to implement the Directive before 31 December 1992. The Directive was implemented in the UK by means of the European Communities Act 1972 and the above Regulations.

Tour operators must provide bonding to protect clients' payments and repatriate clients in the event of the company ceasing to trade. This bonding continues to be provided for ABTA tour operators through their ABTA bond. The Regulations also specify the kind of information which should be included in brochures such as the destination, means of transport and type of accommodation. The tour operator should also give the client any necessary information with regard to passport and visa requirements unless the booking is made very late.

Travel agents who organise their own packages as well as sell those of others are in exactly the same position as any other organiser. It should be noted that for the purpose of the Regulations a package is defined as a trip which is prearranged and sold on and involves at least one overnight stay with the all-in-price covering at least two of the following:

- transport
- accommodation
- other tourist services, such as excursions, which account for a significant portion of the package.

If the viability of the trip is dependent on a minimum number of clients booking, then this should be made very clear in the original literature about the trip. This legislation is quite complex and yet to be tried in the courts but the above Regulations attempt to outline some implications for both tour operators and travel agents.

Negligence

The modern tort of negligence stems from the famous case of *Donoghue* v *Stevenson* (1932).

Mrs Donoghue and a friend ordered a drink of ginger beer in a café in Paisley, near Glasgow. The drink came in an opaque glass bottle so the contents could not be seen. When Mrs Donoghue was in the process of pouring her second glass of ginger beer, out came the decomposed remains of a snail. Mrs Donoghue subsequently sued the manufacturer of the ginger beer who then claimed there was no contract between himself and Mrs Donoghue. However, the Law Lords ruled that there was a duty of care, which had been broken. Mrs Donoghue was unable to inspect the contents of the opaque bottle, but she was entitled to assume that its contents were fit for consumption.

Since that case it has been established that a consumer who wishes to claim for negligence has to prove three points:

- that the manufacturer owes the consumer a duty of care
- that the duty of care has been broken
- that as a result, the consumer has suffered damage or injury.

We saw above that the client booking a package holiday must rely on the care of the tour operator and the travel agent. The average holidaymaker is not in a position to go and inspect the hotel abroad and must depend on the selection made by the tour operator and the advice offered by the travel agent.

Damages

Damages are awarded in civil cases in an attempt to compensate the person who has brought the complaint. There are two types of damages which can be awarded:

- special damages
- general damages.

Special damages

These are easy to measure because they relate to out-of-pocket expenses which might be incurred if for example telephone calls have to be made or alternative accommodation has to be found.

General damages

These are awarded as compensation for disappointment or mental stress and are more difficult to quantify. The court will consider if the client received any physical injuries, as in *Wall* v *Silver Wing* (1981), or if the client suffered mental stress and disappointment, as in *Jarvis* v *Swan Tours Limited* (1973).

The court will ask if the clients have attempted to mitigate their loss. This means did they attempt to enjoy themselves and, if things went wrong, did they approach the tour representative to try to put things right.

I once saw a family who did not like their hotel in Torremolinos and insisted on sitting by the pool in their English heavyweight clothing in 90 degrees of heat rather

Figure 15.4

than attempt to enjoy the holiday in any way. They could hardly be said to have mitigated their situation (Fig. 15.4)!

Compensation could range from a small amount to even double the original cost of the holiday, as in *Jarvis* v *Swan Tours Limited* (1973). However it is unusual for the total cost of the holiday to be awarded as damages because it is difficult to prove that the client received no enjoyment whatsoever. Damages generally depend upon the importance of the lost facilities to the holiday. For instance the lack of skis on a skiing holiday is drastic, but having to use the swimming pool in the hotel next door may not be regarded in the same category.

Ultimately the court will consider the exact wording of the brochure which forms the basis of the contract with the client and the price paid for the holiday, because the price can be expected to reflect the quality being offered.

The role of the travel agent

Although the client has a contract with the tour operator as regards a package holiday it should be remembered that the ABTA Code of Conduct for Travel Agents states that agents 'shall ensure that their counter staff carefully study all tour, holiday and travel programmes and brochures'. The travel agent would in fact be liable for any misrepresentation of the contents of a brochure or indeed for any mis-statements which they detected but did not bring to the attention of the tour operator and client.

Whatever the client's complaint, the travel agent is very likely to be the client's first line of approach on returning from holiday; agents should remember that they have two major roles to play with regard to complaints and legislation:

- the first role is that of the client's own agent who is prepared to listen, sympathise and advise as to whether or not there seems to be genuine cause for complaint
- the second role is that of agent for the tour operator, who should always be represented in the best possible way.

The travel agent's place is not to take sides in a dispute but simply to take an impartial view and advise an appropriate course of action.

Employment law

As an employer the travel agent is subject to laws which relate to the duties of employers and employees, including health and safety at work.

Duties of an employer

These duties are implied in law by all employment contracts and they include the duties to:

- pay wages
- provide work
- cooperate with the employee
- take reasonable care of the employees
- allow time off for public duties, trade union activities and ante-natal care
- allow holidays
- comply with laws such as the Race Relations Act 1976, the Equal Pay Act 1970 and the Sex Discrimination Act 1975.

Duties of employees

The main obligation of employees is to attend work and do their job according to their contract. They have duties to:

- cooperate with the employer
- obey lawful and reasonable orders
- be loyal to their employer in that they should not 'moonlight' doing other part-time work which might harm the employer's business
- not disclose confidential information
- take reasonable care in performing their duties so as not to harm clients or their fellow employees.

Health and safety legislation

The Health and Safety at Work Act 1974 was passed to strengthen the protection of people at work. Older legislation such as the Factories Act 1961 and the Offices, Shops and Railway Premises Act 1963 remain in force. In order to reinforce protection for employees two bodies were set up by the 1974 Act, namely:

- the Health and Safety Commission (HSC)
- the Health and Safety Executive (HSE).

The HSC has a full-time chairman and representatives from both sides of industry and local authorities. Its duty is to promote the objectives of the Act and formulate policies. The HSE has powers to inspect premises, to issue improvement and prohibition notices and to prosecute.

The Act imposes a duty on employers to provide a safe working environment and it protects employers, employees, self-employed people, clients, passers-by and neighbours.

Revision Questions

Primary level

1 At what point does a contract in law exist between a tour operator and a client booking a package holiday?

2 Where a problem arises with a holiday, suggest TWO possible sources of the problem other than the tour operator or the travel agent.

3 Briefly describe the advice which ABTA gives to the public with regard to problems on package holidays.

4 What TWO types of courts are there in the legal system in England and Wales?

5 State the Act of Parliament which would be breached if a brochure advertised the availability of a hotel with a swimming pool but the pool had not been built when the client arrived.

6 How can tour operators ensure that the day-to-day running of a particular hotel abroad is up to the standard they expect?

7 State the Act of Parliament which would be breached if a travel agent were to consistently display late availability cards which related to holidays which had already been sold.

8 What TWO types of damages could be awarded in the courts in England and Wales?

9 State the Act of Parliament which would be breached if a member of staff tripped over an electrical cable left lying across the floor by another member of staff in a travel agency.

10 If Mr Walsh goes into the Trendy Travel travel agency and books a holiday from the Happy Holidays brochure, with whom does he make a contract?

Advanced level

1 State THREE types of contracts which are recognised in law.

2 List THREE items which should be submitted for a client's complaint about a package holiday to be considered under the ABTA conciliation scheme.

3 In what form should evidence be presented to the ABTA arbitration scheme?

4 What do you understand by the term 'tort'?

5 What do you understand by the 'small claims procedure'?

6 What do you understand by case history?

7 State the Act of Parliament which would be breached if a tour operator stated in their booking conditions that no complaints would be considered more than 24 hours after the completion of a holiday.

8 Give an example of when the EC Directive on Package Tours might be applicable to a travel agent.

9 Which THREE conditions must exist for a claim of negligence to be successful in the courts in England and Wales?

10 What, according to the ABTA Code of Practice for Travel Agents, is the responsibility of a travel agent who finds mis-statements in a tour operator's brochure?

Tailor-made arrangements

Sometimes travel agencies act rather like a tour operator when they prepare tailor-made arrangements for individual clients. To prepare these the travel agent uses commission rates from principals in hotels and transport. Like the small tour operator, the travel agent would add a mark-up to cover fixed costs and some profit.

The production of tailor-made arrangements builds on the knowledge and skills in all the previous chapters and in this short final chapter we consider the integrated skills through a series of six worked examples. The first and second examples are concerned with hotel accommodation alone in the UK; the third and fourth with European trips involving a ferry crossing and hotel accommodation with some currency conversion; and the fifth and sixth examples are more complicated trips involving flights to the USA, multi-centre accommodation and excursions.

UK accommodation

Using Fig. 16.1 and assuming that the travel agency requires a mark-up of 12%, rounded up to the nearest £.

First example

A client wishes to book three nights' bed and breakfast in a single room at the Hotel Grand.

basic single	3 × £21.50	£64.50
travel agent's commission of 10%		−6.45
net cost		58.05
mark-up of 12%		+6.97
		£65.02

The selling price, rounded up to the nearest £ and excluding VAT, would be £66.00.

Notice that the cost of accommodation is calculated at the advertised rate, then the travel agent's commission is deducted. The rate of travel agent's commission is shown in the hotel entry next to the • symbol. The net cost is the price of the accommodation minus the travel agent's commission and to this is added the mark-up which is required by the travel agent. The mark-up is used to cover fixed overhead costs in the agency

---

•Hotel Grand -250R- 125 Promenade, Restonsea   01704 23456
  Fax: 01704 34567 B SB 21.50, TB 40.00 •10% cc A,D,E,X

Figure 16.1 Hotel Grand

and some profit. The travel agent can adjust the mark-up according to the desirable profit. In a competitive situation where the travel agent is seeking business the profit margin may be quite low but where there is a great demand and plenty of clients the profit margin may be greater, leading to a higher percentage rate for the mark-up.

Second example

In this example the same principles are used but calculations for two types of rooms are included. The system of calculation of the commission and mark-up is the same as in the first example.

A group of four people wish to book a twin and two single rooms for seven nights.

basic twin	$7 \times £40$	£280.00
basic singles	$2 \times 7 \times £21.50$	301.00
		581.00
travel agent's commission of 10%		−58.10
net cost		522.90
mark-up of 12%		+62.75
		£585.65

The selling price, rounded up to the nearest £ and excluding VAT, would be £586.00.

European holidays

Using Figs 16.2 and 16.3 and assuming the travel agent requires a mark-up of 15%, rounded to the nearest £. The ferry company offers 9% commission and the Rate of Exchange (ROE) is FF 7.77=£.

		Standard Return
Car, motorhome, minibus	vehicle + driver	126
motorcycle combinations	vehicle + 2 persons	149
up to 5.50m long	vehicle + up to 5 persons	159

Figure 16.2 Dover–Calais ferry crossing

> •Hostellerie du Golf -55R- 780 av de la Mer, Mandelieu-la-Napoule 06210
> [in suburbs] . . 93.49.11.66. Fax 92.97.04.01. E SB FRF 350, TB 430 ●8% cc A,B,D

> •Hotel La Ferme D'Augustin -34R- Ramatuelle-Plage De Tahiti [Seasonal] . .
> 94.97.23.83 Fax 94.97.40.30 E SB FRF 760, TB 870 ●10% cc A,B

Figure 16.3 Two French hotels

Third example

A couple wish to take their car on the ferry and stay at the Hotel La Ferme D'Augustin for seven nights in a twin room

basic twin	7 × FF870	FF6,090	
travel agent's commission of 10%		−609	
net cost		FF5,481	
divided by ROE 7.77			**£705.41**
basic ferry	vehicle + 2		£149.00
travel agent's commission of 9%			−13.41
net cost			**£135.59**
Therefore			£705.41
			+135.59
Total net cost			**£841.00**
mark-up of 15%			+126.15
			£967.15

The selling price, rounded up to the nearest £ and excluding VAT, would be £968.00.

In the third example the cost of accommodation has been calculated as in the previous examples but this time the cost of the ferry has been added. Notice that the hotel and the ferry company give different commission rates to the travel agent. It is useful when a currency exchange has to be worked out to keep the answers in a different column which is used for all sterling costs. It is then easier to identify the net costs and add them together. The mark-up is calculated only once on the final total net cost. It is a waste of time to keep calculating the mark-up in the course of the calculations and indeed such a method would introduce numerous possibilities for error.

Fourth example

This example will build on these principles with calculations included for two hotels, each offering different commission rates. It is important to keep the French franc calculations in one column and the sterling calculations in the far right column.

A family of five wishes to book a ten day holiday with a standard return ferry crossing and five nights in each of the hotels in Fig. 16.3 using one twin and three single rooms each night.

basic ferry	vehicle + 5		£159.00
travel agent's commission of 9%			−14.31
net cost			**£144.69**
Hostellerie du Golf			
basic twin	5 × FF430	FF2,150	
basic singles	3 × 5 × FF350	5250	
		FF7,400	
travel agent's commission of 8%		−592	
net cost		FF6,808	
divided by ROE 7.77			**£876.19**

Hotel La Ferme D'Augustin

basic twin	5 × FF870	FF4,350
basic singles	3 × 5 × FF760	11,400
		FF15,750
travel agent's commission of 10%		−1,575
net cost		FF14,175
divided by ROE 7.77		**£1,824.32**
Therefore		£144.69
		+876.19
		+1,824.32
Total net cost		**£2,845.20**
mark-up of 15%		+426.78
		£3,271.98

The selling price, rounded up to the nearest £ and excluding VAT, would be £3,272.00.

USA trips

Using Figs 16.4, 16.5 and 16.6, and assuming the travel agent receives 9% commission on scheduled fares, 10% commission on charter fares, the rate of exchange (ROE) is $1.56 = £ and the travel agency requires a mark-up of 17.5%.

Fifth example

A couple wish to book a two centre holiday in Los Angeles for two weeks followed by six nights in Las Vegas at the hotels in Fig 16.5, departing on 25 May. They would prefer scheduled flights to Los Angeles (assume they qualify for the Apex fare) and a hired car (CCMN) for the three weeks of their stay. They will return to the Los Angeles hotel for the last night before their return flight home.

scheduled fare			
basic	2 × £429		£858.00
travel agent's commission of 9%			−77.22
net cost			**£780.78**
Los Angeles (15 nights)			
basic	15 × $70	$1,050	
travel agent's commission of 8%		−84	
net cost		$966	
divided by ROE 1.56			**£619.23**
Las Vegas (6 nights)			
basic	6 × $75	$450	
travel agent's commission of 12%		−54	
net cost		$396	
divided by ROE 1.56			**£253.85**
car hire (21 days)			
CCMN basic	3 × $145	$435	
travel agent's commission of 14%		−60.90	
net cost		$374.10	
divided by ROE 1.56			**£239.81**

Manchester – Los Angeles

Scheduled Weekend Flights

Apex Fare	£429 1 Apr – 15 Jun
Application	Y RT/CT/ Single or Double open jaw
Fares	Only applicable if purchased before departure.
	Open jaw: charge half RT for each leg.
Children	No discount *Infants* Pay 10%
Routing	Direct to gateway
Min Stay	7 days *Max Stay* 45 days
Stop overs	Not permitted
Re/Payment/Ticketing	Deadline: 21 days

Los Angeles Charter Flights

UK AIRPORT	GATWICK	GATWICK	MANCHESTER	MANCHESTER
VIEWDATA CODES	LGW	LGW	MAN	MAN
DAY	FRI	SAT	THU	SAT
DEPART UK	1030	0830	1030	1015
ARRIVE UK	0700*	0430*	0610*	0430*
STOPS	NIL	NIL	NIL	NIL
FLIGHT CODE	AB21	AB22	AB31	AB32
20 MAY–31 MAY	349	359	359	369

Flight prices are in £s per person up to 14 nights. LONGER DURATIONS SUPPLEMENTS Los Angeles max. 21 nights £27, 4 weeks £55. Child discount 2–11 50%, INFANTS PAY 10%

Manchester – Los Angeles

Consolidated Net Return Fares ex UK during the month of May

TO USA
CURRENCY GBP

From MAN to:	via Gateway	M/W	W/E
HONOLULU	IAH.EWR	420	445
INDIANAPOLIS	NON-STOP ONLY	225	260
JACKSONVILLE	IAH	245	270
KANSAS CITY	IAH/EWR	230	255
LAS VEGAS	IAH	240	260
LOS ANGELES	IAH	260	280
No child discounts			

Figure 16.4 Flights to Los Angeles

Therefore	£780.78
	+619.23
	+253.85
	+239.81
Total net cost	**1,893.67**
mark-up of 17.5%	331.39
Clients would be charged	**£2,225.06**

Notice that for accommodation in the USA, 2PRS means a room rate for two people sharing and 1PRS means only one person in the room. We saw in Chapter 3 that North American rooms are very often large enough to accommodate four persons and in fact in Las Vegas the charge per room is $75 regardless of whether there are one, two or four persons in the room. The E indicates European Plan, which means room only with no meals and again this is common in hotel and motel rooms in USA.

Sixth example

In this example we shall build on the skills already learned and consider a potential booking where the client expects the travel agent to give advice as to the best means of transport.

A family of three adults, one of whom is aged 68, and two children, aged 8 and 10, wish to book a three week holiday departing on Saturday 23 May. They want to spend

---

●Bay View Hotel -350- 1250 Long Beach Blvd, Los Angeles   310 499 6666
Fax 310 499 7777   E   1PRS $65   2PRS$70   ●8% cc A,D,E,X

●Main Strip Hotel -700- 1450 North Main Street, Las Vegas   702 382 5477
Fax 702 382 5478   E   1PRS $75   2PRS$75   ●12% cc A,D,E,X

SEE THE GRAND CANYON FROM THE AIR THE GREATEST THRILL ON EARTH			
	1 hour	*half-day*	*full day*
Helicopter Flights	*$120*	*$250*	*$500*
Fixed Wing Flights	*$175*	*$350*	*$550*
No Child Discounts			
Agent's Commission 20%			

Figure 16.5 Tourist information in USA

USA – all prices in US$						
Rental period		daily 3–5 days	one week	extra days	2–4 weeks	extra days
MCMN	MINI	25	96	23	90	22
EBMN	ECONOMY	27	110	25	103	25
EDMN	ECONOMY	29	120	27	113	25
CCMN	COMPACT	35	153	31	145	30
ICMN	INTERMEDIATE	37	166	33	155	33

Rates include: Unlimited mileage, CDW, PAI, Theft Protection and Local Tax

Extra charges: Luggage rack $1.00 per day, Child Car Seat 25cents per day,
Airport Charges may apply for rental commencing from airports – please check at time of reservation

Surcharges: for drivers under the age of 25 $5.00 per day

Agent's Commission 14%

CONNECT-SAFE INSURANCE

Net Premiums

Period up to	USA, Canada, Caribbean	
	Net	*IPT*
5 days	18.70	0.47
8 days	26.50	0.66
18 days	30.90	0.77
32 days	40.70	1.02

IPT = Insurance Premium Tax @ 2.5%
Infants under the age of 3 at the date of departure – free, provided accompanied by an adult whose name appears on the same Policy
Children under the age of 16 at the date of departure – 50% of the above premiums
Persons aged over 65 at the date of departure at double premium in excess of 17 days in Area 2, and all duration in Areas 3, 4 and 5, but no loading for Area 1

Agent's Commission, exclusive of IPT, 37%

Figure 16.6 Car hire and insurance rates

most of the holiday at the Bay View Hotel in Los Angeles but want a four night trip to the Main Strip Hotel in Las Vegas. While in Las Vegas they want to take the half-day trip to the Grand Canyon by helicopter. They wish to book two double rooms and a single room in each hotel. They have asked the travel agent to price the holiday including insurance and car hire for 21 days in an intermediate car, for which they will require a luggage rack. All flights are available so the costing for the holiday with scheduled, charter and consolidator fares is as follows.

Accommodation

Los Angeles (17 nights)

basic 2 PRS	2 × 17 × $70	$2,380.00	
basic 1PRS	17 × $65	1,105.00	
		3, 485.00	
travel agent's commission of 8%		−278.80	
net cost		$3,206.20	
divided by ROE 1.56			**£2,055.26**

Las Vegas (4 nights)

basic 2PRS	2 × 4 × $75	$600.00	
basic 1PRS	4 × $75	300.00	
		900.00	
travel agent's commission 12%		−108.00	
net cost		$792.00	
divided by ROE 1.56			**£507.69**

Car hire (21 days)

ICMN	3 × $155	$465.00	
luggage rack	21 × $1	21.00	
		486.00	
travels agent's commission of 14%		−68.04	
net cost		417.96	
divided by ROE 1.56			**£267.92**

Grand Canyon

basic half-day	5 × 250	$1,250.00	
travel agent's commission of 20%		−250.00	
net cost		1,000.00	
divided by ROE 1.56			**£641.03**

Insurance

basic adult	2 × £40.70		£81.40
double premium	1 × £81.40		81.40
basic child	2 × £20.35		40.70
			203.50
travel agent's commission of 37%			−75.30
net cost			**£128.20**

*IPT to be included after the travel agent's mark-up

basic adults	2 × £1.02		2.04
premium adult	1 × £2.04		2.04
basic child	2 × £0.51		1.02
			£5.10

Flights

Scheduled Apex

basic	5 × £429	£2,145.00
travel agent's commission of 9%		−193.05
net cost		£1,951.95

Charter (Saturday)

basic adult	3 × £369	£1,107.00
basic child	2 × £184.50	369.00
		1,476.00
travel agent's commission of 10%		−147.60
net cost		£1,328.40

Consolidator

basic (net)	5 × £280	£1,400.00

Each of these would then have a mark-up of 17.5% but it is clear that the cheapest will be the charter flight, followed by the consolidator and then the scheduled Apex fare. The travel agent could point out the benefits of each to the client. The cheaper price is obviously an advantage with the charter fare but the consolidator fare will not be much dearer and for that the clients will have the comfort and services to be expected on a scheduled flight. However the consolidator fare will involve them in a change of aircraft at Houston in Texas and of course as with all consolidator fares they will have to be sure to reconfirm their flights before the journey. The scheduled Apex fare will give them the comfort and services of a scheduled airline with a non-stop service from Manchester to Los Angeles but it will be dearer than the other two options.

If after discussion with the travel agent the clients decided to book the charter flight the complete costing would be

Total net cost	
accommodation	£2,055.26
	£507.69
car hire	£267.92
helicopter	£641.03
insurance	£128.20
charter fares	£1,328.40
total net cost	**£4,928.50**
mark-up of 17.5%	+862.49
*IPT	+5.10
Cost to the clients	**£5,796.09**

*Notice that the insurance premium tax (IPT) is added into the calculation only at the end. This is a tax on the insurance and does not come into the calculation for either commission or mark-up.

The above examples are simple enough to demonstrate a method for calculating both commission and mark-up. However, another factor which is extremely important in dealing with tailor-made arrangements is for the travel agent to use the skills outlined in all the previous chapters. The travel agent should identify the needs of the clients, use benefit statements to help them see the advantages of particular arrangements and then use viewdata and brochures if necessary to put together specific aspects of a business trip or holiday.

Tailor-made arrangements can in fact add pleasure and enjoyment to the client's business or holiday plans and can be a source of both profit and job satisfaction for a well-trained travel agent.

Solutions to the revision questions

Many of the revision questions at the end of the chapters could have more than one correct answer. Below are some suggestions of answers which would be acceptable.

Chapter 1

Primary level

1 see the text
2 transport, accommodation, transfers
3 current research
4 current research
5 English Tourist Board
6 Association of British Travel Agents (ABTA)
7 Institute of Travel and Tourism (ITT) and the Tourism Society
8 Civil Aviation Authority
9 Guild of Business Travel Agents (GBTA) Guild of European Business Travel Agents (GEBTA)
10 English Heritage

Advanced level

1 travel, leisure time, entertainment, travel industry

2 Association of National Tourist Office Representatives (ANTOR) Pacific Asia Travel Association (PATA)
3 clients who are visiting friends and relatives
4 various local attractions
5 royalty, museums, shopping
6 Air Travel Organiser's Licence issued by the CAA to those British tour operators who sell foreign package holidays which include charter flights.
7 Development of Tourism Act 1969
8 Passenger Shipping Association Retail Agents' Scheme (PSARA)
9 British Incoming Tour Operators' Association (BITOA)
10 National Trust

Chapter 2

Primary level

1 Collision Damage Waiver Personal Accident Insurance
2 Compact, two door automatic car with no air conditioning Intermediate, four door car with manual transmission and air conditioning.
3 FRAR, a full size, air conditioned, automatic recreational vehicle to give plenty of room, comfort and ease of use.
4 1 cheaper price for the charter

2 probably more spacious seating on the scheduled flight
3 the scheduled flight is guaranteed to fly at the published time
4 charter flights must be reconfirmed
5 token minimal accommodation will be offered with the charter booking

5 (a) two children with two adults, or one child with one adult

(b) Advanced Purchase Return, either economy or standard, depending on the day of travel. They may also be entitled to a Student CoachCard, if they are studying at least 15 hours a week for 20 weeks in a year.

6 (a) Rapide services should include a courier; hot and cold drinks; toilet and washroom facilities; reserved seats; no smoking area on the bus

(b) approximately 4 hours 30 minutes

(c) Victoria Coach Station.

7
- arrange to meet disabled person at the departure station
- arrange car parking or ramps
- spaces on most trains to carry a standard sized wheelchair
- induction loops at ticket offices guide dogs can be taken into all areas, including restaurants and buffet cars
- special discounts for the disabled person and one companion.

8 (a) Darlington
(b) Liverpool Street
(c) King's Cross
(d) Fishguard
(e) Inverness
(f) Paddington

9 Le Shuttle
Eurostar

10 HSS

Advanced level

1 Liability Insurance Supplement
Personal Effects Insurance

2 (a) 2 weeks @ £94 = £188.00
luggage rack, 14 × 55p = 7.70
£195.70

(b) 1 week EDMN = £110.00
3 days @£17 = 51.00
child's seat, 10 days @ 50p = 5.00
driver supplement,
10 days @ £10 = 100.00
£266.00

(c) 3 weeks @ £89 = £267.00
2 days @ £15 = 30.00
Christmas surcharge,
4 @ £12 = 48.00
£345.00

3 Savannah and Atlanta are both in the state of Georgia, therefore there would not be an interstate drop-off charge if the car were hired in Savannah. Also the rail journey would be shorter and the AMTRAK fare cheaper.

4 (a) Brittany Ferries
(b) Hoverspeed, P&O European Ferries, Stena Sealink
(c) Scandinavian Seaways
(d) P&O European Ferries

5 see the text

6 the season
the time of the sailing
accommodation booked
size of the car

7 see the text

8 (a) £44.40
(b) £31.05
(c) £54

9 see the text

10 AMADEUS
GALILEO
SABRE

Chapter 3

Primary level

1 Modified American Plan means half board or bed, breakfast and one main meal. American Plan means full board or bed, breakfast and two main meals.

2 lounge, desk, fax or fridge

3 see Fig. 3.1

4 see Fig. 3.2

5 5 crowns

6 3 crowns

7 see Fig. 3.3

8 5 key

9 a double room has only one large bed, a twin room has two single beds

10 self-catering accommodation in an approved establishment in France.

Advanced level

1 the highly commended 4 crown has all the required facilities at a high standard

2 grading

3 'red' coats, entertainment programme, fun pool, choice of accommodation arrangements, theatres, and children's clubs

4 see the text

5 Hotelspace

6 Best Western   (813) 261.1148
  Charter Club Resort   (813) 261.5559
  Cove Inn   (813) 262.7161
  Fairways Resort   (813) 597.8181
  Super 8 Motel   (813) 455.0808

The Tides Motor Inn   (813) 262.6196
Trails End Motel   (813) 262.6336
Vanderbilt Inn   (813) 597.3151

7 Trail End Motel

8 English Tourist Board   crowns
  AA   stars
  Thomson Holidays   Ts
  Jersey Tourist Board   suns
  Greek Tourist Board   letters
  Q Scheme for Scottish Holiday Parks   ticks

9 a 3   d 5
  b 4   e 2
  c 1

10 GALILEO, SABRE, AMADEUS

Chapter 4

Primary level

1 (a) peseta   (d) Turkish lira
  (b) Cyprus pound (e) French franc
  (c) drachma   (f) dirham

2 see the text

3 see the text

4 £78.19

5 Form R

6 (a), (b), (d) YES
  (c) NO

7 see the text

8 see the text

9 China

10 see the text

Advanced level

1 £287.29 (charge 1.5%)

2 France

3 (a) Yellow fever
  (b) see the text

4 a 2   d 3
  b 1   e 6
  c 4   f 5

5 (a) Canadian dollar
  (b) US dollar
  (c) Sterling/German mark
  (d) US dollar

(e) Sterling
(f) Sterling

6 Egypt is in Area 3

3 adults @ £15.80	£47.40
1 over 65 (double)	31.60
child under 16 (50%)	7.90
	86.90
+ 35% mark-up	30.42
	117.32
+ 2.5% IPT	2.93
premiums due	**£120.25**

7 The client should take two passports and present the one without the Israeli stamp at the Saudi Arabian border.

8 Flight delay compensation will be a standard amount, whereas the claim for loss of or damage to luggage will depend on the original value of the luggage and will be subject to an excess.

9 (a) YES
  (b) Form C

10 All children, even babies, must be named on a passport.
   Children may be included in the passport of near relatives up to the age of 16.
   Children under the age of 16 may hold their own passport but the photograph must be renewed every five years.

Chapter 5

Primary level

1 7 am

2 International Date Line. From East to West you would lose a day, i.e. if it were Sunday in the West, it would be Monday when you crossed to the East.

3 arrive at 15.05

4 16 hours

5 (a) 2 hours 15 minutes @ 28 mph = **63 miles**
   (b) 63 + 14 = **77 miles**
   (c) 77 miles @ 44 mph takes 1 hour 45 minutes, which is **30 minutes less**

6 e 1   b 4
   a 2   d 5
   f 3   c 6

7 see the text

8 theatre tickets
   airport transfers
   car hire
   insurance
   itinerary
   information about time differences
   information about passport, visa and health regulations

9 Australia, New Zealand, Singapore

10 IATA Area 2

Advanced level

1 9 hours 20 minutes

2 Monday 11 pm. The city is situated on the east (Pacific) coast of USA

3 Saturday 5 February
   11.30 check-in at AA desk at Manchester airport
   13.30 depart on AA flight, via New York
   16.30 arrive Orlando airport
          collect Alamo car
          drive approximately 20 miles to Kissimmee
          check-in at the Granada Hotel

Saturday 12 February
07.00 depart Kissimmee for the 190 mile drive to Fort Lauderdale
11.15 return Alamo car at Fort Lauderdale
12.00 check-in at cruise line desk
14.00 depart on SS *Windswept* cruise for seven nights

Saturday 19 February
08.00 disembark from SS *Windswept* take limousine to Orlando airport
14.00 check-in at AA desk in Orlando airport
16.00 depart on AA flight, via New York

Sunday 20 February
07.00 arrive at Manchester airport

4 The flight via London Heathrow is from Liverpool to Abu Dhabi in the United Arab Emirates and the entire journey takes 12 hours 25 minutes.

5 The flight via London Heathrow is from Liverpool to Amsterdam in the Netherlands and the entire journey takes 1 hour 30 minutes.

6 The flight via London Heathrow is from Liverpool to Bombay in India and the entire journey takes 11 hours 25 minutes.

7 A Pacific Ocean   1 Paris
   B Rocky Mountains   2 Singapore
   C Indian Ocean   3 Miami
   D Caribbean Sea   4 Rio de Janeiro
   E Himalayas   5 Nairobi

8 excellent group accommodation
   accessibility

9 cheap travel
   organised entertainment
   basic shared accommodation

10 Wednesday
   arrival on the third day
   arrival on the following day
   indicates more than eight stops en route

Chapter 6

Primary level

1. Southport — Merseyside
   Torquay — Devon
   New Quay — Dyfed
   Oban — Strathclyde
   Brighton — East Sussex
   Newquay — Cornwall
   Saltcoats — Strathclyde
   Scarborough — North Yorkshire
   Great Yarmouth — Norfolk
   Rhyl — Clywd

2. see the text

3. London Heathrow, Gatwick, Stansted

4. M6 links Preston to Birmingham
   M5 links Birmingham to Exeter
   M4 links London to Bristol
   M1 links Sheffield to London
   M2 links London to Dover

5. Buckingham Palace
   Hampton Court
   Sandringham
   Windsor Castle

6. South West Peninsula Coast Path

7. National Trust

8. see the text

9. Beamish Open Air Museum, Co Durham
   Black Country Museum, Dudley
   Blists Hill, Ironbridge
   Weald and Downland Museum, near Chichester

10. Granada Studios
    Camelot

Advanced level

1. see the text

2. Stratford on Avon
   Black Country Museum
   Alton Towers
   Center Parcs

3. York
   Winchester
   Buxton
   Woodstock
   Manchester
   Stoke on Trent
   Ripon
   Telford

4. Edinburgh
   York
   Bradford
   London
   York

5. National Trust
   Countryside Commission

6. Brecon Beacons National Park
   Snowdonia National Park

7. Countryside Commission

8. Scottish Whisky Trail
   Such trails links several towns which can pool their marketing resources to make a greater impact.

9. Industrial heritage sites often cover a larger area than regular museums and include actual buildings and interpreters dressed in period costume.

10. entertainment is included for an all-in-price
    there is usually the option of self-catering or meals
    secure environment for children
    many such villages are built on the flat giving easy access for pushchairs and/or wheelchairs

Chapter 7

Primary level

1 Benidorm

2 see the text

3 Dover–Calais
Harwich–Esbjerg
Felixstowe–Zeebrugge
Plymouth–Santander
Hull–Rotterdam

4 Nice, Cannes, St Tropez

5 Ipsos, Benitses, Kavos

6 The Alps can be found in Switzerland, Italy and France

7 Eiffel Tower, Notre Dame, Sacre Coeur

8 Athens, Greece
Berlin, Germany
Dublin, Republic of Ireland
Florence, Italy
Lisbon, Portugal
Amsterdam, The Netherlands

9 Corfu

10 Lakes Maggiore, Como and Garda

Advanced level

1 Poland, Hungary, Russian Federation

2 see the text

3 Uffizi–Florence, Italy
Prado–Madrid, Spain
Louvre–Paris, France

4 Costa del Sol   Malaga   Torremolinos
Costa Dorada   Reus   Salou
Costa Blanca   Alicante   Benidorm
Costa Brava   Gerona   Lloret de Mar

5 Toledo, Avila, Segovia

6 Majorca is the largest Spanish island in the Mediterranean
Malta is the island whose capital is Valetta
Corsica is the island where Napoleon was born
Sicily is the island which has a volcano called Mount Etna
The Dodecanese is the Greek island group to which Rhodes belongs
Crete is the largest Greek island

7 Arromanches in Normandy

8 Malaga, Spain
Barcelona, Spain
Charles de Gaulle Airport, Paris
Esbjerg, Denmark
Warsaw, Poland
Bern, Switzerland

9 Canary islands and southern Spain
Malta

10 religious or historical reasons

Chapter 8

Primary level

1 Australia   Canberra
Thailand   Bangkok
China   Beijing (Peking)
India   Delhi
Japan   Tokyo

2 autumn

3 Van Kleef Aquarium
Jurong Science and Bird Park
Haw Par Villa (Tiger Balm Gardens)

4 Walt Disney World
Sea World
Universal Studios Florida
Arabian Nights

5 Los Angeles

San Diego
San Francisco

6 Empire State Building
Rockefeller Center
South Street Seaport Museum
Statue of Liberty

7 Ottawa

8 Pattaya
Phuket

9 Kimberley
Coral islands of the Great Barrier Reef
Tanami Desert

10 Sydney
Melbourne
Adelaide

Advanced level

1   Yosemite is in USA
    Phuket is in Thailand
    Sentosa is in Singapore
    Ayers Rock is in Australia
    Fisherman's Wharf is in USA
    Pattaya is in Thailand
    Bondi Beach is in Australia
    Barossa Valley is in Australia
    Sea World is in USA

2   Temples
    Nightlife
    Seaside resorts such as Pattaya or Phuket
    by air

3   Kathmandu is the capital of Nepal
    Kuala Lumpur is the capital of Malaysia
    Rangoon is the capital of Burma
    Manila is the capital of the Philippines
    Jakarta is the capital of Indonesia

4   Barossa Valley is a wine producing area in
    Australia
    Thailand is a country famous for its silk
    garments
    Hong Kong is the area in the Far East
    which has the highest density population
    Hong Kong is a tax free shopping
    paradise in the East
    Singapore is a small island in the Far East
    which is an independent republic
    Australia is the largest island in the world

Las Vegas is a gambling city built in the
middle of a desert
Rhode Island is the smallest US state
Quebec is a walled city in North America

5   The Freedom Trail is in Boston, USA
    Tiger Balm Gardens are in Hong Kong
    and Singapore
    Raffles Hotel is in Singapore
    A Canadian Cowboy Festival is held in
    July in Calgary, Canada
    The Rockefeller Center is in New York, USA

6   Orlando is the gateway airport for Walt
    Disney World
    Hong Kong is the gateway airport for
    Kowloon
    San Francisco is the gateway airport for
    Yosemite
    Sydney is the gateway airport for Bondi
    Beach

7   Toronto

8   en route to Australia
    English is widely spoken
    mysterious Eastern culture

9   from the blue haze of the leaves of the
    eucalyptus trees

10 Australia   Australian dollar
    USA   US dollar
    Thailand   Baht
    Canada   Canadian dollar
    Singapore   Singapore dollar

Chapter 9

Primary level

1   transport, accommodation, transfers

2   see the text

3   charter

4   low, shoulder

5   costs, photographs, booking conditions

6   costs such as inflight refreshments which
    are incurred for each client

7   transport from the holiday airport to the
    accommodation

8   flight times/days; costs; any penalties

9   types of bedrooms; meal arrangements;
    fire and safety precautions

10 Holiday codes are used in computerised
    booking systems to identify a holiday uniquely.

Advanced level

1   see the text

2   consolidation

3   The release date is the agreed date after
    which an airline is at liberty to sell seats
    to others if the tour operator has not
    taken their full quota.

4   Break even point is the selling price at
    which the tour operator will cover all
    fixed and variable costs, travel agent's
    commission and an element of profit.

5 load factor

6 Mark-up is the percentage added to the actual price of the holiday to cover fixed costs, travel agent's commission and profit.

7 see the text

8 February in skiing brochures because the snow is likely to be at its best at that time.

9 staff salaries, rent, heating, etc. of the office, advertising

10 An empty leg is the flight at the beginning or the end of the holiday season when the aircraft flies empty.

Chapter 10

Primary level

1 golf, skiing

2 A fly/drive holiday is one which includes a flight from the UK and the hire of a camper or car at the destination.

3 the person who is the 'lead name'

4 a deposit is paid to secure the holiday in the name of the client

5 two weeks

6 £350

7 the obligations of the client and the tour operator

8 60% of £450

9 £50

10

basic cost	2 adults @ £349	698.00
half board	2 @ (£2.55 × 10)	51.00
Bristol flight	2 @ £5	10.00
insurance	2 @ £29.95	59.90
total cost		£818.90

Advanced level

1 see the text

2 departure dates; prices; insurance details; booking conditions

3 eight weeks before departure

4 50% of £1,230 = £615.00

5 single room; balcony; sea view; full board

6 lower category of accommodation; inconvenient change to the airport for either departure or arrival.

7 force majeur means a major change to a holiday which is beyond the control of the tour operator, such as a hurricane or an earthquake

8 1 report the complaint to the holiday representative

2 report the complaint to the local supplier, e.g. the hotel

3 make a written complaint to the tour operator's UK office

9

basic	2 adults @ £279	£558.00
1st child	50% of £279	139.50
2nd child	90% of £279	251.11
adult	£279	279.00
single room	(£2.95 × 14)	41.30
sea view	(0.90 × 14)	12.60
Manchester flight	5 @ £23	115.00
adult insurance	3 @ £29.95	89.85
child insurance	2 @ £15	30.00
total cost		£1,516.36

10

basic	3 adults @ £279	£837.00
children	2 @ 50% of £279	279.00
apt supplements	3 @ (£2.90 × 14)	121.80
half board	5 @ (£8.40 × 14)	588.00
Cardiff flight	5 @ £11	55.00
adult insurance	4 @ £29.95	119.80
child insurance	1 @ £15	15.00
total cost		£2,015.60

Chapter 11

Primary level

1 18–30s and 55-plus
2 Lloret de Mar, Benidorm, Magaluf
3 theatres, exhibitions, shopping
4 MetroCentre, Gateshead, and Meadowhall, Sheffield.
5 cheaper cost of living and concerts and operas
6 Switzerland, Austria, France.
7 1 good ski runs
  2 well designed lift systems
8 black
9 discos, fondue parties, restaurants
10 swimming, ice skating, walking, tennis

Advanced level

1 Western Canada, Colorado

2 1 quaint architecture
  2 village shops
  3 the resort may have a congested lift system
3 cross-country skiing
4 a kindergarten and children's ski school
5 A points card gives the holder a limited number of rides on a ski resort lift system and it is cheaper than a full week's lift pass.
6 Jamaica, British Virgin Islands, Sri Lanka
7 Elephant, lion, rhino, buffalo, leopard
8 Kenya   Masai Mara National Park
  Tanzania   Serengeti National Park
  South Africa Kruger National Park
9 a hat, sensible shoes, lightweight brown clothing, a warm sweater
10 Mount Kilimanjaro

Chapter 12

Primary level

1 cabin steward, entertainment, fitness centre
2 Gibraltar, Malaga, Barcelona, Genoa
3 Miami, San Juan, Fort Lauderdale, Port Everglades
4 *Oriana, QE2*
5 port to port cruises, fly/cruises, cruise and stay
6 An inside cabin is one which does not have natural light from a window or porthole.
7 no
8 The midnight sun is the time when the sun shines 24 hours a day in the Baltic for a few weeks at the end of June each year.
9 St John's, Antigua; Bridgetown, Barbados; Ocho Rios, Jamaica; Martinique.
10 Passenger Shipping Association (PSA)

Advanced level

1 Two-bedded cabins have two single or twin beds, but two-berth cabins have bunk beds.
2 deck tennis, shuffleboard, fitness programme, swimming

3 playing cards, sunbathing, computers, library
4 The port of embarkation is the port of departure.
5 (a) 32   (c) 51
  (b) 16   (d) 19
6 see the text
7 The party should be booked on F Deck
  2 adults, double inside
     price band E   2@£1,845   £3,690.00
  2 adults, 4-berth
     price band G*   2@£1,645   3,290.00
  1 child aged 12   1@£1,645   1,645.00
  1 child aged 10   (30% reduction in 4-berth) (plus 75% of this as a child)
  75%(£1,645×70%)   863.63
  2 adults, single cabins
     price band F   2@£1,745   3,490.00
  Total cost for the entire party   £12,978.63
8 shore excursions, insurance, single cabins
9 children, sharing a cabin, early bookings
10 Copenhagen, Trondheim, Narvik

Chapter 13

Primary level

1 Association of British Travel Agents.

2 tour operators and travel agents

3 The travel agent is an agent responsible to both the client and the principal. The principal is the company selling the holiday product - for example a tour operator or ferry company.

4 ISTEL

5 10

6 To be able to find all necessary documentation and to give a decent impression to potential clients.

7 'which means that'

8 window display; brochure display; late availability cards; advertising

9 How many people will be in the party?
Where has she been before?
What kind of accommodation would she like?

10 Either suggest Mediterranean cruises which are slightly dearer or suggest cruises in another area which are roughly the same price.

Advanced level

1 ABTA bonding will assist the client to return home and the ABTA reconciliation scheme could be used if a problem arose as a result of the liquidation.

2 ABTA bond; rental on the premises; standing charge for electricity

3 A 2   D 5
   B 3   E 1
   C 4

4 (a) open   (d) closed
   (b) closed   (e) open
   (c) closed   (f) closed

5 They give the client an opportunity to express their preferences.

6 They give the travel agent an opportunity to control the conversation with a talkative client.

7 (a) closed questions
   (b) listening and agreeing as far as possible
   (c) indication that the holiday may be booking up fast

8 (a) The hotel is on a main road so it is easy to get transport.
   (b) The flight takes one hour so you are there very quickly.
   (c) You will have half board at the hotel so you can have lunch down at the beach if you wish.

9 (a) A coach will meet you at the airport so you don't have to worry if the children have fallen asleep on the flight.
   (b) The hotel has two restaurants and a coffee shop so you have plenty of choice of meals for the whole family.
   (c) The return flight leaves at 8 pm so you gain a full day which you can spend beside the hotel pool if you wish.

10 To give advice to clients and to make bookings for travel and holidays.

Chapter 14

Primary level

1 see the text

2 see the text

3 client's name; date of travel; departure point; destination

4 insurance

5 a higher rate of commission offered to travel agents with a higher turnover of business for a tour operator

6 Connect and Delta
American Express and Diner's Club
Visa and Access

7 • the texture of the paper
• the quality of the print, which should not be raised above
• the paper
• the metal strip, which should appear as a dotted line until held up to the light, when it appears as a solid line

8 card type and number
date of expiry
amount
name of cardholder
address of cardholder

9 stamps, milk, drawing pins

10 balancing the amount taken with the cash, cheques and credit card receipts in hand

Advanced level

1 commission, service charges, interest, referral vouchers

2 see the text

3 Departure dates are used as a basis so that the travel agent can easily check those bookings for which full payment needs to be sent to principals, eight weeks before departure, or those bookings for which tickets need to be sent to the client, two weeks before departure.

4 the information must be obtained and processed fairly
data should be held only for specified and lawful purposes

data should be used and disclosed only in the manner described on the Data Protection Register

5 see the text

6 The travel agent signs an agreement with their bank that unspecified amounts can be taken from their account by the principal on an agreed date each month. The principal should inform the travel agent prior to that date of the relevant amount that month.

7 no personal calls; use the 0800 numbers

8 word processor and database

9 six years

10 care in opening the post
checks on the use of postage stamps
make full use of the agency safe
keep the bulk of tickets in the bank

Chapter 15

Primary level

1 when the deposit is paid and the booking is confirmed

2 the hotel, or the airline

3 Try to resolve the matter as early as possible in the following stages
1 approach the local tour rep
2 approach the local service provider, e.g. hotelier
3 complete a standard tour operator complaint form
4 make known the complaint on return to the UK

4 criminal and civil courts

5 Trades Description Act 1968

6 by making both regular and spot checks

7 Supply of Goods and Services Act 1982

8 special and general damages

9 Health and Safety at Work Act 1974

10 a contract is entered into with the tour operator for the holiday and also with the travel agent for the advice given.

Advanced level

1 written, oral and implied contracts

2 • photocopies of any correspondence with the company involved
• the confirmation invoice
• any photographs or other evidence

3 written evidence

4 A wrong which is serious enough to merit damages being awarded but not actually a criminal offence.

5 A form of arbitration offered in the County Court where the claim must come below a certain limit. The cost is reasonable, but neither side may claim their legal costs.

6 Case histories are judgments which have been made in the past by a judge in a court.

7 Fair Trading Act 1973

8 If travel agents produce and sell their own packages, e.g. a mini-overnight break to a show in London.

9 that the manufacturer owes the consumer a duty of care
that the duty of care has been broken
that as a result, the consumer has suffered damage or injury

10 The travel agent should inform both the tour operator and potential clients.

Glossary of terms

Ad hoc is a term used when reservations are made, either by travel agents or tour operators, as and when required by individual clients.

Allocation is a block of hotel rooms or airline seats which are made available to a tour operator or travel agent. The rooms or seats are reserved in their name until an agreed release date.

American plan (AP) is accommodation with breakfast and two main meals included in the price.

Back to back is a term used to describe the practice of charter airlines whereby an aircraft flies out with a full load of passengers and returns with another full load who have completed their holiday.

Bond is a type of insurance taken out by a travel company, possibly with a bank, so that, if the company ceases trading, costs can be recovered to compensate clients who are stranded abroad or may have lost their holiday or flight.

Break even point is the holiday price which a tour operator needs to charge to cover minimum costs.

Business house is a travel agency which specialises in providing local firms with travel arrangements, visas and currency exchange.

Charter aircraft are commissioned for a specific period of time and usually fly with a full load of passengers to a given destination.

Collision damage waiver (CDW) is an extra insurance cover which clients who are hiring a car should be advised to take. This covers the costs for the client in the event of an accident without prejudicing their own UK car cover.

Commission is payment made to a travel agent by principals such as tour operators, airlines, ferry companies and car hire firms. The payment made is a percentage of the value of the booking. The percentage of commission paid varies from one principal to another.

Confirmed is the term used for a booking for which a client has paid the deposit.

Consolidation occurs when clients are asked to change their flight or hotel arrangements by a tour operator who has poor bookings. For example, bookings may be poor from both Manchester and Birmingham airports and clients from one airport are required to use the other airport so that one full load of passengers can depart on one aircraft.

Consolidator fares are scheduled airline fares which are sold at a cheaper rate. Bookings using consolidator fares should always be confirmed 24 hours before travel.

Continental plan (CP) is accommodation with breakfast included in the price.

Contract is an agreement between two parties. The agreement may be written, oral or implied.

Controllable costs are those such as lighting, heating, telephone calls and stationery items which can be used or abused by the staff of a travel company.

Corporate image is the image or impression given of a company. The impression given can be influenced by its advertising, logo and attitude of its staff.

Courier is a representative of the tour operator who is employed to assist clients on package holidays. For example, a courier will meet clients at the airport, assist with general enquiries, and make arrangements for clients who are ill to see a local doctor.

Density is a measurement of the space available on a ship in relation to each passenger. To calculate the density, the Gross Registered Tonnage (GRT) of the vessel should be divided by the number of passengers to be carried.

Deposit is a small payment per person made by a client to secure a holiday or travel booking. A deposit is normally not refundable. The balance of payment is usually due eight weeks before the departure date.

Domestic is the term applied to flights and holidays in the United Kingdom. It applies to mainland Britain, Northern Ireland, and the off-shore islands.

Empty legs are those flights made by charter aircraft without passengers at the beginning and end of the season. The first flight out in a season will have to return without passengers, and also the last flight out will be made solely to pick up holidaymakers who have completed their stay.

European plan (EP) is accommodation but no meals included in the price.

Ex gratia payment is sometimes made by a tour operator or airline when a problem has arisen for a client. Such a payment is made on the understanding that the principal does not accept any liability or responsibility for what has gone wrong but is simply making the payment as a goodwill gesture.

Expiry date is the date after which an option or booking will not be reserved for a client. It is also used for the date on which the use of a credit card expires.

Fixed costs are costs such as staff salaries, rent or mortgage payments which have to be paid for by a travel company.

Flight series means charter aircraft which are made available to a tour operator at a specific time each day or week for a specific number of flights.

Fly/cruise is a term used to describe package holidays which include a client's flight to the Mediterranean, Caribbean or other area, in order to take a cruise.

Fly/drive is the term used to describe package holidays where the client flies out to a holiday destination and a hire car is waiting for them at the airport. This type of holiday very often involves independent travel making use of hotel vouchers for accommodation.

Force majeure or 'Acts of God' are circumstances beyond the control of a tour operator which may force a change to be made to holiday arrangements. For example, a hurricane, threat of war, nuclear disaster or terrorist activity.

Gateway airport is the airport through which the majority of tourists fly into a resort or area.

Gîtes are self-catering units in France which have been modernised with help from the French government and are supervised and let by the Fédération Nationale des Gîtes.

Ground arrangements are the services provided by a tour operator in the resort for their package holidaymakers. The ground arrangements are usually organised by the courier and include taking the clients to their accommodation and offering excursions or car hire.

High or peak season refers to the most popular dates for flights or holidays. The most expensive prices apply to these dates. The other seasons are called low and shoulder seasons.

IIT means **Independent inclusive tours** and refers to package holidays prepared and sold by travel agents using commission rates from principals in transport and hotels.

Incentive commission is a higher rate of commission paid by tour operators or other principals to stimulate more sales by a travel agent who already has a higher than average turnover of business for them.

ITC means **Inclusive tours by charter** and is used to describe package holidays which make use of chartered aircraft.

ITX means **Inclusive tours by excursion** and refers to package holidays which make use of seats on scheduled aircraft which have been made available to the tour operator at SGITS (see below).

Lead name is the name of the first person on a booking form. This person should sign the booking form and for legal reasons must be over the age of 18.

Load factor is the number of airline seats or hotel beds sold as a percentage of the number available. Airlines and tour operators calculate their prices based on a minimum load factor, that is the minimum number of clients required to break even and cover costs.

Logo is a symbol or design adopted by a company to identify it and distinguish its product from that of other companies.

Long haul describes destinations beyond Europe. For example, the Far East, USA and Canada are all long haul destinations.

Long stay holiday means a holiday of more than two or three weeks. Such holidays are taken by some tourists in the winter and may last for up to three months.

Low season refers to the least popular dates for flights or holidays. The cheapest prices will apply to these dates. The other seasons are called high or peak season and shoulder season.

Mark-up is a percentage which is added to the basic cost of a holiday by a tour operator to cover fixed costs, travel agent's commission and profit.

Medium haul describes destinations within Europe. For example, Rome, Athens and the Costa del Sol are all medium haul destinations from the UK.

Mitigation means making the best of a situation when a problem arises.

Modified American plan (MAP) is accommodation with breakfast and one main meal included in the price.

Option is a term used to describe a holiday booking which has been reserved for a client. The option will be held for a specific period of time, such as 24 hours, to give the client time to send the deposit and confirm the booking.

Option form is used by travel agents to record details of a client's request. Information such as the client's name, the desired resort and hotel, the departure date and airport would all be recorded on the form.

Option reference is the reference number for a booking given by the tour operator to the travel agent. This number should be carefully recorded so that it can be quoted when the client pays the deposit and confirms the holiday.

Outbound tour operators produce package holidays for UK residents wishing to holiday abroad.

Over-rider commision is extra commission paid by a tour operator to a travel agent who does more than average business for them. The over-ride commission could be 2% or 3% over the usual 10% offered by the tour operator.

Package holidays are put together by tour operators who charge an all-in-price for the whole holiday including transport, accommodation, transfers and the services of a courier.

Passenger manifest is a list of names of passengers in an hotel or on an aircraft or ship.

Peak or high season refers to the most popular dates for flights or holidays. The most expensive prices apply to these dates. The other seasons are called low and shoulder seasons.

Pipeline money is money which has been paid to a travel agent by a client but which has not as yet been sent on to the principal.

Principal is the general term used to describe companies with whom a travel agent may do business. A principal may be a tour operator, an airline, a ferry company or a car hire firm.

Receipt is a written acknowledgement of an amount of money received from a client. Receipts should have serial numbers so that each one can be accounted for, and they should be issued for all transactions, whether by cash, cheque or credit card.

Reconciliation is the calculation at the end of a period of time, such as on a daily basis, of the amount of money taken and paid out by a company.

Reference is the identification of the person or company with whom a booking has been made. Very often the reference is the first name of the person dealing with the booking.

Release date is the date after which an airline or hotel is free to sell seats or beds if the tour operator has not taken the full quota of their allocation.

Scheduled flights operate to a timetable and are committed to fly whether or not the aircraft is full.

Self-catering holidays include accommodation with kitchen facilities, but no meals.

Short haul destinations are those closest to the UK such as northern France, Belgium, the Netherlands and parts of Germany and Scandinavia.

Shoulder season refers to the dates for flights or holidays which are neither the most nor the least popular. For example, the shoulder season for transatlantic flights covers the autumn rather than summer or Christmas. The other seasons are called high or peak season and low season.

SGITS means **special group inclusive tour rates** and these are specially priced scheduled airline seats made available to tour operators who wish to offer ITX (see above).

Tender means using a small boat, very often utilising the lifeboats, to ferry from a cruise ship to the quayside.

Time charter means that an aircraft is made available to a tour operator over a period of time, such as six or twelve months.

Tort is a Norman-French word which simply means a wrong. In law in England and Wales the word is used to identify wrongs which are serious enough to merit damages being awarded but which are not actually criminal offences.

Tourist is a person who travels for pleasure staying one or more nights in a place other than the normal place of residence.

Tour operators package and sell holidays which are offered in a brochure with a fixed price for accommodation, transport and ground arrangements.

Transfer is the transport provided by tour operators to take their clients from the airport or port to their accommodation.

Travel agents book holidays or travel arrangements for clients. The travel agent also offers advice with regard to destinations, passports and visas. The main source of income for this service is the commission the travel agent receives from principals with whom the bookings are made.

Variable costs are costs which have to be taken into account by a tour operator when costing holidays, but which vary according to the number of people travelling. For example, these costs include the ticket and inflight refreshments.

Visa is a stamp in a passport giving the holder permission to enter or leave a country.

Index